In Your End is Your Beginning

A Memoir and Spiritual Wayfinding Manual

Elaine Murray

Tehom Center Publishing is a 501(c)3 nonprofit publishing feminist and queer authors, with a commitment to elevate BIPOC writers. Its face and voice is Rev. Dr. Angela Yarber.

Paperback ISBN: 978-1-966655-54-1

Ebook ISBN: 978-1-966655-55-8

Contents

Embracing New Life

Conclusion

*Dedicated to my children
and the adults who picked me up and shone a light
to find my way back to myself.*

Introduction

Preface

THIS BOOK IS A PROMISE—THE WORDS I NEEDED WHEN EVERYTHING fell apart and the words I know others in the world need when life is teetering on the edge. I prayed that someone, anyone really, would tell me what to do, how to get up and live again, how to fix and repair even *one* of the broken, twisted, messed-up things around and within me.

This book is not a fairy tale—there is no happily ever after—but there is new life. There are promises that do not break. This book aims to be the kind of companion I needed in a time when everything went dark—I had cheated on my husband, lost my job and home, gone through a very public scandal and revelation of all my rotten past, and teetered on the edge of losing my children. This book is not afraid of darkness. When I look around at our world today, so many individually sad and hard stories of people coping with loss and change that comes toward them at a rate faster than our bodies and souls can metabolize, I saw the need for a set of powerful tools to help us find our way back to ourselves, our purpose, and our future. That's why each chapter includes a "Wayfinding Practice"—a spiritual tool for metabolizing and alchemizing pain, and for finding our way back to ourselves and the Divine presence within us. When we're in pain, we grasp for whatever will make it stop or numb, but before we make any sudden moves, we ought to revisit ourselves, our hearts, our path and discern the next right thing. This lesson, to stop numbing and escaping long enough to peer into the abyss within and trust the Spirit to pull you out again—that's where the magic happens.

How did *In Your End is Your Beginning* come to be? If I'd had the choice, I certainly wouldn't have picked to be the person who finds new beginnings in the endings of things. But when I look back I can see that this has been who I am—a spiritual wayfinder—for my entire life. From sitting in the branches of an oak tree and learning to talk to God in the silent loneliness of childhood to blazing trails as many people's first experience of a woman in the pulpit of their sanctuary. From ending hobbies and friendships only to find deeper and truer expressions of myself on the other end of them, I have come to know this truth: ***no act of love is ever wasted.*** This book, this story is an act of love from me to myself, from me to the world, from me to every person who has ever wondered how on earth they will get through their hard thing. I love you. There is a new beginning in you yet.

It's Easter morning and the sun is just coming up over a hill. The spring air is crisp as my father and I tumble out of his truck and make our way to the stone benches of the outdoor chapel built into a hillside. The music begins and a small cadre of people in sweat-pants and blankets begin to sing,

In the bulb there is a flower;
in the seed, an apple tree;
in cocoons, a hidden promise:
butterflies will soon be free!
In the cold and snow of winter
there's a spring that waits to be,
unrevealed until its season,
something God alone can see.

The "Hymn of Promise" continues, "In our end is our beginning; in our time, infinity; in our doubt there is believing; in our life, eternity."[1] All good writers borrow from the inspiration of others, and this hymn's author Natalie Sleeth is no different. Repurposing the words of T.S. Eliot "In my end is my beginning," she points to a reality of life after death. The worst things that happen to us are not the last things that happen to us.

"I came that they may have life and have it abundantly"[2] is an affirmation, a promise from the New Testament that guides the telling of this story.

Life will break your heart, but it will break it wide open for love, for truth, and for freedom. Parker Palmer tells a story in *Hidden Wholeness,* claiming there are two kinds of broken hearts: the first is one that is an unresolved wound we carry with us for a long time, sometimes tucking it away and feeding it, sometimes trying to "resolve it" by inflicting the same wound on others. The second is different—imagine this broken heart is a "small clenched fist of a heart, broken open into the largeness of life, into greater capacity to hold one's own and the world's pain and joy." I write now from the other side of pain and loss, with this clenched fist that has become an open hand, knowing there will be more things in this world that bring me to my knees. But I have confidence, and dear reader, you can too, that whatever destroys your spirit or wrecks your carefully

---

1. "In the Bulb There Is a Flower" words by Natalie Sleeth
2. John 10:10

crafted world will ultimately lead you to more understanding, more depth, more joy, more compassion, more connection…just so much *more*.

"Let the redeemed of the Lord say so,"[3] the psalmist writes. Their redemption didn't come from the church or the community. Their redemption came from God. Throughout this story, you will find scripture of the Old and New Testaments woven throughout it, plus other writings that are part of my personal canon of holy works. This is the script I've been handed, the spectacles through which I interpret the world. Yours may come from elsewhere. The words of scripture for me are a balm, not a weapon. I know this has not been true for everyone. I hope these references may ground you rather than trigger you, perhaps even pique your curiosity enough to encourage you to give the Bible a chance one day, or if it has broken you, courageously try again. Its collection of stories and poems and prayers have made a place for me to belong more deeply to myself, more profoundly to an infinite universal force of love that stuns and empowers me to live with courage and joy.

The most profound story that calls me back over and over again with wonder towards the Bible is the resurrection of Jesus. I'll share more later about why Easter is the absolute best day of the year. Many have wondered, joked, and doubted what really happened with the body of the political enemy of Rome and Palestinian Jewish teacher some 2000 years ago. The doctrines are of little importance to me compared to the certainty of what a resurrection means, that what comes after the finality of death *is* new life.

What if resurrection is the deep old magic of grief? What if every time someone close to us dies, there was a small sense of gladness in us too, because we knew that death is the necessary step towards an experience of new life—both for the dying and the grieving? We never live without the ones we lose, but the life we continue living is forever changed.

My sense of resurrection has changed over the years—no longer

---

3. Psalm 107:2

some Santa Claus type holiday magic, but more akin to the "old religion" that Aslan, C.S. Lewis' Christ-like figure, quoted in *The Lion, The Witch, and the Wardrobe.* Aslan is an enormous lion, who is neither safe nor tamed, but gentle in his powerful command of the animal kingdom in Narnia. When Aslan sacrifices himself in order to break the evil curse that makes Narnia a land where it is "Always winter and never Christmas" he defeats the White Witch who has ruled for many years. In explaining Aslan's own resurrection he describes it as such:

It means that though the witch knew the Deep Magic, there is a magic deeper still which she did not know...a little further back, into the stillness and the darkness before time dawned.[4]

We begin from our endings, trusting this deeper magic at work that has been at work even in the stillness and darkness where time began. In every ending, there is a new beginning.

This is a story about grief. About grieving a relationship that perhaps never should have been, but that created two perfect children, and whose ending changed the adults forever. This story broke through a facade of achievement and revealed for me who I really am: a beloved child of God, resilient, deeply compassionate, who leans on her joy for strength.

There are tender parts of our selves and our experiences which confuse and confound us. Without meaning or purpose or story to make sense of them, we feel lost. Like children making our way through a maze of clothing racks looking for the pair of legs that is our mom, our parent, our person—without a sense of orientation, every sweater or pair of slacks begins to look like hers or like she has left us there.

As adults experiencing this confusion, we are led to construct elaborate lists of qualities that define us as "toxic" or "pathological" or "narcissistic" but the truth is that we are all fighting for our lives and our goodness out here, fighting to protect what is good and right and generous within us.

---

4. *The Lion, The Witch, and the Wardrobe* by C.S. Lewis

Each of us longs to be known and to be seen; to live a "Life that truly is life."[5] But we are not born recognizing this experience for ourselves. We must pilgrimage there as an act of faith, an act of healing, an act of accountability and love for ourselves and our place in the world. This book is a testimony and a guide to deeper, wiser, more compassionate life that leads to joy and abundance. I started writing to explain myself and my behaviors and where I ended up was in a silent state of forgiveness and peace with my intuition, richer from all the tools I found to help me along the way.

Trouble and Grace

The first seven years of my professional life were spent in pulpits all over Texas. I'll let you in on an industry secret of preaching—many sermons can be boiled down into four parts: trouble in the text (in the scripture passage for the day), trouble in the world (a situation facing us currently that corresponds to the text), grace in the text (where God's action is saving and remaking the action of the text), and grace in the world (where God's action is saving and remaking us in the world).[6] Now that you know, you'll start seeing this pattern everywhere. Even when your uncle starts "preaching" around the Thanksgiving table, you can keep your cool by analyzing his speech—where's the trouble? Where's the grace? Every good story begins with trouble or a question, such as "Where's God when I'm scared?" or for this one, the question is "What happens when everything falls apart?"

In a flurry of words and directives, the big trouble in my life arrived on August 30th, 2019, when my husband came home to have lunch with me, walked in the door and said, "We're getting a divorce. You're out of the house. Now."

In a moment, I lost my home. I lost my job. I lost access to my children. I lost a husband. I lost my sense of safety. I lost money. I

---

5. 1 Timothy 6:19
6. *The Four Pages of the Sermon* by Paul Scott Wilson

lost dignity. I lost face. I lost friends. I lost a vision for the future to which I had clung quite deeply.

The psychologists would say these are serious risks for a nervous breakdown. When the hits just keep coming, one wonders, at a certain point, will I just waste away? Will I have anything left to sustain all these losses? These are the questions at the beginning of a powerful story of resilience, change, and new life.

By some miracle of divine accounting, there is more of you than you think. The thing that threatens to undo your everything will not.

"Weeping may linger for the night, but joy comes in the morning"[7] is the pattern for how these life-wrecking moments go— although one thing this scripture misses is that things don't always literally get better overnight. One big bang, with lots of aftershocks, and then, in a whisper, piece by piece (and peace by peace), joy worms its way through the wreckage into a new life.

Often the trouble alerts us with anger or a disturbance in the force. A child throws a tantrum, an adult begins slamming cabinets or marching around in a huff. A quake echoes through the shadows to alert us that something is amiss. Much of our communication is nonverbal—our senses are trained to pick up on these cues all around us.

Often such a disturbance is a response to signaling we haven't yet picked up on. When a person's behavior surprises or stuns, it is commensurate with the situation at hand. We often haven't *seen* the situation fully— there are layers and histories at play. The alcoholic after an unwanted intervention (is there such a thing as a *wanted* intervention?) may lash out or shut down, not because of the actual words being said, but because they have been transported to the first hurt, or the biggest hurt, the layers of pain that numbing with booze has covered up for them until now. As it is with pain, perception plays a bigger role than reality does. Our senses are signals to us, yet we gloss over and ignore what they tull us in favor of going

---

7. Psalm 30:5

with the flow and not raising alarm "unnecessarily." The intensity of emotions like anger and sadness shock, scare, and overwhelm us before we even get to the story we're telling ourselves beneath them. When things fall apart, it all seems so overwhelming. Eventually the rebuilding affords you the capacity to take responsibility and understand the context behind your overwhelm, ultimately leading to forgiveness and self-compassion. But not at first.

Years of being hurt, exploited, and ignored (first by myself!) led me to find a secret way to survive—through my career and the eventual intimacy I found through it. This secret I held nearly broke me, as secrets often do. Through the shards, I found new life. In new life, secrets cannot survive. Come with me into the deep pain, where those secrets once living and into the singing darkness, all the way through to the light of a brand new day.

The Singing Darkness
Filled me with melodies
until I became a song.
The Singing Darkness
carried me into the dawn and
sent me forth to sing my own song.

— *Macrina Wiederkehr* "The Singing Darkness"

Orientation

So, what'll it be then? You can go back to your regular life and forget any of this ever happened, or you can know the truth about the universe. The choice is now yours.

— *Weird Barbie*

I'M DAYS AWAY FROM TURNING SEVENTEEN, PRACTICALLY HOPPING across the linoleum to the barricade of the Security Checkpoint at the San Antonio International Airport, laden with a gigantic hiking backpack, trailed by my parents and sister. It's time. The day is finally here when I will set out for a student exchange program in Germany to spend the ten months of my senior year of high school. I am thrilled. The activities, classes, and headache of navigating peer relationships in the halls of my high school had exhausted me. Eight months prior, in the midst of burnout, I dreamt of what it might be like to go somewhere else for the capstone of the American high school experience. *What if I could be anywhere but here?*

After a thorough application process, recommendation letters, group and solo interviews, I'd been selected to be part of the Congress-Bundestag Youth Exchange Program, sponsored by the

U.S. State Department. Two hundred ninety-nine other American teenagers and I were setting off for a year in Germany. I would live with a host family who was counting down the days for me to arrive. *Ecstatic* was too soft of a word to describe how I felt leaving the U.S. eighteen months after Operation Iraqi Freedom had begun and before George W. Bush was elected for a second term.

I zigzagged through the empty barricades of the security checkpoint and turned one last time to wave goodbye while taking off my backpack to go through the X-ray machine. That's when I lost it. The reality of change hit me—not only that I was embarking on this epic adventure, but that now a gulch existed between me and the ones who had seen me through up to this point. I waved and sobbed while gently and firmly taking the steps towards my next big step, into an unknown future. One path of life was ending, and a new one just beginning.

Even change we hope and yearn for has some element of surprise. Not all surprises are wonderful.

How we respond to surprises can tell a lot about a person, about what they keep hidden from polite company, and what within them is nurtured and has a place of belonging. In the TV show, *The Good Place*, Kristen Bell's character who has died and ascended to heaven/"The Good Place" but spent her life on earth with a colorful vocabulary finds herself unable to utter a profane word. Her favorites at the element of surprise come out as "Holy Shirt balls!" instead of the more vulgar alternative. Where do you go when you are surprised? The therapists tell us our responses can be sorted into four "F" words (ok, not that one!)—fight, flee, freeze, or fawn.

I tend to *fawn*, that is, remain calm, and slowly, methodically obey whatever the scary thing is in front of me, whether it be a bear or a Transporation Security Agent. On that day in the airport, the scariest thing was life apart from all I held dear. Even though school and my peers were exhausting, leaving them behind also meant leaving behind the known, the settled, the secure. Before me was a yet unscripted adventure that I would come to discover.

At another time in my life, the scary thing before me was my then husband, X, telling me to leave, that I no longer had a home there, and that he didn't care where I went, but I couldn't stay. I obeyed.

I grabbed my things and left. I couldn't even call it escape, just obedient departure. Even as I write these words six years later, with so much between me and that day, my heart pounds fast.

These fight, flee, freeze, and fawn responses are inherited from our ancestors—from way back. When we were hunters and gatherers, nothing could trigger us like a predator attack.

It seems a more common occurence now, as we behold the state of things, for words to fail and those familiar F's come into play. We run, we act out, we shut down, we distract, we dissociate. My prayer in situations like these is "To know the next right thing." Asking for guidance toward the next right thing has led me to wonderful, rich, fulfilling places. But not at first.

Words I am known to utter in such times, in addition to Kristen Bell's "Holy Shirt Balls!" —when the state of the world around me is too much— are these: "I fucking love Jesus." They usually accompany a sigh or a shake of the head. I've learned the only reasonable response to the absurdity of the world is to state the claim yet again, that a 33-year-old Palestinian Jewish man changed things for me long before any of my known ancestors were twinkling in their parents' eyes. The cussing is a necessary part of it too —passion and reverence are intertwined together. A former boss (not the one I married!) told me once that "If it's not empathy, it's bullshit" and that seems to be a cornerstone for where I begin in finding my way through life's surprising changes.

Perhaps you are reading this because you find yourself in a change. Has God closed a door and not yet opened the window, or the bottle of wine? Is it dark and scary where you are? Have the tides changed in a way that you cannot find your way back to where you came from and the new way forward has not yet emerged?

Welcome, fellow wayfinders.

I am here. The wilderness sent me here, to shine a light, to go with you to the next right thing.

Many of us have found a sudden end on the path we thought we were on and had to find or make a new beginning. Life changes like marriages and divorces, job changes like layoffs or promotions, or identity changes like pronouns or religious traditions are just some of the impasses we find ourselves at in the need of something new, something "not that" from how we lived before. When I became a parent, along with many others on this journey, I was dismayed to find there wasn't a manual for this, nor could I trust much of the so-called "instruction books" on the market for this odd and wondrous calling either. Without a manual from the end of one thing to the beginning of the next, we must find something to aid our navigation.

A map of some kind is essential. The map may exist inside your brain, or your phone, or within the wisest person you know. But where we are going, there is no room for backseat drivers or Monday morning quarterbacks. If it were up to my dad, the map would be paper because you never know when your memory or phone battery will fail you. We need different maps for different destinations of course, but even the same long journey may require more than one means.

We have so many violent and militaristic terms for what we use to make our way in the world. Arsenal, tool chest, rig, tackle—all describe things we use to conquer something. What if the goal is not to overcome or "beat" a disease, a setback, or the thing that takes our breath away? But what if we were looking to befriend our grief, make our way through the wilderness of the unknown, and reorient ourselves in a new direction as we receive a new life?

This wondering may seem like too much too soon if you are at the beginning of this and the trauma is too fresh. Trauma is anything that is too much, too soon.

It's okay if it feels like too much all at once. What you have in your hands is a wayfinding manual. I won't tell you the way, but I'll be beside you as you discover it. We are going on a journey, whether it's one you sought out or not, and most likely this journey is one you never expected to take. I find the most worthwhile journeys rarely appear on someone's five-year plan or long-range strategy. They emerge more organically, that is literally, from the shit we endure.

On this journey you will want a guide—you may beg and plead with the universe to send you someone or something who knows with exact certitude what to do every step of the way. I hate to break it to you, but this guide does not exist anywhere outside of the skin you are in. You are the guide and lemme guess, you have no idea what the $&#% you are doing! This is an exciting place to begin. None of our growth occurs within our zones of genius or comfort. Knowing now, even if you're afraid to admit it, that you are the guide you've begged the universe to send you, it's time to pull out the maps.

I want to say a word about sacred texts at this point. A map can be hand drawn on a napkin or handed down on an old piece of vellum. It can be up to date from the latest cartography software or street views. All kinds of maps exist to guide people. Here's where I would plop down and say "My map is the Bible" and then just smile awkwardly while you plot your escape plan. But it's more than that—I am guided by the collection of maps that includes a deep and wide variety of sacred texts. So often what keeps us afraid of the dark is a lack of compass—no system of orientation guiding us to where our True North is. For me that system has been a rich spiritual life and rootedness in an inner world, fueled by community and many sacred texts. Belief and trust in something bigger at work in the world and in us has been the compass, showing me where I am and what lies in each direction. A map does not give us directions—navigation software does, but a map shows us what we might expect to see along the way, what roads we might not wish to go down, or what destinations to avoid to get to where we'd like to arrive.

In times of disorientation, a map can help us determine where we are, but there are times in which a map may not be helpful at all.

One of my maps is a love for the Hebrew Bible and Greek New Testament. My love for and fascination with the Protestant Bible began in a United Methodist sanctuary when I learned I could read the Bible they gave me in third grade instead of listening to the preacher's boring sermon. The book of Ruth, when read silently to one's self in the pew, is about the length of a white Anglo-Saxon protestant sermon.

My love for scripture continued as our family became Presbyterian and I was a whizz at memorizing the books it contained during one special summer when I heard the story of Exodus for the first time—the Bible transported me to a magical world of frogs, locusts, rivers of blood, and one brave soul speaking out for a people's freedom. The Bible was something I could be good at—comprehending complex stories, taking in information, and then spitting it out as was useful or impressive to the adults around me.

I learned the Bible is beautiful—a tapestry of stories from different periods and perspectives—even the texts we think of as one cohesive unit—the book of Genesis for example, beneath its hood is composed of multiple sources and voices trying to present a poetic message about where we come from. The Bible has been weaponized against me too—a pastor once sat across his huge desk and calmly, respectfully walked me through how as much as I may sense a call from God, it couldn't possibly be to preach because, tapping his fingers on the very big leather-bound volume, "The Bible forbids it."

Some of my colleagues and peers who know this gorgeous, diverse collection of poems, stories, teachings, and letters used it to condemn me, charging me with adultery (a violation of commandment number seven), but refused to also find the good news within it, to lift out the words of Jesus for adulterers, "Go and sin no more" or the welcome of the prodigal son. Many who have loved and found meaning in this big volume of stories have also been hurt by it, broken by its judgment. But that judgment does not come from the words themselves. Like money, the bible is neutral. It can be a powerful force of healing and reconciliation. It can also be used to hurt, oppress, and ostracize. I have encountered both, but enduringly I can claim that the Bible helps me to see the world new—the sunrise has new meaning against the backdrop of Psalm 19,

> *The sun is like a groom*
> *coming out of his honeymoon suite;*
> *like a warrior,*
> *it thrills at running its course.*

The Bible has helped me to see myself anew, in the face of shortfalls and mistakes and in the promise of new life against the backdrop of 2 Corinthians 5:17:

> *So then, if anyone is in Christ,*
> *that person is part of the new creation.*
> *The old things have gone away,*
> *and look, new things have arrived!*

The Bible helps me to see the world being loved all over again, even in its worn-out, corrosive state. I hear promises of transformation:

> *Look! I'm doing a new thing;*
> *now it sprouts up; don't you recognize it?*
> *I'm making a way in the desert,*
> *paths in the wilderness.*[1]

And yet, I cannot make a case for the Bible for you—but instead, I offer room for lots of sacred texts. In this brutal and beautiful life, the sacred will be the rocks we cling to along the way. During a season of letting people break me with this big book of stories, I

---

1. Isaiah 43:19

needed other stones. Literally, crystals became part of my canon. Even as I write, I carry a Tiger's Eye and Citrin in my pocket, reminding me to boldly tell the truth and confidently accompany you through your hard thing. There's a little plastic owl on the shelf, reminding me to communicate assertively and not shy away from the hard truths. Along with astrology, moon phases, Stevie Nicks, and Tarot, I believe it all works together, and anyone who claims a wide chasm between the "sacred" and the "profane" has not experienced the thin place where all of it converges—where the medium and the priest meet, where the seer and the imam find common ground, where all the world's holy people and sooth-sayers speak a truth that goes beyond dogma and denomination.

In this book, I rely heavily on sacred texts. Sometimes those quotes come from the Bible. But sometimes they are experience-based. All are valid and welcome along the way.

I invite you, gentle wayfinder, to hold these sacred texts with an open hand. If something is new to you, take on a posture of curiosity and wonder. If it is old hat or a place where you have been wounded, dare to hear it in a new way. I can promise I do not take the sacred lightly but take it up with the reverence of a skilled swordswoman.

Throughout this book are stories and reflections, but also invita-tions to practices that will accompany you towards a new begin-ning from some other beginning's end. This book can be read straight through or like a manual, jumping to the chapters most timely to your situation. You already know your wounds and your failures; skip over chapters if you find yourself needing help with a particular aspect of this journey. The book is structured in three parts. We begin with accessing joy, even when shit falls apart; the messy middle helps us to name our losses but not live there; and we conclude by embracing new life. Along the way are both metaphors and practical tools and experiences for finding your way through change and growth. It is a gift to move with you through these periods of transformation. I can promise you won't be the same person at the end of it that you were when you started.

Wayfinding Practice: Find Your Sacred Text

It could be a book, a deck of Tarot cards, a favorite astrologer, or some rocks/crystals that have special meaning to you. In the Christian tradition, we practice "Sacred Reading" or *lectio divina*, in which you choose a passage of scripture, which could be a verse or a mantra, and read it aloud several times slowly, letting the words massage, comfort, or challenge you. Each time you read it, take a moment or two to bask in the verse's meaning and listen for how it is speaking a truth to you in this time.

If you're using something physical and tangible like a crystal, hold it. Let the warmth of your skin heat the stone. Close your eyes and allow it to orient you to the next right thing. Does it have rough edges? Or smooth grooves? Feel its textures and let them shape you.

Many of the steps in finding one's way are made one at a time—we cannot skip ahead to our ending without going through the messy middle. A blessing for your sacred reading: *May the Divine reveal the next right thing on your journey.*

For My Kids

Finding the good inside can often come from asking ourselves one simple question: "What is my most generous interpretation of what just happened?"

— *Dr. Becky Kennedy,* Good Inside: A Practical
Guide to Resilient Parenting Prioritizing
Connection Over Correction

IT'S HARD TO WRITE FOR AN AUDIENCE OF JUST ANYBODY, ESPECIALLY when enough people have nudged you over the years that "you need to share this story," sitting at the keyboard is like serving a penance of thanksgiving to the community who has loved you back to life. The worst mistake I made in laboring with this book-child was to tell my children that I was writing it. "Oh, Mama! Can we read it? Will it be kid-appropriate?" Um, no. Never.

Except, while parents ought to protect their babies from narratives that will hurt them, we cannot protect them from truth, from pain, at every age. I've learned what matters more than scary or mature content for kids, is that they are not left alone to understand and make meaning out of it by themselves. I've often wondered

27

what age will be the appropriate age for my darlings to read the story of their mother emerging from life with their dad in all its messy scandal. Right now they are living this story—and maybe when they are in college, or starting out as young adults they will find this a helpful companion as they build their lives and begin to make new beginnings out of endings. Until then, the book's themes are an ever-present ticker tape of our life together.

This story is *my* story, but it is also theirs. Eventually, the pain of not letting our children know and see us outweighs the fear of what they will see. In these pages, I hope to give my kids a sense of who their mom is as a person, as a flawed and redeemed human being who loved them so much and never as much as they deserved. Some writers think their kids are bored by their stories — perhaps their brokenness and redemption are intertwined so closely that it doesn't delight, fascinate, or enrapture them. Not mine. And if my mother were a writer, I wouldn't be bored by it either. Are our pupils trained from the very beginning to be starving, not for light, but for information about this mother creature whose voice stirred us into being?

A Letter to My Babies About This Book:

Dear Darlings,

There are parts of my story that I am afraid for you to see. In our day-to-day life, I tried to shield you from the anger and hurt I felt towards your father, the prayers I prayed for his untimely death or sudden combustion. But I also want you to see, from a safe place, like watching a fireworks display or a bomb detonating — you are safe, that anger cannot hurt you or those you love. And anger can dissipate. Anger is not forever. Anger is but one voice in the cacophony of human emotions, and I want you to hear the others too. There are laugh lines on my face from the humor I still appreciate in your dad and which you now carry within you. There is pride and so much joy, a deep fountain of it that never runs out for you.

So much of the work of this journey is not sugar-coating the healing process, but it is telling the truth, the godawful bits enveloped in shame, and telling it in a way that sets a path for you through whatever the worst and hardest mistakes are that you will eventually make. And you will make mistakes. Big ones! There is always another side. Your mom is a fire sign, born to a fire sign, who was also born to a fire sign, *and* the youngest child, born to a youngest child, who was also born to a youngest child. That's three generations deep of big, bold, fiery spunk that persists. I want you to hear in these pages that you too know how to persist. Already, you have. I hated breaking your hearts when your dad and I told you we wouldn't be together anymore. You were freshly four and pushing six, and sat on our laps and cried, then asked if you could play *Connect Four*. Everything was no good, horrible, very bad that day. But you persisted. You went back and forth between Dad's house and the air mattresses at Grandma's before we had a place of our own. You persisted.

Before I knew you could persist, you did. You persisted in being born, despite my reservations. Your dad took you on a trip to Dallas recently and showed you White Rock Lake, which is where it began. We walked and walked and he talked and talked about kids, about *his* kids and how important it was "because he loved me" for us to have kids *together*. I didn't want to have children, at least not yet. I still had so much growing up to do. I was twenty-five then, and twenty-two when we were married. I was just in the first months of my first career job as a pastor — a vocation I had dreamed about since childhood, worked towards, prayed about, and felt finally, I was in a place to start on what I hoped would be a long ministry in God's church. I love children, but I didn't see myself as mothering them.

This is an important distinction to make about bodies and autonomy. Never ever should a parent hear "You're pregnant!" and

29

it is not good news. If it's not a "Hell yes!" over-the-moon, best news ever excitement, then it's a no. For me, it wasn't a "Hell yes." It was hours and hours of walking around the lake and listening and allowing my 28-year-old desperate husband to convince me that "Okay. We could do this." Maybe I gave up a part of myself and my wishes too soon. Maybe I wanted your dad to be happy so much that if it meant giving up my body and soul to do it, I would. Once I say "Okay" there is no holding back for me. I am all in. I am ALL IN for being your mom. I know you *know* that, but that day, around White Rock Lake, is when you were born in my mind and heart. You weren't even conceived yet, but in my mind, you existed. And I was your mom. It felt like unlocking a part of myself that not even your dad could access. It was you and me on a journey that hadn't even biologically begun yet. Even if I let a man convince me to go on this adventure — you see, it doesn't matter *how* you arrive at something when it is true and real. You got there. We got here.

And it makes me cry to think about how women's reproductive rights are so much more under attack than they were in 2012 when your dad convinced me to have his babies. I gave in and freely — not under duress. Out of my autonomy, I chose to become your mom. This is rare. What is even more rare is that after I made that choice, getting pregnant was so easy. You already existed in my mind and then boom! You existed in my body and grew. You persisted. Maybe your father's dogged persistence is also what summoned you into the world. You are people who persist.

I didn't know when I started that this book was for you. Not for who you are today or who you were when things fell apart, but for you to see and interpret who you and your parents are as human beings doing their very best to love. I want to insulate you; I have cried many an hour on a therapist's couch to protect you, and do you want to know what she said back to me?

"Why? Why would you want to protect them from this pain? Hasn't this pain made you grow? Why would you hold them back from growth?"

Not all pain makes us grow. Some pain kicks our teeth in irreparably. Some pain cripples us, denies us our inherent right to thrive. But this pain helped us grow. This pain helped us grow and that makes this story one worth telling. In some ways, it is putting our family stuff out in the world for others to see, but this is why I think it's worth it: you remember that book *Everybody Poops*? It's real. Everybody poops *and* everybody messes up at some point in their life, more than once. Some of the mistakes are big and some are not so big. Some are financial, some are spiritual, some are sneaky, some are loud, and just like there are all different ways to get excrement out of your body, you will be surprised as you grow to learn all the ways people can mess up and hurt others, including you! I share our story to help somebody who has messed up or who has been hurt by others' mistakes to know how to go on and be free, to experience joy again and again. I want them to know they can laugh until their faces hurt and their bellies are sore again and that the pain they endured on the way will never not hurt, but it will not always hurt as much or in the same way. We got to learn these truths together and it has made all the difference. These truths are so compelling, they have to be shared with others. So they know and so they can laugh and love and delight in the world again.

All stories start out terrible. We wouldn't like them if they started out great and then it was really bad and then it just sort of never got as great as it was once. That is a crappy story. In this story, some would say I play the victim. At parts, yes, I'll admit that. But not the whole time. Victim stories aren't very good if they're just telling you how bad everyone was to them. But it isn't a hero's story either. I began a fool, and perhaps I end that way too, but in a transformed and beautiful way. This story ends with me as a happy, wise fool, beginning again.

I want you darlings to know that your mama doesn't know everything. I want you darlings to know that joy is possible to be shared with others. That your dad is worthy of joy. I want you to know that I'm sorry that your dad and I couldn't have joy together with you in the same home. There is something truly beautiful about family joy together and I wish I had given it to you in this way. But sometimes we don't get what we want and we learn to feel the disappointment and make the joy with the thing we did get and parenting you has been all joy (and at times, no fun)—so much more joy than I could have imagined. You have taught me that I am stronger, kinder, and braver than I ever thought and that yes, I could do it alone and it is a sign of that courage, kindness, and strength that I chose not to do it entirely on my own.

Is that too much to ask of one book? To be a story for everyone, for anyone, and most especially for two siblings to see their mom as a human being?

Kids, here are some rules for reading this story:

1. **You get to judge me.** I am big enough to handle your hatred and loathing and shaking your head. Whatever your reaction is to the things you will read in these pages, I love you. And I love me enough to share them even if you react in a way that hurts.

2. **Promise me you won't let this story isolate you from the people who love you.** I told you this the day we announced we were getting a divorce, but it bears repeating. There are lots of people who love you. Your connection to the truth doesn't make you deserving of exile. The right people love you more for owning your identity and standing by the ones you love.

3. **Your people will love you fiercely, even when you're wrong.** No matter what mistakes you make, there will be scores of people who will be in your corner, even if they're disappointed in how you eventually make a mess of things (because life is full of messes, and making them is part of how we are human). How do I know? Trust me, I know. There will be people you thought were your people, but how they deal with your truest truths disappoints you and it will be painful to find that they

are indeed, not your people as you thought. But there will still be scores of people who show up in your corner and stay there and love you there.

4. **You have a life that is your very own.** I got the privilege of bringing you into this world, and I hope I'm dead in the ground for a long long time before you take your exit out of it. But I bear no ownership over your life or your choices. Yes, people tell you at every opportunity how much you look like me or how similar our mannerisms are, but baby that's just proximity and strong genes. Genes don't tell you who you are. You get to find that out and tell the rest of us. My choices have had an impact on you, but they are not a determinant for your future, your love prospects, your chances at living and loving whoever you want to and for however long.

You are more than I ever could have imagined. May this true-telling of how I found a new beginning right smack in the middle of what felt like an ending for us be a tiny glimmer in your wonderfully shining journey of life.

Love,
Mama

Wayfinding Practice: Write a Letter to Who or What You Love

Who or what is the deep love of your life? When we go through endings and navigate new beginnings, letter writing is a way to express our hopes, dreams, and fears to an object of our affection beyond ourselves. Pull out a piece of paper and write—what are you afraid of? What does this person, identity, or thing mean to you right now? What do you hope for as you get to the other side of this thing? You don't have to send this letter, but the act of articulating it gives you something to go back to when you are in the middle of transition that can be a sort of "North Star" on your compass.

Circles

And the seasons they go round and round
And the painted ponies go up and down
We're captive on the carousel of time
We can't return we can only look behind
From where we came
And go round and round and round
In the circle game

        — *Joni Mitchell* "The Circle Game"

THE HULA HOOP, THE RINGS OF TREE TRUNKS AND ONIONS, THE HUSHED zinging sound of the mechanical spiral art machine my sisters and I used to go round and round at the kitchen table, making pages of circular designs with awe and wonder— these are the patterns we see in nature, and moments of childhood boredom that remind us of the truth: life is one big circle.

Walter Brueggeman describes humanity's fluctuations between three realities: orientation, disorientation, and reorientation. The times we feel most out of control and like we are "spiraling" are more aptly described as cycling into or out of a phase of orientation, disorientation, or reorientation. The transition is rocky, even if you don't realize at the time that this movement is even happening. We have been conditioned to empathize with others but not with our own experiences—and acknowledging that you deserve grace when orienting to a new job, school, or life situation is hard.

To "Orient" means to point yourself in a particular direction. Orientation is at the root of life, whether it is an orientation we previously held that is going away or learning to see our situation in a new way—reorientation. Orientation is always occurring.

Have you ever had the stinging realization that your life is out of balance with the world around you? My washing machine has the loudest, most noticeable "out of balance" indicator ever—it wobbles with great intensity, making the walls shake, and then a little chime plays that has a small note of panic in it, but seems to sing to me, like a little electronic flute, "Whenever you get the chance, come put me right, so I can make your laundry dance like an Irish spring, which is also the genre of this playful little tune." Life doesn't come with load-off-balance alarms, and if it did, I suspect they wouldn't be nearly as cheerful.

Nevertheless, in the words of Robert Frost who summed up everything he'd learned about life: "It goes on."[1] As it does, each passing day, month, and season give more space and opportunity to see the patterns emerging from our behaviors and habits. Themes begin to emerge from the material of our lives, not to imprison us as victims of circumstance, but to be rich earth from which we grow.

---

1. Robert Frost , on his 80th birthday, speaking to journalist Ray Josephs, 1954

Shell fossils from Morocco, attributed to Alexander Schimmeck,
Unsplash license

Plato taught there was an ideal form that life, art, and beauty
ought to take. Everything in the world is a spin-off or less desirable
dupe of the perfect ideal, spinning out like a spiral. We get more
distant from the model of perfection on an incremental level,
according to Plato. But if we can get farther away, we can also get
closer to it. If a spiral can descend into so-called rock bottom, we
can also spring up from there to rise.

Everything, absolutely everything comes around again. Old
friendships never really die. We carry the gifts, the learnings with
us into new chapters. We came from the soft earth of the ground
and to it, we will return to let new life sprout from our dust. In a
trillion years or so we become stardust in another universe. On a
two-dimensional plane, like a sheet of paper, spirals that have
depth and dynamism to them look like circles. Life is a big circle
through which we grow.

How would our perception of struggle or success shift if we
knew that the farther we get from the things we love, the closer we
were to our true desires? Our truest truthiest truth is on the other
side of releasing the things we depend upon so much, and its often
the thing we resist releasing the most. I wanted to love being
married so much, that I couldn't see how much my marriage to a
person who was not good for me was hurting me and I, him.

Elaine Murray

Circles are everywhere—the circle of life; the cycle of breath and air communing us with the trees; flowers dying and becoming the matter from which new seeds grow; The orbits of the planets around the sun moving in ellipses, getting closer and further away, yet always returning to the same place. When we are born, we are helpless and need someone bigger and stronger to do everything for us; when we die it is the same. "In my end is my beginning," wrote T.S. Eliot. I am at peak adulthood today, the farthest from death I can imagine, and yet from what I've observed, the back half goes faster than the first.

Learning to adjust and assess when the distance from things you care about feels far is part of the task of resilience. So much of our suffering is caught in the web of evaluating every experience as good or bad, then justifying the evaluation, which builds up our egos, exacerbating suffering. When we experience our lives first through the lens of judgment, we become fragile victims to whatever that judgment is, before experiencing it first for what it is, without evaluating it. Recall for yourself the first time you did art as a child. Maybe it was a coloring page or finger painting and with reckless abandon, you scribbled put your mark on the page, thinking, "This is really fun! I love creating!" And then maybe an older child or an authority figure in your life looked at it and began critiquing it: "You should try to stay inside the lines," or "That's not as good as what someone else did," etc. Or maybe they said, "Wow! That is incredible! You are such a talented artist!" We learn from an early age to accept or reject ourselves based on the evaluation of it, which makes us suffer. Even the *good* and positive receptions of our offerings eventually lead to suffering because we learn not to do art for art's sake, or life for life's sake, or love for love's sake, but to seek either reward or punishment as a result of our actions. When we do well, we want everyone to recognize how amazing we are at coloring or public speaking, or counting to a thousand. When we do poorly, we want to protect our tender hearts, which leads to defensiveness and retaliation. At certain points in my own journey, I realized nearly every action I took in a day, was for the purpose of evaluation by me or someone else. It takes a lot of undoing and deconstructive work to get to a neutral perception of an experience I was having—I had to slow down to receive it simply as it was.

Circles are neutral. They neither hope nor despair. Circles remind us that judgment has its limitations. As the Tarot Card, *Wheel of Fortune*[2] shows us, what goes up must come down.

And as Jesus taught, we are to "Give, and it will be given to you. A good portion—packed down, firmly shaken, and over-flowing—will fall into your lap. The portion you give will deter-mine the portion you receive in return."[3] Whatever the content, whether it is material goods or a heavy hand of judgment—this teaching encourages us to enter our pursuits carefully.

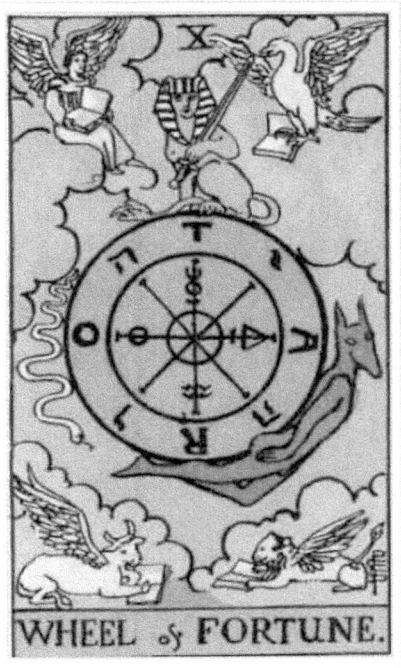

WHEEL of FORTUNE.

---

2. https://pixabay.com/illustrations/tarot-tarot-cards-wheel-of-fortune-6129686/ Used with permission.
3. Luke 6:38

No one can stay at the edges of life's big circle for long. Step on the merry-go-round, carefully, and keep your eyes fixed on something steady lest you lose your way. I have felt that shaken sense of doom like I was the one *inside* the off-balance load in the washing machine. It's disorienting—you cannot find a fixed spot on which to focus and the ground beneath your feet gives way. If you've ever spun around in a circle on a dance floor, without fixing your eyes on an unchanging spot on the wall, your body quickly falls into disorienting dizziness. Within any circle, identifying a fixed spot will keep you grounded.

The fixed spots still move, albeit slowly. The universe is constantly in motion, and if we felt every dynamic sensation, we might all be sick to our stomachs. Gratitude is the practice that's helped me find my still spot on the wall. I begin the day writing a few things for which I am grateful, and noticing. Part of what got my load off-balance was expecting everything to be constant and taking the solid forces for granted. My house may have a firm foundation, but titles transfer and assets are numbers on a page when it comes down to what's real. "The earth is the Lord's and all that is in it,"[4] the psalmist recounts as if to say they are delighted with all that is seen around them, though cognizant it does not belong to one individual or entity apart from the Source.

What will be the fixed spot for you? For some the fixed spot is God, or belief in a divine source of order, goodness, and care. My faith affirms a God who does change, who dances with us in the sea of chaos and energy. God, for me, is *not* a fixed spot on a wall, but a traveler, animant; a dancer in the hula hoop with me.

Losing our way as we move through life's circles is not always a result of error, losing focus, or taking things for granted. Circles come around again. Circles give us new opportunities to show our learnings. While mistakes and grief never fully vanish, the sweetness of wisdom discovered in its time is unmatched. Divorce taught me and my now husband many things about the value of family

---

4. Psalm 24:1

and partnership, but those lessons were not without profound loss, including the casualties of loss experienced by our former spouses.

We lost friends and community, and our relationship with our children and our parents changed profoundly.

And yet, the exhibitions of what heaven is like, what redemptions and healing are like that Jesus proclaims in the New Testament, are of estranged and lost people reunited, lavish, prodigal love poured out—an unbroken circle authored by the divine.

When the sacred silence overcomes my husband—the raucous roar of lament heaves deep inside his chest when his son will not answer him— within him are deep sobs of a father whose child has been taken away. I know the farther the son goes away, the quicker he will return and Rob, like the prodigal father, will wait with the light on and never give up, even though he might say he's done in this moment of anguish.

Like an orbital ellipse, the farther the son goes, the closer he is to his joyful return.

It seems counter-intuitive to enter into and engage your suffering more deeply to get to the other side. We would much rather use any preposition to save ourselves from the agony. But you can't go over, under, around, or beside it. There is only *through*.

There are entire industries built on the belief that we humans are too cowardly to face our own feelings of inadequacy, abandonment, and uncertainty (see: diet culture, payday loans, convenience services and subscriptions who make it hard to cancel). I believe we are more than what we have been underestimated to be. There is no product, drug, or relationship that saves us from catching up to ourselves. Circles are everywhere and the farther we get from ourselves, the close we are to our own return.

Elaine Murray

Circles. (A poem)

In our end is our beginning.
We become again like little children,
Shitting our pants and toddling about
(if we are lucky)
The Wheel of Fortune
And the law of gravity
What goes up must come down
What gets cast out will be brought again to shore.
The most faithful way to live
follows the force that draws us out and away,
trusting it will pull us back again.

Circles are not just shapes; they are life's rhythm, echoing through every experience and emotion. We return to the essence of our beginnings, evolving through the trials and joys that life bestows. Like the Wheel of Fortune, we rise and fall, each movement a necessary part of the grand cycle.

Wayfinding Practice: Scavenge for Circles

Go on a scavenger hunt for circles. Where do you see them in nature? In your home? Where do you come across them? Hold one in your hand.

What's it made of? Copper? Stone? Mineral? Glass? Consider how it was formed. What had to be beaten or melted or given time to settle and become, even fossilize to take the shape and form it has now. What, do you imagine, it is in the process of becoming? If it's a coin, it will be spent for something, I'm sure. What kind of new life or lives could it have? Carry this circle or draw it or take a picture of it to remind you that whatever dead end you find yourself in right now will begin again, will take new shape and form with time.

The Uppity Inside Voice

Have patience with everything unresolved in your heart and try to love the questions themselves... Do not now seek the answers, which cannot be given you because you would not be able to live them. And the point is, to live everything. Live the questions now.

— *Rainer Maria Rilke*, Letters to a Young Poet

THE 1990S PURITY CULTURE STRUCK THE BIBLE BELT WITH SUCH ferocity that it didn't matter if you were an Evangelical Christian or not, at some point you were going to question, as a young woman, if and how everything you did was a temptation for a man, causing one of your "brothers" to stumble. At the same time, our moms were counting points on *WeightWatchers* and we were binging Snackwell's Devil Food Cakes while working out with Richard Simmons and Denise Austin on TV. "Nothing tastes as good as skinny feels" is still an annoying mantra I occasionally excavate from the back forty of my mental landscape. Where's the spiral eyes emoji when you need it?

As an adolescent, I looked at my parents and longed for the peaceful, settledness that came with finding "The one my soul loves"[1] —*the ONE*, the man I would marry, all while navigating how to live in this body of mine, how to find a place in the world that was constantly growing and expanding, even as society and culture encouraged me to shrink and take up less space in it. Joshua Harris' *I Kissed Dating Goodbye* and the follow-up memoir about meeting, courting, and marrying his now ex-wife Shannon in *Girl Meets Boy* shaped my sense of order, achievement, and "arrival" into adulthood. I thought a God-fearing husband would fix me, with the same desperation I believe a perfect cup of coffee might now.

When I entered college, I had the intellectual capacity and passion for changing the world, but beneath it all was a secret yearning to meet *The One*. Never one to miss a goal or a deadline, I found him. X was an admissions counselor at my small liberal arts college with whom I immediately became smitten —he was tall, nerdy, and liked yoga and organic vegetables. At 23, he was barely not a student himself and we shared an awkward sense of humor and tender outlook towards the world. Our courtship was stunningly romantic—the friends I called as soon as he left my apartment at the end of our first date referred to him as *"The Notebook guy"* after the popular Nicholas Sparks novel turned film during our college years. He swept me off my feet. If my heart had been something to possess, when I met X, it was *begging* to be bought, owned, and cared for. Many young women raised around more traditional gender roles and households felt this way. Cole Porter's song, "My Heart Belongs to Daddy" summarized the patriarchal dynamic many of us Bible Belt girlies felt, that we first belonged to our fathers until a suitable man entered our lives who proved he could take over the care and keeping of us from there. This order of things, that "First comes love, then comes marriage, then comes the baby in the baby carriage" was the standard I held myself to, even subconsciously, as I searched for my own compass through adolescence and into adulthood.

---

1. Song of Solomon 3:4

In the absence of a compelling counter-narrative, we go with the ones we've inherited.

My charmed childhood came with stability and privilege; I never went hungry and my homes were always comfortable and safe. This firmly upper-middle class existence also included a set of tacet rules I'd learned to follow in my conditioning. Even with the inherited generational wealth of quality healthcare access, warm and nurturing homes, and enough money to buy a lot of choice in life, our society is still built on a framework which convinces women that taking up less space increases your value, and speaking kind words softly without ruffling any feathers makes you palatable and desirable. Some of this I learned through church, but most of it I learned through being socialized in the time and place that I did.

When you've been given so much, a nagging sense of guilt accompanies any temptation to find your voice or your truth. Why go looking? Meaning has been handed to you. Just take your nice house, paid for car, and determined path as a teacher/subservient pastor/wife and be grateful. That wasn't enough for me. It wasn't truthful enough. I thank God for that uppity inside voice that resisted the scripts I'd been handed. Even if I didn't feel brave enough to always listen to that voice, it was that voice inside that helped me torch the old life and embrace something new.

That uppity inside voice led me to get out of my small town and go abroad in high school. The uppity inside voice led me down less conventional paths than the ones laid out before me. The uppity inside voice woke me from the numbing slumber of my early twenties when I had been going through the prescribed steps of "First comes love, then comes marriage" part of my inherited life script. After graduate school, the questions and the begging eyes began from the man I loved, longing for me to fulfill the next piece of the chant, "then comes the baby in the baby carriage." The question "Can we have kids now?" plagued our every interaction. The uppity inside voice tried to show me I didn't have to follow a prescribed path in this marriage thing. There was a truth inside of me, shaking the walls of my being, saying, "I'm alive in here! Stop talking over me!" The cajoling for children got my attention. That's when I started to see that none of my other desires mattered in this marriage. It didn't matter how I wanted to grow professionally, or where I wanted to live, or what kind of dining room table we had or what kinds of clothes I wore or car I drove. What mattered was would I be willing to procreate with him, to do my duty as a Christian wife that all my life had been building me up towards. This wasn't just a question from X, this was a question from my entire upbringing. How could I say no?

I know now that the correct answer when someone asks if you will have their babies is either, "Hell yes!" or "No." If they ask again, the answer is still, "No." No is a complete sentence. You do not owe them your storied past with eating disorders and body dysmorphia. You do not owe them stories from your childhood or your doubts and fears that you might not be a good mom or will screw up the hypothetical offspring. You don't owe them anything except an honest "Hell yes!" or "No." Even if you present these other offerings, they will not honor them. These are really good discoveries to make before you decide to get married.

While I followed the life plan of love/marriage/baby carriage, what wasn't as neatly scripted for me was the discovery that I carry the BRCA-1 genetic mutation, making me a zillion times more susceptible to contracting breast, ovarian, pancreatic, and colorectal cancers. I didn't know this when I was asked, "Would you have our baby?" but I would add it to the things my body knew when I overrode its internal "Hell no!" answer.

We each carry something. Whether genetic or circumstantial or environmental, there is no such thing as a perfect life. Often our "hards" come to us by chance more than choice. We might never understand why we had the disability or generational trauma or abusive situation that happened to us.

A Church History professor from seminary once explained that every one who has ever been ousted by the church's leadership and declared a heretic, was someone *impatient with mystery*. For example, one of the early church's first disagreements was in trying to determine if Jesus was fully human *and* fully God. How does that work? How could it possibly? Rather than sitting with the question and working it out together, the Docetists, eventually declared heretics (people whose beliefs opposed those of the church's majority), voiced their conviction that Jesus couldn't possibly have *really* been a human being. His earthly body was an *illusion* and they leaned hard into the divinity of Christ instead. Being patient with mystery and developing the capacity to hold on to life's "whys" without a clear explanation is something we grow into—we are not born with this inherent ability. And yet, every time we draw a line around ourselves and our beliefs, over and against someone else's actions and convictions, I firmly believe the presence of God is on the other side of that line.

While my small, squeaky, 25-year-old voice finally submitted to bearing the children of the forlorn man in front of me who wanted to procreate more than anything else, I believe God's presence was stirred on the side of the uppity inside voice I overrode—the one that was screaming "Hell no!" while I held a hand over her and went X's way on this choice.

Where have you heard your truth speaking inside of you? Do you recall a time when you ignored or denied it in favor of something or someone else? Ignoring my uppity inside voice had consequences that would come later. But at the time, oh it felt good to please the voices outside of me.

In Bible Belt purity culture, we love to blush at the sensual verses in *Song of Solomon*. The writer compares his beloved's breasts to "two fawns" and "clusters of grapes"—I can hardly write these words without turning a little crimson. But amidst all the sexy language delighting in bodies and physical intimacy, the chorus of women chimes in throughout the book, warning, "Do not awaken love until it desires!" Whispering for us, to be patient and let mystery unfold. Turns out there's an uppity inside voice in scripture too. This voice longs to be heard and will make itself known.

Wayfinding Practice: Live Into Your Questions

Make a list of your questions. Don't answer them. Next time a child or someone who looks up to you asks you a question, practice taking a pause before answering. Let's retire the phrase "because I said so." I mean really, it just perpetuates a sense of false confidence, right?

Learn to love your questions. Carry them with you. Add to the list. Question the choices you made that led you to the place you are at this point in your life. Writing down and learning to love the questions will lead you to be curious and curiosity is a form love takes. Learning to love your questions will make you more compassionate.

The Ticking Time Bomb

What we're seeking is an experience of being alive, so that our life experiences on the purely physical plane will have resonances with our own innermost being and reality, so that we actually feel the rapture of being alive.

— *Joseph Campbell,* The Hero's Journey

HOW MANY UNPRECEDENTED ECONOMIC DOWNTURNS CAN ONE generation live through before they become "cyclical" or "expected" or "precedented"? In 2008, during one of my generation's first economic downturns, a pastor told us we were "Hogging all of the grace in the universe" when we were offered full rides to continue our education in a new city together. While hints and red flags popped up like wildflowers in that season, I think back to it as a time of innocence and sunshine. He would become a clinical psychologist, I would become a pastor. We would take on the world's traumas as a team, transforming the church, transforming the field of mental health *together*.

Around the time our second child was born, a family cancer

diagnosis led my sisters and I to get the BRCA genetic testing, and all three of us had the BRCA1 mutation, making us more suscep-tible to breast, ovarian, and pancreatic cancers. Our grandmother died too soon from ovarian cancer, and our beloved older cousin was being treated for cancer in her breast. It was like swallowing a ticking time bomb receiving the news. You know how Captain Hook goes into that anxious spin every time the crocodile who swallowed the clock comes near? We heard the "tick tock tick tock" all day and all night inside our own bodies.

When I met with the genetic counselor, she kindly and boldly shared a piece of paper with charts on it that explained my risk for developing cancer from now (age 28) to 88. It was no longer a ques-tion of *if* I would get cancer, but at what age the diagnosis would come. I felt my body betrayed me. My genetic inheritance had doomed me. My gender identity seemed off—why was I born a woman if my woman parts would ultimately kill me?

"Out, out, get out!" is what I thought when I looked at my breasts, when I held my abdomen. As if periods and cramps and PMS and milk stains were not enough of a curse, now this? I was already low on sleep parenting a two-year-old and a newborn while pastoring a church full time. Now my mortality tick tocked through my insomnia. I couldn't get the prophylactic surgeries soon enough.

The google searches that had once been:

- *When will my pregnancy show?*
- *When will I stop feeling like I got hit by a bus (first trimester)?*
- *What if I don't do the 12 week genetic test?*
- *What is normal pregnancy discharge?*
- *Tips for giving birth without drugs*
- *Midwife vs hospital delivery*
- *Hypnobirthing*
- *When will this pregnancy end?*
- *When will my milk supply come in?*

- *Should I wake the baby every two hours?*
- *How do I know my baby is getting enough milk?*
- *Cluster Feeding*
- *Pumping*
- *Low milk supply*
- *When do the 4 am feedings stop?*
- *When will the baby sleep through the night?*
- *Foods to boost milk supply*
- *Faster ways to wash breast pumps*
- *Sample schedule for breastfeeding and pumping while working*

Were now:

- *Right age for preventative double mastectomy*
- *Hysterectomy side effects*
- *Removing fallopian tubes to prevent ovarian cancer*
- *Ovarian cancer symptoms*
- *Breast cancer symptoms*
- *BRCA age recommended surgeries*
- *Mastectomy and reconstruction*
- *Will I still have sensation after mastectomy*
- *DIEP flap reconstruction*
- *How much time off for DIEP flap?*
- *DIEP vs implants*
- *How to prepare for DIEP and mastectomy*
- *How soon can I hold my kids after double mastectomy?*
- *Recovery time from salpingectomy*
- *Sample letter for medical leave for prophylactic surgery*

As soon as I was able, when my son was about six months old, I started with getting my fallopian tubes removed. The research was still in process, though leaning in a positive direction, that ovarian cancer likely begins in the little finger-like ends of the fallopian tubes, where it is hard to spot or feel any tumors. We didn't have exact numbers of how much it would cut my risk, but it would at least make the ticking time bomb a little softer in my mind, and end my child-bearing days, which was a relief. X was with me through the surgery and through the genetic counseling after my BRCA testing. He insisted that this was my body and my choice with his words (finally), but I think my insistence on being done having kids stung a little.

I was fortunate to be close to the best plastic surgery specialists in the country whose expertise was in deep inferior epigastric perforator (DIEP) flap reconstruction, which meant after the removal of my breast tissue and mammary glands, the microsurgeons would spend eight hours relocating fat, skin, blood vessels and nerve endings from my belly to where my breasts had been, resulting in a naturally warm, soft breast that fluctuated in size the same way my body had once stored fat in my belly, and in place of my "mom pooch," I had a scar from hip to hip reflecting that I had been a woman sawed in half who survived. The recovery time from the first surgery was eight weeks of not picking up or holding my one- and three-year-old. At the same time, we were in the middle of a kitchen renovation, so the walls of our home reflected what was taking place under my abdomen concurrently: "Closed for Remodeling."

When you look back at the wreckage, it's easy to spot the parts where things went off course. I believe couples are capable of surviving lots of things together. Things like chronic illness, children's health troubles, death of loved ones, moves, vocational crises, etc. are not death sentences for the relationship. They are navigable storms, but with a big warning: you may not like or recognize who you become on the other side of them. Maybe if we close our eyes and rip the bandaid off all at once, it will be over and we'll get back to the way things should be or were before, or where the happy ending is. But in the remodeling stage, whether physical, relational, spiritual, or other kind of reorienting undertaking, we're getting to know our new selves in real time while the old is going away and the change is happening.

"Speed thee slowly" or *festina lente*, if you need a cryptic tattoo idea. In such moments we both grieve what was and welcome what's to come. The speed of this change can splinter us in a second. "Let's just get it over with" is not the wisest motto for such experiences, as I came to learn.

Wayfinding Practice: Practice the Pause

Pump the brakes! Whatever you are going through, take a pause, take a moment to allow yourself some nostalgia. Memorialize it. Light a piece of paper on fire or burn a picture of what is going away. Write it on a plate and take it in the yard to break it into pieces. When I prepared for my mastectomy, I had a "boob cake" made by a local baker with the blessing "Thanks for the mammaries!" to celebrate with friends this big undertaking— the end of a literally life-giving chapter and the openness to what was on the other side. Make art to symbolize the transition you are in. One of my favorite ways to slow down and allow for an ending to end and a new beginning to begin is to pay attention to the dates on the perishable items I buy. For example, the ketchup in my pantry expires in 2027. Where will I be then? Where will this book be by then? Dear God, hopefully out in the world. When I got laid off from a job, I went to the store and began stockpiling enough coffee and collagen to get me through the severance they offered. Each morning when mixing my beverage I imagined, "What kind of work will I be doing by the time I have to buy more coffee and collagen?" These tangible practices empower us to practice *wonder* while time ticks on. Practice completing the sentence, "I wonder…" like "I wonder if it will rain today" or "I wonder where this walk will take me." "I wonder what these lab results will tell me." Practice saying or writing these phrases with as little anxiety as possible. Even allow a smile to form while you imagine not just the worst, but what the best possible outcomes could be.

Grow, Grow, Grow Your Boat

A ship in its harbor is safe; but that's not what ships are built for.

— *John A. Shedd*

Writing this story, I wanted to speak truthfully about resilience—not as an abstract idea, but as the deeply personal journey it is, one tied to faith, identity, and transformation. This story is about how, through the unexpected, I found my way through spiritual turbulence and personal loss, toward something new. It's a journey that involves mistakes, pain, and infidelity—but also growth, healing, and a mystic understanding of God's presence.

It might hurt to read. Infidelity affects 1 in 4 marriages,[1] which means the lives it touches are much more than that. You may have been cheated on, or been raised by people who cheated on each other or one person left the other before the relationship had ended. It may be your family's big secret. Or maybe it just makes you feel ick. Hold those feelings and honor them. And enter with me into

---

1. "Predictors of infidelity among couples" in *The Journal of Sexual Medicine* (2024) Charlene F Belu, PhD, Lucia F O'Sullivan, PhD

this true thing, that on the other side, you might take with you a blessing for your own truth.

Spring brings new life, a giddiness that makes us want to escape routine and embrace the world with energy and wonder. It's a season of blooming, of renewal—and a time to reflect on our own spiritual growth.

Spring gives us a hunger for something more than the dregs of winter. Easter is the cornerstone of a pastor's Spring. The forty days of Lent are like a great purple drape we drag over the congregation if only to pop out on Easter with a "Hallelujah!" Jack-in-the-box, the-tomb-is-empty surprise. Lent comes from the old English word for "lengthen"—corresponding to the lengthening of days that occurs in the springtime, where perhaps we ought to give some thought and attention to our spiritual growth. On a practical level, that looks like giving something up (fasting) or taking on a new practice (like participating in a Lenten devotional).

All this seasonal change can be exhausting too. On one of these Spring days I was so exhausted visiting a saintly old choir member that while she chatted away, I accidentally dozed off in her apartment recliner. I'm not sure if she noticed, but the sun was so perfectly warm, the chair so cozy, and I had not slept in so long.

It was in this blur of sacred ordinary days, that the day's work called me to a presbytery meeting—a quarterly regional gathering of church elders and pastors to do things like commission one another for special mission projects, hear reports on the good we'd been up to in our corners of South Texas, and sneakily read the list of everyone's updated salaries to measure where we stacked up compared to our colleagues. This isolated extrovert pastor longed for opportunities to gather with colleagues and the larger church who knew me well. Even when the meetings were in unfamiliar contexts, the community gathered there was like an oasis; just to *be* present with my thoughts in worship I wasn't planning was a respite.

Just as spring is a season of new growth, so too can moments of spiritual awakening come after periods of deep personal struggle.

For me, that awakening came unexpectedly in the midst of a professional and personal crisis. During this time I found myself at a crossroads, where I could either continue down a path of frustration and doubt—or allow myself to open up to something new.

The opportunity was rare in those days, for neither of us to be surrounded by other people. Yes, we were in plain sight, in a church lobby with multitudes around us, each of us in our way was experiencing a momentary stay against the confusion of the world, and spotted the other. "Rob!" I said with a warm smile washing over me. My little introverted pal was seated on a cast-aside pew in his tie and khaki slacks, canvas satchel next to him. He sheepishly grinned and responded familiarly, "Kid!" As he rose from his seat, we stood with knowing looks for the other as if we were two comrades peeking in from battle for a moment.

Pause: One might suspect that was when we were falling in love, but it couldn't be farther from what was happening. We were colleagues; friends. No "just" implied. Collegiality and friendship were the fullness of how we related. Our spouses and our kids were protected, walled off, in another world of domestic intimacy. Not something cast aside, but a precious flower to be protected and fought for, within its castle walls.

As we caught up on the latest in each other's church lives, I nodded understandingly while he shared what a pain it had been to document the office manager for her infractions in anticipation of her resignation. He knowingly smiled as I conveyed the exhaustion of developing a weekly sermon wondering if I was wasting my passion and skills in this little country church. Our interaction was so innocent—like how I imagine it was for Adam and Eve in the garden, before sin entered the picture, to take in each plant, each natural cycle of creation, and each animal's unique, and at times laughable nature.

While we laughed and wondered at what was going on in the lands that God had shown us of church vocational life, my colleague floated that there was an opening for an Associate Pastor to come to work with him at the church in my hometown. Was I interested? Did I know anybody? Another colleague had messaged me a week before to express her interest in applying for the position herself. But no, I didn't think I could ever go back to the church that raised me.

We had a female Associate Pastor when I was growing up. Kind of a hippy, who wore Birkenstock sandals, and woven stoles, and was the least feminine person I could think of. She played guitar, preached blissfully short sermons, wore transition lenses and a butch haircut. I shook my head. "Not me, pal. I don't wanna be a Verna."

Verna was a second-wave feminist—a divorcee, single mom, whose parents were members of the church. Everybody knew that Verna didn't get along with Tim, the dry, academic Senior Pastor. It almost seemed like her lack of femininity was *on purpose*, which I've since learned is a tactic many "lady" pastors have used to survive the inherently sexist dynamics of ministry in the church.

I used to see Verna as a model of who I didn't want to be, but in hindsight, I realize her courage to be herself helped me embrace my own uniqueness.

A few weeks later, I met with Rob in town to discuss the church's needs. As we talked, I admitted, "Sometimes I just say things without thinking." He smiled, "I know."

Within months, Pastor Rob was standing at the front of the chapel with his acoustic guitar, an old Martin he's had since his seminary days, gently plunking out "This is the day that the Lord has made" before and alongside the voices of delighted and squealing preschool children, of whom Pastor Elaine's kids are a part.

The task for the church was simple: grow.

The task for the pastors was to grow the church spiritually, numerically, and financially.

What we know now is that those areas of growth are sometimes in conflict with each other. You challenge people to grow spiritually and they may cut you off at the knees financially (chances are high that they will). You grow a church numerically and struggle to meet its spiritual needs or keep up with what the Mystery of God is stirring up. Jesus' Great Commission to "Go therefore and make disciples of all nations" doesn't always align with capitalist aims.

And yet another possibility is that God's Spirit *does* take hold of a congregation and leads them far away from their pastors' convictions, or takes hold of the pastors' lives in a direction few are comfortable with.

But how it began was in the sunshine. The field was wide open, including the one we walked across to meet one morning for our first "Pastors' Retreat," a quarterly day we took away from the church building to plan, dream, scheme, and take the "balcony view"[2] of what all was going on with those we were called to love. The first day, meeting at a local park in the heartbeat of our small town we said, "This feels big. It could be heaven or it could be hell, but we're up for God's adventure." We thought the heaven or hell piece was about what God was doing through us in ministry, with no thought or nod towards the fact that he was a guy and I was a girl, or how affairs happen, or that we could relate at all on a sexual level.

When I called my pal, C, after I was kicked out of my home, she said "What disturbs me the most is that you think this shit is the will of God." I nodded through tears.

Me too, sister. Me too.

How did we get to thinking this was the will of God?

In the ravishing tale, *If You Give A Mouse A Cookie*, children learn what we humans know to be true about ourselves: way leads on to way. First the cookie, then the crumbs, then the milk, the napkin, the cleaning, the bath, the nap, and so on. First comes love, then comes marriage, then comes the baby in the baby carriage, then things fall apart, then there's an affair, then comes the decision to

---

2. "Balcony View" is a concept that refers to getting above the noise of a particular context to be able to see far—like going up to the balcony to look down on the dance floor for a different perspective of what needs to happen from Ron Heifetz and Marty Linsky's *Leadership on the Line: Staying Alive through the Dangers of Change.* Harvard Business Review Press, 2002.

stay together or split, and so on. We make our way towards solutions we never could have imagined for ourselves one little step at a time. Each step chips away at the strong walls we put up that say "Oh I would *never* cheat on my spouse." But boundaries—these walls around ourselves, our relationships—when so rigid have no give to them. They crumble. A healthier image for a boundary is more cellular membrane than castle wall. There is some "give" in all of us—we don't always say no to our children's requests for a treat, but we don't always say yes either. Affairs begin long before a boundary is crossed. They stem from inner pain, a longing for something outside ourselves to fix what's broken within. We often think rescue will come from a change in circumstances—but it's not the fix we imagine.

We often think rescue will come from somewhere else—a move, a baby, a new job, an award or recognition. I can say that X and I had all of those things and none of them were a salve on what had broken between us. It was much easier to focus on the brokenness everywhere else and be a fixer than to question and self-reflect on what was not right within me and where my own pain lived. I imagine Eve in the Garden of Eden—what if she had taken a moment to herself after the serpent beckoned her towards the tree of knowledge of good and evil? What if she had asked, "What in me is missing?" My own answer was safety, courage, and love. I didn't feel safe with X, after being manipulated into birthing children, after many nights waking up realizing we were in the middle of intercourse during which I was asleep. I didn't feel brave anymore when the same concerns were met with disregard and a shoulder shrug but no meaningful solutions or empathy. I didn't feel loved anymore, but that was too scary to admit aloud. To answer my friend who said she hated that I thought this affair was the will of God, I turn again to a children's book: *What is God Like?* By Rachel Held Evans and Matthew Paul Turner.

"Whenever you aren't sure what God is like, think about what makes you feel safe, what makes you feel brave, and what makes you feel loved."[3] As Rob and I navigated our friendship and professional collaboration, something profound began to emerge—a recognition of the importance of safety, courage, and love, not just in the context of our work but in our own lives. These were the qualities that I had been yearning for but had been unable to name until I encountered them in the raw honesty of our connection. In many ways, this was the beginning of a spiritual awakening—a wayfinding toward healing that wasn't about finding perfection, but about embracing the brokenness and letting that become the catalyst for transformation.

It wasn't right for Rob and me to turn to each other before communicating that our prior marriages were done. What we learned about ourselves while trying to "grow, grow, grow" a church was that growth is messy, uncomfortable, and complicated. Couples who begin with infidelity fear their relationship will suffer the same fate. Two broken people who used one another to deal with the stress in their lives, could one day turn to another when the source of their stress is the marriage itself, or the primary relationship. Rob and I began not with any kind of passionate encounter, but as one safe space for the other one. We fell in love one meeting, one drive, one training run, one bike ride at a time.

Often the pastoral vocation is a public one, but securing the space away from others to think, strategize, and listen to God's voice is key to meaningful ministry. In a two-pastor model, building in alone time and together time apart from meetings, committees, and observers is necessary. Our custom was to drive to a country road outside the city limits to do our long training runs for the half-marathon which sounded better in theory than in practice. We would pound out the miles on our hot feet and pavement, avoiding cow-patties and leaping, or cautiously tiptoeing over cattle-guards. For hours, the conversation meandered between crappy emails we'd received, dreams we had of kickass worship services (I know, pastor fantasies, right?), weird insights we had in

---

3. *What is God like?* By Rachel Held Evans and Matthew Paul Turner

prayer or bible study that we'd never share from the pulpit, but experienced as foundational or pivotal for our faith journeys.

Be careful who you pray with. Who you study scripture with. It's a great way to find a friend, deepen a friendship, or even destroy a marriage. I hate to blame Jesus for the destruction of my first marriage, but something was born on that road, grafted with each footfall and moment of splendid stupidity. Rob and I fell into one another along the way.

After the race, we needed an excuse to continue these holy escapades: really, just exercise for the body, mind, and spirit. We started road-biking that same beautiful country road, learning the gears and delicate balance of "clipping in," feeling like Lance Armstrong but much, much slower. I craved those times. People aren't delicacies to be devoured, but the heart is ravenous. The heart wants to love and be loved in return. To love should be life-giving—not easy, but it should feel like breathing deeper. Like exercise, the practice of loving another person should be good for your metaphysical joints. Yet something is disturbing about real love—perhaps why we keep ours hidden behind marital fences, so as not to blind one another all the time, and experience that beautiful brilliance like a controlled burn, safe for neighborhoods and living communally.

Some of our deepest vulnerability sharing began on Sunday afternoon bike rides. After church and lunch with our families, most warm afternoons beckoned us onto the bikes.

In the deafening silence from those I considered friends and peers in this wreckage after being discovered, I recognize their silence as the fear that I carried some sickness, an "infidelity influenza" that would come for them next. Myriad reasons exist as to why someone, especially someone who never saw themselves as "the type" to cheat, does. There are lots of different types of affairs. When X and I were preparing for our marriage, we said an affair wouldn't ever break us—we'd work through it, like my parents had and like we'd seen was possible, particularly with the older couples in our lives. Perhaps he would have been more understanding if it had been an actual affair, a one-night stand, or a drunk meet-up in a hotel. Is what Rob and I did worse or less honorable because we actually love each other? I wouldn't throw this away for a one-night stand, but to recognize that enough to say, "Yes, I love him, and not you" is perhaps a marriage worth leaving. I thought I was willing to love X too, though now I know this was another instance of me plastering over that uppity inside voice that had told me to run before. Finally, it was X realizing that he was not willing to love me which was a catalyst for change.

When I moved back to my hometown, so many thought it was coming home, coming full circle. The reality looked more like a burned-out psychologist and a minister clanking into town with a not-yet one-year-old baby, an almost three-year-old who peed all over the place because her kidneys didn't work right, trying to hold that shit together with duct tape, and a moving van. I wanted to be somewhere safe—and of the places I'd been so far, I had, on a level, felt compromised in one way or another.

At the country church before now, my body and family were not mine. If I breastfed my baby, it was an offense (yes, even on Christmas Eve—when Christians celebrate the *birth* of a *baby* to a *human Mother*). If I didn't make it to the hospital in the next town over, I was neglectful of my people. If I stayed too late finishing bulletins, I would be negligent of my family. When Rob floated the Associate Pastor opening at the church with him in my hometown, X happened to find a tenure track professorship in his field at the local college, exclaiming, "Elaine, this is my *dream job*!" I banked on the safety of home.

Resilience isn't about avoiding pain, but about learning to navigate our vulnerability, trusting that God's presence is with us even in our brokenness. For me, it meant embracing love, accepting my mistakes, and knowing I was never alone on this journey.

Wayfinding Practice: Focus on the Physical

Often when we are on a spiritual path, we approach it at the expense of our physical health. No, this practice isn't about finding someone to have sex with! But here is an invitation to invest in your physical embodiment. "The body keeps the score" trauma therapy tells us and our bodies often possess a level of wisdom our minds and emotions come around to later. Where is your body aching? What would give it what it needs?

Sometimes aching bodies need a good soak in the tub, but sometimes our bodies are restless and need to go pound some pavement. Do you long to be touched? Explore your own body. Close your eyes. Touch your skin, and give yourself a warm embrace. Move around, if safe to do so, with your eyes closed. Put your hand on your heart. Can you feel your heart beating? Your breaths going in and out? You are alive, and that is a miracle.

Drink a glass of water in silence. Let its cool refreshment enter into and nourish your body and cells. Plant your feet in a wide stance, if possible while barefoot and touching the earth. Close your eyes and breathe, while your toes squeeze the ground between them. You are at home in your own body. Your body is yours and belongs to no one else. You are growing at a particular rate, yes even as an adult, your cells are renewing and new life is entering into you even now. You are becoming and while you are becoming you have a home in your body where you are safe, brave, and loved.

The Journals

Write what disturbs you, what you fear, what you have not been willing to speak about. Be willing to be split open.

— *Natalie Goldberg*

I AM A JOURNALER. SINCE MY EARLY TEENS, I'VE SCHLEPPED A SMALL notebook with me to chronicle my observations, questions, and deep thoughts that the world showed me were too deep, too probing, and unwelcome for polite company. My first journal started while camping out on a church balcony on the south side of Chicago during a church youth group trip. I was the youngest student on the trip, and in a moment of desperation realized I had to write down all the things running through my head if I was going to get any rest.

Since then I've filled fifty some-odd books with to-do lists, devotionals, prayers, musings, poetry, and various stages of preaching. My journal is the place where I process anything that feels too big to solely rely on my senses to understand. Way leads on to way in the writing process. I found the more I tucked away to jot down a thought or two, the more my mind would wander to what else I could note for future me to peruse or ponder in days, weeks, years to come.

Many people have engaged the practice of journaling at one time or another. Like running, or any other form of discipline, once people find out I'm a "journaler" I often hear about their poor experiences with it, or why it wasn't a practice that stuck. One of the most common refrains is some variation of, "I started, but then when I looked back at what I wrote it just felt silly and stupid." Oy vey! Yes, absolutely. I still have the first journal I started at fourteen. I actually looked back on a sheet of yellow legal pad I started on much earlier than that—even at age six, where I chronicled my experience of watching Richard Nixon's funeral processional on TV in our church basement while the adults showed what were to my child brain out-of-character emotional reactions. Writing has helped me process the things I see with my eyes and feel deeply with the heart. Some of those observations seem stupid or silly in hindsight, but all of them were allowing me to absorb something true.

Sometimes it is the feel of the pen stroking the page and the unique movement of my wrist, bobbing up and down, especially when something is emotionally charged or I'm feeling feverishly creative. Typing on a keyboard doesn't do the same thing, although the loud clacking of typewriter keys has a similar catharsis.

Journals are precious to me. I never keep them under lock and key, and have been known to abandon an open one on a table to fill another cup of coffee, wipe a toddler's bottom, or answer the door. In my home, I keep completed ones on the bookshelves, right next to my volumes of Emily Dickinson, Brené Brown, and *Harry Potter*. They are part of the hygge aesthetic, a subtle nod to the vulnerability I feel when inviting others into my home. To invite them, even to see the spines on the shelves, is to usher them into the reality that I am a soft, squishy human. One day while at my home, Rob asked, "You don't think X ever reads your journals, does he?" Knowing my stream of consciousness style before the blank page, I could sense a note of worried questioning in his voice. "Of course not!" I casually laughed it off.

Boy was I wrong.

On August 30th, when I scrambled to pack a bag and leave, go anywhere but there, my current journal was in my gigantic mom purse, but on a whim, I thought I'd grab the most recent few from the last year and a half to look over while, in my mind, making the irrefutable case for why X should give me another chance. Our kids were four and almost six then, so the house was a typical mess of clutter and piles—I assumed the books were somewhere lost in the shuffle and shrugged it off.

As the weekend unfolded, I became more desperate to get my hand on the old evidence—to reflect on how I got to this place of suddenly being *without*. Without spouse, without home, without a place to belong.

Finally I asked X directly—"Have you seen my green journal? I thought it was on the dresser shelf, but I can't seem to find it and I'd really like to have it."

He knew exactly where it was, along with four others.

He'd stolen my journals—five of them. I honestly couldn't imagine a world where someone would intentionally want to hurt me like this, much less the person I'd spent my adulthood beside, who had watched babies come out of my body—surely not him. He said he was making copies and that he would return them. Making copies? Why would someone want to copy the contents of my stream of consciousness daily reflections? I had sermon snippets in there, copious reflections on my own self-doubt and imposter syndrome and of course, a few spicy bits about the great sex I was having.

He held them captive for weeks. Copying them at his attorney's office, he said. Paying someone top dollar to run page by page through a Xerox machine, and then to catalog the contents of them by theme.

I have no idea who all they were shared with except for Rob's wife. And I can imagine, two lonely, betrayed people with copies of some juicy accounts of their spouses' dalliance would be irresistibly difficult not to share beyond that.

Later I learned that extended family saw them and heard accounts of the juicy snippets X saw fit to categorize into subheadings like "Abandonment of the Family" and "Intensely Cruel/Vindictive." One excerpt from the cruel and vindictive bit was where I wrote that I had come to realize, even if my mother in law *died*, I would never be free of her power in our family, in our relationship. In "Abandonment of the Family"—all the times I ranted about how noisy my kids were or that trying to find some peace of mind when I could still hear the pitter patter of their little feet was pushing me to the edge.

I'm proud of what I wrote there. Sometimes the prayers of the faithful are ugly and hard, but they are true and real. I stand by what I said. In those pages are life and truth. It is *damn* hard to be creative when your kids have needs that only you can ease.

X swore my journals would "never see the light of day" but they—he and Rob's wife— "needed to hold on to them for collateral" they said. Collateral is what the bank wants to guarantee that you'll repay the loan they give you. What did I owe to get those journals back? The journals that were…mine? It turns out, it would cost about $45,000 in legal fees. At the time, the grief-monster of divorce had me spinning down a rabbit hole of paranoia. What if he went to the papers with them? What if I never got them back? Was he sitting around the fire at night, reading excerpts to his friends and laughing? Were these pages being devoured to feed the angry monster he had kept jailed inside him until now?

That's what we had become: two monsters fighting back and forth, while beneath them, our humanity was scarce to be found.

I continued journaling every day. Journaling gave voice to the tiny, wounded human living under the weight of the grief monster. If someone really wants to read what I'm writing, they can do it, with as much ease as before. The content of those pages has changed. If I need to rant, I usually go for a walk or lift something heavy instead of writing it. I try to begin and end the day with gratitude, even through gritted teeth. These books are within unfettered access of my husband now. But it's because I realized that a) I didn't marry an asshole a second time and b) my journals are mine. I am proud of them. I stand by each prayer, each careless word and doodle. What exists in those pages is the evidence of what keeps me loving the world and approaching it with wonder, curiosity, and delight. When I was a child and learning math, we were taught that more than the right or wrong answer, we were to show our work. The journals are my work being shown for the paths I took in life. The extramarital affair was a wrong conclusion to reach, but the work was faithful to get there. Of that I am not ashamed.

Wayfinding Practice: Stick With What You Promised Yourself

There are plenty of things to quit that make sense: disgusting or harmful habits, behaviors that hurt or destroy our environment or people we love. But oftentimes in a fit of self-improvement or on a wild hare to change something, we abandon things that give us joy or that make us truer to ourselves. This invitation isn't simply habit tracking, it's nurturing a spiritual connection with our own souls. There are so many things that threaten to undo us, burn us out, and continue fracturing us to pieces. Ask yourself, "What promise have I made to myself, and how can I honor it today?" You can check in by lighting a candle, holding a special rock or stone in your hand, or putting your hand over your heart as a tactile indication that you are "all in" on keeping this promise to yourself. At the end of the day you can check in again and ask, "How did I show up for myself today? Where was it hard to do that? How can I return to myself with grace, not guilt, tomorrow?"

Poisoned Mashed Potatoes

What I don't understand about myself is that I decide one way, but then I act another, doing things I absolutely despise. So if I can't be trusted to figure out what is best for myself and then do it, it becomes obvious that…I need help!

— *Romans 7:15-17, The Message*

IMAGINE YOU SPEND YOUR EARLY LIFE, EVEN FROM BEFORE YOU CAN remember—your very first experiences of food, sitting in a high chair, being spoon fed mashed potatoes. Your mom pours gravy on them and smiles as she brings the airplane spoon towards your mouth. "Mmmm yummy!" The years go by and you grow—at every holiday the potatoes come out with the tasty gravy on them, surrounded by your family and all those who love you. There may be screaming or yelling, but it's home, and it's tradition. Only later when you leave do you realize, perhaps well into adulthood, that the gravy was *poison*! And yet, every holiday you gather around the table and crave those creamy mashed potatoes swimming in savory brown sauce that tastes "just like home."

We get conditioned to what's normative for us in childhood.

Even if it's unhealthy or abusive—our young minds can't tell the difference. As adults, we have to work hard to reprogram our taste for what is good, healthy, wholesome. Sometimes literally with real food, but often with the hidden, unspoken rules and scripts we've learned from those we love the most. A child raised by an abusive, addicted, horrible parent, will still, on some level love them. And usually hate themselves for loving them.

X's mother poisoned him with the belief that he was the only one who could take care of her and attend to her needs, and that attention to those needs was his life's highest purpose. He was aware of it as an adult, but awareness wasn't enough. For a decade, he poisoned me with these "comforting truths" and by the end I was severely malnourished. I had literally gotten so skinny, obsessed with my weight and body fat percentages. I thought if my physical presence could just waste away I wouldn't hurt anybody.

At the same time that I was trying to waste away, anger surged within me. Anger is a powerful emotion, signaling to us that something is not right. Being forced out of my home led me to face the anger; now I know how to recognize the malnourishing messages and the poison behind them. They still make a showing at family gatherings —you see, everyone has some poisoned food on their table—and a little bit at a time doesn't hurt too bad, especially when you have years of resistance built up. But to an outsider? The toxins could be deadly.

What is it in us that finally switches and recognizes we can't live that way anymore? I twisted and contorted my body and soul to accommodate the truths that were so dissonant with my reality. There is a will to survive in all of us, an evolutionary force like water that will find a way to not stagnate and turn to poison within us. I call it love. Powerful divine love and powerful love of self. Love led me out. Love was both the antidote to the poison and the bridge out to a new table, to a new life.

But what does it feel like in the messy middle? I borrow from Gary Nicholson and Stephen Bruton's song in the movie *Crazy Heart*:

I was goin' where I shouldn't go
Seein' who I shouldn't see
Doin' what I shouldn't do
And bein' who I shouldn't be
Funny how fallin' feels like flyin'
For a little while

It's fun to sneak around, to get away with something and avoid the hard truth fighting its way to the surface. I found and made a quiet space where no one could find me except my beloved. Rob and I built our little world brick by brick, text by text; one church crisis at a time.

It was in the Fall that we began "The new adventure in being" as we called it; life in a "Covenant that's not a covenant." Calling it an "affair" seemed so base and unbecoming of the spiritual intimacy we felt with each other. We didn't enter this way of life carelessly, but it was as if we were two knights fighting battles on the same side, and we backed into one another, recognizing the other's face as beloved. The emotional part happened gradually, and the physical part emerged rather suddenly, like the keystone brick in an archway pinning the whole thing together.

I felt seen by Rob and like I truly saw him for who he was. I admire his faith and ability to deeply listen to the rhythms of life in poetry and prayer. A big smile would spread across my face as I got little glimpses into what was really on his mind, or what scriptures were shaping the way he saw things that day. Nothing is simple with Rob. There's no such thing as just firing off an email or letting him know about a situation that's brewing. He likes to hold the thing in his hand, admire its shape and its limits, ponder and reflect and contemplate. He is unlike any man I've ever known. Delicate and complex; I imagine this is what it must be like to love a dancer. Their bones dainty, their muscles strong and intricate. It takes a lot of strength to move through the world with such finesse and graceful intention. I often feel gangly and awkward, like I am gallumping through daffodils and crushing each one inadvertently, whereas Rob moves, both literally and figuratively like a small flowing stream—trickling, dancing in a playful way that refreshes, renews, and delights.

He referred to us as "The river and the sun—" like a poet would. He, the river, steady, flowing, quiet, with edges and banks, containing multitudes beneath it where it could get dark and brooding, but reflective too; and I, the sun, shining wherever I went, inviting others to play in my light and warmth, beaming down to brighten what was dark and moody in the river's shadows. For some I burned and was too bright—they wanted to cover me with clouds. My energy brightens rooms; his mystical flowing calms and steadies. Is there anything more beautiful than the sun setting on a river?

When our adventure began I thought I could live with no regrets. I thought it was either something broken within me—this inability to experience regret or something my stubbornness had fixed in on and set itself on decidedly not experiencing. Now I see, it was immaturity. I believed the key to a successful, happy marriage was as simple as committing to being married rather than to the person you're married to, and I became convinced that no matter what we do or what happens to us, we can simply choose not to experience regret. Even the mistakes are part of growth and progress. Now I know there is another wrinkle to this: regret is unavoidable. Instead of denying our regrets, we must learn to metabolize them—learn from our missteps, let them nourish us with their bitter goodness.

Our pasts do not define us, but they do shape and inform us. We cannot doggedly insist on living in the present with "Good vibes only." The future creeps in on us, thankfully, so that we may gain a wise heart. Because my marriage to Rob began as a secret, we each know the power secrets hold. We do not live together as ones without secrets, but we know how secrets are like fire—they have the power to make us warm, but also the danger to destroy. It was not the secrets that brought us together, but it was the Spirit.

When we understand another fully and there is no frontier left in them or us, boredom seeps in, and resentment, callousness. We must work on ourselves to safeguard, perhaps reserving some 10% like a savings account, that we do not meld entirely into another, and we must allow the other to hold back a part of themselves. There is a difference between secret and private.

"Our hearts are restless till they find their rest in thee," Saint Augustine claimed, and within each of us contained a restlessness whose balm was faith, was God. Had our spouses also found their rest in God, we might have seen them there, but I trust and hope the restlessness within them leads them to find someone else.

In the healing and reflective time between divorce and deciding what was next, I explored the possibility that I might be codependent. Codependency convinces us that someone else's pain is all our fault and responsibility. The truth is that pain comes from a lot of places. We don't get to claim it all ourselves, but we do take responsibility for our part. Codependency develops out of experiencing significant rejection from a young age and failing to develop appropriate attachment to reliable caregivers. Codependency is rooted in abandonment. We learn to find comfort in the misery of feeling left behind. If our loved ones do not abandon us, we will continually abandon ourselves. While we never get our early childhoods back, we carry within us the earliest version of ourselves, that small, vulnerable child and promise never to leave them. I'm an adult now, and the child I was goes with me. She longs to connect to the two children I have in my care now. She longs to be known and loved and welcomed. How can we practice hospitality with others if we have been so inhospitable to ourselves?

Therapist Pat says you gotta follow the rule of the Three C's—if you didn't CAUSE it, you can't CURE it, and you (sure as hell) aren't going to CONTROL it.

"What did it *feel* like?" I want to inquire of myself. Was the torrid affair with Rob romantic, like fireworks and lightning? No, it came on more subtlely. Like the earth groaning its way towards equilibrium. When Rob looked at me across a table, I didn't feel like a girl or like a sexy woman, either. I felt like a peer, an equal, a conversation partner worthy of his time and like I was looking back at one worthy of mine. We were not, nor are we now, "best friends." There is a mystery within him that I will never fully understand, and I believe, one in me too that eludes him.

Before this crossroads, I had viewed others through the lens of achievement. Every relationship was a prize to be won. First comes love, then comes marriage, then babies, and home ownership, and excel, excel, excel! Until you WIN at the game of life, right?

Those poisoned mashed potatoes that fed me as a child were being served up out there in the world—I could win at a poisoned game, a game that might kill me in the process.

My therapist drew a map for me once, a depiction of my home and a store not far away. She said the patterns I'd learned had been like a route from home to store filled with potholes and jagged, broken glass that kept giving me flat tires and messing up my car. But now there is a new, paved road that doesn't hurt me between home and the store. Learning the new way takes effort though, and occasionally I go on auto-pilot, ending up on the jagged, potholed road without realizing it. It takes work and attention to leave the harmful thing for the thing that heals and gets me where I need to go.

It is a brave thing to adopt new patterns. It takes courage to say no to the things that harm you, and yes to the things you aren't accustomed to but nourish you anyway.

I don't know how to convince someone else to go to therapy or to dig in and get curious about the patterns in their lives that are not helping them, but I do know how to be where I am, to root myself in the present and speak the truth, even when my voice shakes. Christians love to quote the Apostle Paul who wrote, "Speak the truth in love."[1] But we either tell lies in love or speak truth with venom. It's better to stay silent than throw something out in venom. Truth comes through more gently. Rarely have staged interventions been successful in getting people to change.

---

1. Ephesians 4:15

Instead the one being targeted feels betrayed and like they cannot trust anyone. Without a support system, they are left only to their addiction and self-soothing, sending them deeper into the hole.

My dad reminds me that, "The first law of holes, is that when you find yourself in one, *stop digging*. And the second law is like it: *put down the shovel*."

I didn't believe in myself enough, so it was truly surprising to have *won* at nabbing a boyfriend, then a fiancé, then a husband, that it never occured to me to ask myself if that was what I truly wanted. Winning still guides me in the present. I am coming to terms with this beast of perfectionism. A therapist once invited me to give this perfectionistic drive a name: Betsy. Perfect Betsy insists on everything being done just so, otherwise it must be thrown out. Sometimes Perfect Betsy is invited in to evaluate and sharpen, but not all the time. Play is an uncomfortable activity for Perfect Betsy. She has to stay at the door while I build lego towers with my kids or let my fat roll over the top of my jeans. Perfect Betsy isn't allowed into the drafting process for writing my first book. But she will make me shine when I need to.

Perfect Betsy wasn't part of the new adventure in being with Rob when it first began, but she has been in every marriage. She is the hands behind the poisoned mashed potatoes handed down in every generation of our family. I just hope the recipe I am handing my children is weaker and less potent than the one I was given.

Elaine Murray

Wayfinding Practice: Find Your Poison and Its Antidote

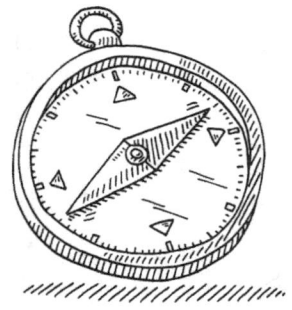 Every spiritual path has some means of recognizing when things go sideways and develops a means for absolution and starting over again. Some call it confession/forgiveness, teshuvah/atonement, penance, Ardaas, Prāyaścitta, and on and on. Here I call generational patterns and trauma my "poison" but there are lots of things we carry that poison us. What are you carrying that's continuing to hurt you, even if you're used to it? What can you affirm that is its opposite? In my example, the poison was the belief that in order to get ahead, I have to abandon myself and my desires. Its antidote? *I'm not leaving little me behind. She gets to want things. My desires are sacred too.*

What is Joy and How Do We Access It When Shit Falls Apart?

Accessing Joy

I've got joy like a fountain,
I've got joy like a fountain,
I've got joy like a fountain in my soul
I've got the joy, joy, joy, joy
down in my heart—where?
Down in my heart!

JOY IS WITHIN US AND JOY IS A RENEWABLE RESOURCE.

Many people have studied happiness, satisfaction, and content-ment. Sermons have been preached about joy as a fruit of the spirit. What's the difference between joy and happiness? The wisdom about happiness is that if you go looking for it, you'll never get it. But if you are still and you let it come to you, its delicate wings will land on your shoulder like a butterfly. But what happens when you move? Must we maintain rigid, still postures of waiting and missing other opportunities in order to be happy?

Joy, in contrast to the elusive happiness, is dynamic; joy has movement to it and exists within us wherever we go. Joy cannot be stolen or go extinct. We can feel distant from it, like its warmth is buried beneath cold, mysterious pain and must be excavated. Joy is not spiritual bypassing or optimism or positivity. Joy runs deeper than those superficial things. Joy holds reality in her hands, having dug something substantive from the mire and rubble of life, and then throws it like a snowball to elicit laughter and delight. Will the journey to joy break us? We may wonder, especially when the symptoms of depression and brain chemical imbalances wreak havoc on our perception of reality.

Joy doesn't have to be elusive. Even amidst life's more painful parts, joy is available to us. Joy came to be personified through the hopeful, gutsy voice of Amy Pohler in Pixar's *Inside Out* movies, which tell the story of 11-year old Riley through her personified emotions: anger, fear, disgust, sadness, joy, and eventually the addition of anxiety, ennui, and envy. While joy is something we feel, accessing it is a discipline; there is a spiritual practice to it. Joy is our purpose. When we are most fulfilled and most aligned and in tune to the next right thing, there is joy. People who struggle to access joy as often are not less faithful or less valuable, but our primary purpose as human beings comes from question one of The Heidelberg Catechism: "Q: What is the chief end of [humankind]? A: To glorify and *enjoy* God forever" (emphasis mine).

When everything in life comes to a screeching halt, joy falls down the rungs of prioritization, but what if we lifted it up? What if in those moments, accessing joy became all the more important? It is said that Martin Luther spent an hour in prayer each morning, but on the busiest days, two. Our hunt for joy becomes all the more necessary when it is scarce to be found.

How do we find joy? Can we dig for it? Do we reach for it? Search for it? Joy cannot possible be happenstance, like whether a property has mineral springs or doesn't. If joy is our purpose, it cannot possibly be limited to those who have the right mix of serotonin in their brains. Joy is not something to mine or extract, but a practice and a habit we strengthen and nurture in our lives.

I grew up in the drought-riddled Texas Hill Country on a limestone lot with cracking caliche, held together with railroad ties. It was a far cry from a lush paradise until my parents envisioned something different. Over the thirty years in which my parents lived there, they slowly made changes that held our little hill together. The vision they sketched out on some graph paper included a small water feature where the two stone walls met at a corner. What came to fruition was not a sweet babbling brook but a 15-foot waterfall flowing into a small pond! Our first observation was "Wow it is so LOUD!" What had been a silent, dusty and oft-forgotten backyard had turned into a roaring oasis. The waterfall ("Murray Falls") has remained, and when I visit I see an emblem of joy. This joy was crafted through human hands—not extracted from nature. It has a pump and a filter that has to be cleaned and main-tained. It gives life to fish and algae, and frogs (oh! the frogs!). It has delighted grandchildren from infancy to teenage years. It has been the centerpiece of farewell parties, birthday surprises, and it's where Rob and I said our marriage vows to start our new life. But if we were waiting for a spring to burst forth and bubble to life in drought-ridden crusty Texas, it wasn't going to happen.

Accessing joy isn't a privilege for the able-bodied or the neurotypical. Accessing joy is not a matter of wealth, status, or identity. Accessing joy is a practice.

Part of accessing joy means opening ourselves up to receive it—crafting the necessary infrastructure for it to grow roots and bloom. We excavate, we pluck up and dig trenches in ourselves to find it. Our joy requires care and attention. We wouldn't look at a xeriscaped "lawn," set down a pot of basil we picked up at the store, and then lament when it withered and died, would we? Plants need soil, water, proper sunshine, and nutrients to grow. Some of us find joy easily like desert blooms or the flower that grows through concrete. Maybe your joy is like a hydrangea, blooming big in its season of sun and warmth but requiring tons of hydration to shine so beautifully. Or your joy is like a bleeding heart flower, growing best in the shade and under a protective canopy away from an audience but whose dark delicacy is blood red with passion and for savoring. Accepting who and what we are while releasing what we are not or hope to be is part of the discovery towards accessing joy. There's a process of self-inquiry, too—why do I wish my joy came another way? Would life be easier if my joy didn't require some pharmaceutical intervention? I love the idea of camping, but I have accepted that I don't enjoy it, and it is much more delightful to think about the romantic idea of sharing quality time outdoors overnight with loved ones than it is to execute.

Wayfinding Practices in this Section:

When you grow a garden, you might need things like shovels and gloves and a watering can. For accessing our joy, these are the tools that will lead us towards that flowing stream:

- Sourcing Joy
- Rest
- Befriending our darkness
- Building your ark/Helping Hands
- Meditation
- Affirmations
- Letting Out/Morning Pages
- Naming our Saints and Angels

Defining Joy

I call it Joy, which is here a technical term and must be sharply distinguished both from Happiness and Pleasure. Joy (in my sense) has indeed one characteristic, and one only, in common with them; the fact that anyone who has experienced it will want it again... I doubt whether anyone who has tasted it would ever, if both were in his power, exchange it for all the pleasures in the world. But then Joy is never in our power and Pleasure often is.

— Surprised by Joy, *C.S. Lewis*

WHEN THE SHIT HITS THE FAN AND YOU HAVE HIT ROCK BOTTOM, OR whatever other fitting idiom describes being in a place far from happiness, it seems particularly calloused and insensitive for someone to write about accessing joy. But from a sister who has been there—homeless and jobless with kids to feed and legal bills piling up—trust me when I say nurturing your ability to access joy is the difference between life and death.

Billionaires know that money cannot buy happiness. The poorest people on the planet know that no paycheck is worth the fulfillment that comes with good health and being "This side of six feet under." Joy is not economic reality, health status, or tied to any other kind of external metric of success.

I once worked with a church volunteer who chaired the deacon board; for context, the deacons in my tradition are the volunteers with particular gifts of care and compassion—they visit the homebound, extend the sacrament of communion to people who cannot make it to worship, write cards and pray for those who are going through something. Deacons have the kind of hearts that break over and over again for their neighbors and community sob stories. The chair of the deacons, we'll call her Marion, was a retired kindergarten teacher and elementary school principal. Her organizational skills were top notch, and she led the deacons like a flock of migrating geese, intimately aware of where the holes and weak spots were, and who needed to fly in front. She did not care for or respect pastors too much, especially young women in this role. Marion signed all her correspondence with (all caps) "JOY!" before signing her name as if it was an order. With three little letters, it was as though she was saying, "Even if you hate what I'm saying or find it vile and unchristian, I'm closing out with JOY! so you have to smile before I slit your throat!" She soured me on the word for a bit, like being in the constant presence of someone who keeps telling you to smile.

But I found it is particularly in moments when joy seems so far away, that a reminder for where it lives and how to find it can be a comfort and inspiration.

Joy is within us and joy is a renewable resource.

Joy does not come down from above. Joy cannot be pressed upon us. While precious, it is not a jewel to be mined, but a movement to tap into. Joy flows.

Accessing joy when everything around you is all wrong has an element of exploration to it. Release your desperate craving to be rescued. Set down the shadows of what will happen if you don't make rent or the next opportunity doesn't come through or if the toxic relationship patterns continue. Close your eyes and breathe. We must dive to the depths of the hurt. Let the hurt bleed inside you to the rhythm of your heart beating. It is just you and a tiny spring of joy whose waves you cannot hear yet. But we're convincing joy that our bodies can be safe enough for the spring to come up within us. We must befriend joy. We must ask it what it needs and be willing and strong enough to wait for its answer. Joy is not something you make, it is a strength you possess already within you. It is a depth you must access.

Sometimes joy and external validation feel the same way inside. The true test for me, as this sensation grew stronger and louder in my soul, was to imagine, "What if I were a deaf, blind refugee in a foreign prison camp? Could I find joy then?" If not, then it probably wasn't joy but the old habit of people pleasing at it again. Joy does not depend on our ability to achieve or communicate with others. Joy is not a sales threshold and it has no stock price. In Nehemiah, God's people had been crushed by exile. Their entire world had been turned upside down by their enemies—perhaps they were close to this test image of the deaf, blind refugee. It was only the ancestors among them who could speak of what tradition had meant in prior days. For generations, they had no homeland and no sense of belonging. All their rituals and tools had disappeared or been stolen. Their place was disorientation. Their home was displacement and exile. But Nehemiah spoke a new truth to them, a return to the city, to the place where God dwelt. It was not political prowess that restored them. It was not their ability to summon a mighty army. They didn't earn this victory through military defeat. But it was their ability to access their joy in all circumstances, even the tough ones. "The joy of the Lord is my strength"[1] became the banner that guided them through the trials of rebuilding. Their return to Jerusalem, to their identity as God's people in God's place would be marked not by their righteousness or their suffering, but because they had accessed the place beneath the rubble within them to nurture joy. Even when circumstances have not yet been made right, even when the process of restoration is one that takes a

---

1. Nehemiah 8:10

long time—many coats of paint and many sanding sessions, it is God's joy implanted within us that will see us through to the other side.

This section of the journey is devoted to accessing joy. There is no one practice that leads you to the inner spring. But you will use many tools: gratitude, meditation, mentorship, examen are a few. If joy is an aquifer, we are learning to be spiritual hydrologists—who use a whole library of tools: magnets, drills, and maps, not to mention an old-school divining rod. Don't be afraid if these sound cheesy or intimidating. No explorer just uses one tool in their collection. Have courage because what remains to be discovered will quench your thirst.

Wayfinding Practice: Sourcing Joy

Where have you found joy before? Make a list. Even if right now, it feels so far away, start a list of joyful memories. Even something as simple as splashing in puddles when you were five, or letting ice cream drip down your chin. If some of your joyful moments are associated with moments of achievement or big milestones, like a graduation or a wedding, dig a little deeper. Where was the joy? Was it being surrounded by your loved ones? Was it how beautiful you felt? Some places where joy once ran, right now are covered over and tainted with pain. That's okay. You can list them anyway, or leave them off the list.

Soup Season

New life starts in the dark. Whether it is a seed in the ground, a baby in the womb, or Jesus in the tomb, it starts in the dark.

— *Barbara Brown Taylor,* Learning to Walk in the Dark

WATERY CHAOS AND DARKNESS IS WHERE THE WORLD BEGAN. Regardless of the continent or creation myth you draw from, the chaos and darkness is where it begins. That's where human life begins too—in a womb too dark to see. If you find yourself wrapped in blankets and tears, not knowing when or if the sun will come out again, trust that this is a **brilliant** place to be. You are hibernating. You are caterpillar-gooing, going into the transformation, wending your way to the river of joy that is there beneath all of the overwhelm. In my own goo process, I was wrapped in a weighted blanket on the bed in my parents' guest bedroom, doom-scrolling and ignoring texts from well-meaning colleagues and neighbors checking in on me, sending out vague social media broadcasts that indicated something was afoot that I wasn't ready to share yet.

I was so afraid. I was afraid that the only true thing about me was that I cheated on my husband and I got caught. That truth existed and felt so large, that none of the other true things about me could even hold a candle to this big, LOUD and obvious and not-going-anywhere truth. None of the other truths could exist until I gave this one time to breathe and to shrink, and to find its proper place in my life.

One day I drove over to my old house, the day we told the kids that we were getting divorced, I drove my little Prius over to what had been our home and loaded it up with the things I would need to live elsewhere while my kids watched cartoons and my soon-to-be-ex-husband told my parents what a horrible person I was. Dear reader, telling whoever will listen what a horrible person your soon-to-be ex is is one of the tasks of divorce. The only part of this I hold against X is that he tried it with my parents. On the way out of my old neighborhood, I stopped at an intersection and I just cried. Before this day I had been The Reverend Elaine Murray Dreeben, wife, doctoral student, mother, pastor, woman who did it all, just like Ginger Rogers, "Everything the men did, just backwards and in high heels."[1] And here I was: no longer a pastor, not sure about the whole "Reverend" part, shedding the "Dreeben" and the "wife" parts of my identity. I would be quitting that doctoral program too. Who was I now? Through tears, I white-knuckled the steering wheel. At that stop sign, I gritted my teeth, claimed a blessing and now I knew I was simply "a child of God." Wasn't that who I had been all along?

I'd become so convinced that the labels and the titles and the achievements is what made up the fabric of me. That those were the parts that were loveable and acceptable to the people around me, to being admitted to human existence and polite society. But now was a stripping down to the essentials.

No matter where you are or what you have done, you are still and always God's child.

---

1. Attributed to another great lady, Ann Richards, former governor of Texas

So back to creation. Earth was a soup of nothingness, a bottomless emptiness, an inky blackness.

When God made the world and spoke it into being, it was watery, chaotic soup. The light and the dark and the waters and the lands and the things that creep and fly and do all the wonderful things that the

"God's Spirit brooded
like a bird above
the watery abyss."
- Genesis 1:1, *The Message*

created world does didn't exist yet. It started out as chaos soup. This is where I was beginning again too—a soupy caterpillar claiming "Child of God" as title, vocation, and life plan.

I want to tell you that when **you** are in soup season, there is this really nifty tool that can get you out of it, it's called…a FRONTAL LOBOTOMY! A SPACESHIP! A DISSOCIATIVE IDENTITY "DIS" ORDER!

Just kidding. It is none of those. It is also not drowning yourself in booze or spacing out on drugs, or running up your credit card bills with retail therapy. I do think therapy is one of the tools that brought me at least back to jello-solid instead of just goo under a blanket, but that comes with a big disclaimer that finding a good therapist is hard and there are so many societal *gestures hands wildly* barriers that keep therapy from being the sole tool you can rely on in this season. So the next best thing is a blanket and the "Do not Disturb" function on your phone. Please find one person that you covenant to check in with at a mutually agreed upon interval. This person cannot be your ex (if that applies to your goo situation). Mine was my mom. She made sure I was eating. And kinda let me be to do my goo thing in the blankets otherwise. Soup season doesn't last forever.

I am also not going to include a recipe in the "Soup Season" chapter. Other people can make you things in soup season. Because YOU are the soup.

From the chaotic creation soup, God made darkness and light, and day by day or eon by eon,[2] brought order from the chaos, putting everything in its proper place. But at the heart of the speaking light and beaches and clouds and butterflies into being, there was Divine acceptance and love, even of the chaotic darkness.

Something profound happens when we begin with self-acceptance. It was God's own self-acceptance within the watery chaos that led to the order and the light and the dark and the days and the invitation to be fruitful and multiply. Before there was creation, there was acceptance.

The thing that will help you find your way out of soup season is to accept your belovedness even now. Even when you are incapable of being productive or measuring up to some externally imposed beauty standard, you are beloved. You are accepted. There is nothing, no horrible, awful, terrible, very bad thing, that you have done that can make you less than beloved and worthy of love.

So once you have accepted where you are, spun around in a circle three times, and sprinkled the blood of an innocent on the bathroom mirror,[3] your soup season is over right? You will wake up and go back to life as it was or as it should be?

No, no, my friend. No life coach is coming to rescue you. Your hair isn't long enough for you to be Rapunzel, and I hear the Prince Charming supply is on backorder. You're coming to save yourself. You're coming to create yourself.

One of the basic things about believing the creation story as it is told in Genesis is that God created everything that is, *ex nihilo*, a fancy Latin cocktail party phrase that means "Out of nothing." God

---

2. This should be a "duh"but in case it's not I'll attempt to use a footnote to describe a very thoroughly studied theological concept in Genesis: the gregorian calendar (what we earthlings use today) didn't exist yet when Genesis was written, much less when it occurred. The concept of days, months, years as we now know them cannot be applied in retrospect, so the "seven" days of creation could more rightfully be understood as seven "clumps of time" or phases of this evolutionary process that goes in the direction of chaos → order.

3. This is a playful reference to some of the childhood sleepover games used for summoning scary things or fixes—none of which will help us through the real life goo, unfortunately.

didn't use a hack or a cheat code or ChatGPT. There was no ultra-processed food version of the universe that God could put to work as a starter pack. The whole everything was made from scratch.

You, in your goopy pile of tears and blankets will be made anew too. There is no starter kit or shortcut. If it looks like a shortcut, I promise it will take you somewhere you do not ultimately wish to end up.

Even here, wayfinder, there is joy. There are little drip drops of it. You are free from the situation that brought you here, for one. You will never find yourself here again, for another thing. Even if something else in life breaks you, you can never be broken in this way again. Like a piece of pottery that is being mended, it never shatters in the same spot. "Oh great, so I'm in shards and now you're telling me I will break again?" Yes, of course you will. Life is too beautiful and terrible, or "brutiful" in the words of Glennon Doyle for it to not break us. If it does not break us again and again then we are not paying attention.

Even when we are breaking, God is creating. Creation begins in self-acceptance. Become the goo. Own the goo. And then from there, the pieces will come together.

Wayfinding Practice: Rest

Choose someone to tell that you are going to rest, and you don't know for how long. Shut off your phone. Close the door. Get rid of all the sharp objects and things that could cause harm and put the world on hold for a while. A day? A week? No more than that. Make sure your person knows a mutually agreed upon time to come find you and ensure you have not actually turned to physical goo. Rest is what you need. Get the comfy blanket, the stretchy pants (or no pants!) and disappear for a bit. Everything you are evading will be there for you when you return but for now, shut off.

Befriending The Shadows

"I could tell you my adventures—
beginning from this morning,"
said Alice a little timidly:
"but it's no use going back to yesterday, because I was a different
person then."

— *Lewis Carroll,* Alice's Adventures in Wonderland

IN THE QUEST TO ACCESS JOY WITHIN US, WE DISCOVER SHADOWS THERE too—a darkness within that is undeniable. Poet Maggie Smith describes it in "Good Bones"—her poem that went viral in 2016:

For every loved child,
a child broken, bagged, sunk in a lake.
Life is short and the world is at least half terrible,
and for every kind stranger,
there is one who would break you

The evolutionary biologists describe how the human spirit is relentless in its quest for survival. Every feature like our tongue's ability to discern in seconds whether something is food or not, or our center of gravity's ability to freefall for only a moment before our reflexes pop limbs out to catch us—each of these is a feature of our desire to ultimately stay alive. And yet, there is another part of us in the shadows, a part that would choose sabotage, unaliving, giving into the voices of jealousy, greed, and malice. We don't want to give into these powers, but to deny their existence is to block the way to true joy.

Just a chapter after the gorgeous Creation story in Genesis, when Adam (which literally means "dirt man") and Eve ("the mother of all living") are given dominion, the responsibility to care, for the trees and plants and animals in the lush garden God spoke into being—just after that, this shadow part comes on to the scene. Some might call it "sin" or even personify this shadow in the serpent character who asks Eve, "Did God really say that you shouldn't eat from any tree in the garden?"

My children's story bible called it "The Really Sad Day" and it was marked with black pages and cartoonish representations of sin. Many interpret this scene as the entry point of the shadows—as if before that, humankind was perfect without a spot or a blemish. This concept is rooted in white supremacy. The work of Sue Monk Kidd in *Dance of the Dissident Daughter* dives deep into the image of the serpent in feminine mythology. The snake is a neutral symbol of wisdom—think Medusa's hair, or why the serpent in Genesis found Eve instead of her male counterpart.

The shadows have always been a part of us. Even creation had shadows from its inception. There was light and darkness, would there not be some in us too? I don't equate "shadows" with sin— but it can manifest itself that way. Shadows are the part of us that hold in tension what is good and kind and faithful. Even God had shadows—it was that part of Them that came to regret making humankind at all and destroyed us in the flood. God's shadows wrestle with how to love, how to not be entirely consumed by their love for creation. After the garden and the serpent, when Adam and Eve procreate, they have two sons: Cain and Abel. When God expresses preference for one brother's offering over the other, They warn Cain, "Sin is crouching at your door, and you must master it." The shadows are always in us, calling us to fall into them. This was the same force that the Adversary wanted to spin Job into, wiping out his family, wealth, and health.[1]

I thought for most of my life that resisting temptation meant ignoring the shadows within me, or turning the opposite direction when I encountered temptation, shoving them under the rug, ignoring, and pretending they weren't there. Like when you wake up from a spicy dream and you're already blushing before the day has begun. I wouldn't dare tell anyone about the dream, or even allow myself to admit that I dreamt it.

It was motherhood that gave me permission to see my own darkness. I didn't recognize at the time that I was impacted by Post-Partum Mental Health challenges. It felt like a lonely fog. I knew how to set alarms for every two hours and could see clearly my way from baby to breast, through bottle and pump-part washing drudgery rituals each evening. But I could not see myself as a person anymore. I had become the mama machine. It didn't matter how many afternoons I spent doing things that I loved, or how much "self-care" I indulged in. There I was, always alone, in the fog.

The night I became a mom was magical. I prepared for the birth by practicing hypnosis throughout my pregnancy. Using my mind and creative visualization, I traveled to "laborland"—a meditative cave that looks very similar to the natural entrance to Carlsbad Caverns, a winding path down into cool darkness. I met my baby in "laborland" for months. I talked to the baby and encouraged them to grow and keep hibernating in my safe womb. There in the cave, I could lay down the anxiety I felt about labor, or if I would be a good mom. There in the cave, Ollie already existed and already knew everything they needed to know. I could dance in the cave.

---

1. Job 1:8-10

No one went into the cave with me—just me and my baby becoming ourselves.

Baby came earthside with no meds and almost no pain. I birthed Ollie from the strength the cave had helped me find and quickly. X's mother was waiting outside the doors to the birthing suite, ready to pounce, as if this precious bundle now belonged to her. It was O and me for a few minutes. Just beholding the other, chest to chest. The midwife's assistant gently taught me how to help the baby root around and find the breast. It was not easy, but it was reflexive. We were having a moment, and then, like the presence of a crone, X's mother descended over us, looked down, and immediately said, "She looks just like him!" (referring to X). It was like a knife to my chest. I hadn't felt a need to have a child. I hadn't felt the primal urge to procreate, but I did so, out of love and devotion to my partner. And there in that holy place, it was like a monster had revealed their true selves, as if to say, "Ha! I got you! And now the child is MINE!"

There are no purely perfect moments. Every occasion is tinged with shadows because every occasion involves human beings and we all carry our darkness—some within, safely tucked away and some right out on our sleeves for the world to see. I began to notice a pattern though—all the joyful moments I had created, when this person was involved, were awash in shadows. Shadows bled all over the pretty pictures I had made.

We all have darkness within us. It's not good to sweep our shadows away or insist they be light. We must face them, befriend them, get curious about them. But we're also responsible for ensuring they don't go too far beyond us. This is what it is to live a boundaried life, a protected life. We have a responsibility to care for our joy and our exuberance and also our heartbreak and inner darkness so that one does not deny the humanity of another.

What do shadows have to do with joy? Barbara Brown Taylor tells a story of interviewing an Indigenous person about his religion. She asked him what his people believed about creation, and he described their belief that the earth sits atop a giant turtle's back.

"What's under the turtle?" Taylor asked, and he responded,
"Another turtle."

"And under that?"

"Another turtle...it's turtles all the way down."

I believe we were spoken into being by the God who came from watery chaos. Within that God exist both shadows and light, joy and sorrow. Created in God's image, we are bearers of light, but also holders of shadows. We cannot deny a part of our existence because we've been conditioned to believe it less favorable. Beneath the shadows, like the turtles, is more truth, and more joy, and yes, even more shadows.

The psalmist proclaims, "Even the darkness is not dark to you; the night is bright as the day, for darkness is as light with you."[2]

The night I became a mama, we left the birth center near midnight. I stepped out onto the sidewalk with the baby in the carrier. While we took in the September air, we both gazed skyward, beholding the big, bright, orange Harvest moon, lighting our way to the next phase of our adventure. Even in the darkness, there is magic to behold.

The magical feeling of giving birth and nurturing life was muted at times by the loudness of culture's expectations of mothers. Becoming a mother was not just a change between me and my baby, but I suddenly became present in the world in a different way. I no longer had a name or a self—I had a role. The role became my name and I, whoever I was, ceased to exist. The shadows of lostness I felt stayed with me through another baby, through a couple of moves, and when the fog began to dissipate, around my youngest child's second birthday, I realized I was home again in my body, but I didn't know who she was anymore. I was no longer afraid of the darkness I had found within and wondered if perhaps my shadows could become my friends.

Around this time in my life I began to crave the ocean. Have you ever stood there and let the waves tickle your calves,

---

2. Psalm 139:12

beckoning you to go deeper? I get a craving for the sea to set me right, to remind me of shadows' proper place and where my goodness is. Watching the white foam come in and go out teaches my heart how to beat in rhythm. Holly Golightly in Truman Capote's *Breakfast at Tiffany's* describes "The mean reds"—when "Suddenly you're afraid and you don't know what you're afraid of." I began to get the mean reds around when the postpartum fog faded. The springtime made me antsy and I figured out how to make a mad dash to the ocean, just to squish the sand under my feet and watch the waves tickle my toes. Just to lose myself in a wave, to celebrate my baptism and the watery chaos of ocean coming over me one time.

We called it "Beach Day" and loaded our car the night before with snacks, towels, sunscreen, and suits. We set our alarms for 4 am and scooped our two babies out of bed, strapping them directly into car seats. Then we drove. We drove 250 miles down to the closest stretch of beach we could get to. With Whataburger breakfast biscuits in hand, we'd spend the morning splashing and napping and delighting in each other. What marvelous, adventurous parents we were! How full of surprises our children's childhoods would be! The hope and the laughter kept my shadows at bay. If only I could hold on to the feeling of Beach Day forever.

Holding on to a feeling forever is also not how accessing joy works. Joy is dynamic; joy is energy; joy has flow to it. Joy cannot be captured, but it can be accessed and beheld. Shadows led me down to the ocean and there I glimpsed joy, letting it run through my fingers like sand. I followed the joy out farther and farther into the Gulf of Mexico, letting each wave carry me, even until it would bring me down into the shadows of myself, giving me space to explore my own darkness, and then summon the strength to swim those waves back to shore.

Once we were all tuckered out and sufficiently starved, we lunched at a surfside shanty and made the 250 mile trek back home. It was one magical, long day. Two kids slept all the way home and two parents crashed soon after bedtime. The mean reds were vanquished for another season.

But pushing the shadows away only makes them grow. If I could go back with the courage I have now, I might have asked my shadows, "What do you want from me? What do you long to hear?" They might have told me to look around. To take inventory of the conversations and interactions I was having in my marriage. They might have asked me in turn, "Where is your joy? We want to see joy!" I was bereft of joy. I couldn't find it anymore after the babies and the moves, and the constant navigation of inlaw relationships. There was a looming presence between us that was X's mother. When we went on vacation, it was traveling to see family. When we planned the holidays, it was the question of how we would appease the dragon in the basement that was her. When I raised issues, challenged tradition, or proposed more distance, X became a child brought to his knees, curled in the fetal position, torn. Or with the sullen reply, "You don't have to go nuclear, Elaine."

I retreated into the shadows, not for curiosity, not for friendship, but for protection. I shut down emotionally. I found reasons to be away from home or miss out on "special time" that involved X's mom. It was great for my career. For a minister, there are a thousand reasons to be more involved with your community. There is always someone to visit in the hospital, a committee meeting to step into, a meal to share, a study to lead. I threw myself into them all as the shadows overtook me. My light was dimming and life was out of balance. The first of the Twelve Steps toward recovery is to admit, "We were powerless over [the shadows] and our lives had become unmanageable." Before I befriended them, I let the shadows take me under.

On the outside, it looked like I had everything perfect. A house, a spouse, two beautiful kids, and a dog. On the inside I was just beginning to wake up to my real self and I felt less and less like there was a place for her in this so-called "perfect" life.

I often wonder what the shadows are like in X's mother's life.

She grew up in a traumatic situation, married young, divorced young, met X's father, married again and raised two sons. No one is free from pain, nor are they responsible for what happened to them. But everyone has a responsibility to heal from it, and we owe it to ourselves to keep our pain from hurting others.

We do this by befriending our own darkness. We ask the unhinged parts of us need and gently, lovingly, provide for it. My shadows needed space to be honest about what was happening. I resisted. I wanted anything but honesty about how unmanageable life had become. I wanted anything but to admit I had abandoned myself. Why? Because I thought to be honest meant telling my spouse everything.

Honesty starts with ourselves. Sometimes it ends there. Within each of us is the capacity to hold it all —our shadows and our light. We must admit to ourselves our fantasies and desires, even when they scare us. We must admit our spicy dreams and morbid thoughts, because to admit them is to turn towards them for a moment, long enough to vanquish the fear and access the joy.

Wayfinding Practice: Make Friends with Your Darkness

Sit in a chair and set an empty chair across the room from you, but within speaking distance. Close your eyes and imagine all that is unsettled within you coming together in a big person-sized clump. With your mind's eye, watch the clump of shadows take shape and move over to the empty chair across from you. Now, open your eyes. Look at the chair, that physically is still empty, but in your mind, holds all that is too heavy, to unsettled, too anxiety producing, too sad, toc everything-but-joy. Welcome it. Thank this shadowy blob for showing up. And ask it what it needs. Then listen. Write down what comes to mind if you need to. Say it out loud. Practice all your active listening skills by repeating back to the blob what you hear it say. Ask clarifying questions. When you feel like you have heard enough (and there may be tears), thank your shadows for speaking up. Close your eyes, put your hand on your heart, and release the shadows and unsettled bits from their throne.

Flood

Life can only be understood backwards; but it must be lived forwards.

— Søren Kierkegaard

I see the awakening of consciousness as a series of spaced flashes, with the intervals between them gradually diminishing until bright blocks of perception are formed, affording memory and a slippery hold.

— Vladimir Nabokov, Speak, Memory

IT'S WORTH ACKNOWLEDGING THAT SHIT DOES INDEED, FALL APART. WE aren't even through the first few chapters of Genesis, when God looks around at all They made and experiences regret at the reality of what destruction humanity had wreaked. God's regret drove a dismantling of all the order back into watery chaos through the flood in Genesis 6-9.

Do you ever imagine what it was like the first day the rain fell during the flood?

I imagine it's like watching all the ideals you hold dear quickly signed away into Executive Orders banning gender identities and safe harbor as a new administration takes power. A collective sigh, battening down of the hatches and a prayer for mercy. We want to believe that our carefully crafted worlds are impervious to the will and contempt of others, but they are not. The flood waters began to rise for me the day I returned home from a routine salon appointment and started to reheat lunch for my spouse and me to have an at-home lunch date. He texted that he was on his way, and I continued to stir the leftover pulled pork in the cast iron skillet. The house had that musty old house odor and was stale from the thirty or so undergrads we'd hosted the night before. The sun was shining, which I would feel on the tops of my sandals feet on the dusty gravel driveway I would walk down that afternoon.

But for the moment, I'm standing in my dream kitchen. I'm reheating the pulled pork from our party the night before. I remember a day from our early courtship at the beginning of my twenties. One day we found an island in the middle of a creek, just big enough for two young, agile bodies to stand beneath a tall cypress tree. We fumbled with the pebbles and sticks as the sun glimmered through the branches onto the water.

Like a miniature "Teribithea," we claimed our own place in time and space—like we were conquerors, uncaring about what this place had been before here and now.

If you know then what you now know, would you shudder and run for cover at the ego it took to face the world so brashly? Or would your older, wiser self stand on the shoreline smiling at the joy such naïveté allowed you in the moment?

Maybe it's a little bit of both, but I choose to lean into the latter.

I'm still standing with the pork when I hear the familiar crunch of tires on gravel. The burner is off; I go to meet him at the door. The shades are partially drawn, so the sun is casting afternoon shadows on the floor. He walks in and before the door is shut says, "I know about you and Rob."

My hearing and vision go hazy. Adrenaline pulses through my

veins. Everything that follows is a blur, ringing through my head as if in slow motion. I cry. I apologize for not admitting it when pressed. At some point, I hear,

"It's not the affair; it's that you lied."

The sun was shining.

But in my carefully crafted world, the pieces were being washed off the walls and there was no way the structure could withstand the storm that had begun. The island we'd found in that creek so long ago was being washed away.

He said, "I want a divorce; I want you out of the house."

I begged. We sat on the couch and I asked if it meant anything— all that we had built? Our careers, our fixer-upper home, our two children? He was stoic and resolved.

When I shifted into logistics—what about picking up the kids today?

He would handle it and I should be gone by the time they return.

And one more thing: "Rob needs to tell his wife."

It was like getting fired from a company you dedicated your adult life to and on a Friday afternoon you find you've been locked out of the projects you'd been working on and completely shut out. He walked out the door. The pork never left the skillet. I sat dumbfounded in the shadows and mustiness of that 1950s bungalow. My body would pack a bag, text Rob, "SOS 💩 " and find a place to spend the night.

Pupils dilated, it felt like I was trudging through smoke and rubble, although the floor was clean except for a little dust and dog hair. The sun was shining.

Questions that would come:

Who am I?

What do I do now?

Who can I trust?

May we all face these questions at some point in our lives. I wish facing them came without the traumatic experiences that shock, scare, and hurt us. But are the shock, fear, and pain side effects from the life-changing magic of facing your own demons?

The rest of the afternoon was like moving through a shadow. I don't know where I left my body, but it drove a car, made some phone calls and somehow eventually ended up on my sister's doorstep as my niece arrived home from school.

You remember that scene from *Peter Pan*, when he asks Wendy to reattach his shadow to him? Now picture, if the shadow had been able to dance, fly, walk and talk while Peter's body and soul were shut up in Wendy's sewing box. I was a walking, talking shadow, clutching a bottle of wine, my phone and my journal like life depended on these three things.

The shadow missed so much of the blessing on this day. I had a sister who would open the door, no questions asked, who would accept my bullshit excuse of "I just wanted a slumber party."

Incredible clarity arises out of such moments if we are tuned into it. Even if not in that particular moment (which is rare), the replay helps to catch our attention, like spotting the thief's sleight of hand on the security tape.

On the replay, I see the things that I missed in the moment: that my husband had asked that morning for the security code to our kids' investment accounts; that four of my journals and all our personal documents were missing from the house already.

On the replay, I learned the girlfriend I thought I could call when the floodwaters rose, was really just a person I'd maintained a perfunctory relationship with over the years. She couldn't handle other people's relationships going any differently than she saw fit. I realized quickly that there were few who could handle the devastating shame I felt facing the consequences of my actions.

It's much easier to live in illusion; think about the joy you felt playing house as a child compared to the real chores your parents enlisted you to do. My security tapes going farther back than just this day revealed I had been playing at lots of serious things: marriage, community, my relationship to myself. Now reality was crashing in on me.

This flood would prepare me for how to navigate future life disasters. I know now how to recognize, before I get too far down the road, how a person acts when they aren't able to support what you're telling them. I learned to trust my intuition and shut down a conversation quickly, calmly and to keep my secrets for those with the capacity and who earn the right to your story.

Compared to how quickly the ringing in my ears began and I dissociated from myself, the rest of the day moved agonizingly slow. It was just me and my Prius. Those who had no idea what was going on continued to text about funny memes and when I'd return the chairs we borrowed for the party. Dear reader, I returned the chairs that day, by the way.

I talked to my best friend, I strategized with Rob on the side of a country road like we were in a movie. Was this the end? I'll confess, I wasn't even thinking of the kids yet. The "D" word was too big. I was still under the illusion that my marriage was worth fighting to save.

We look back at such scenes with the clarity we didn't have in the moment. I yearn sometimes to reach out to her, the woman crying in the dust next to her car. I want to say, "Abandon the hope —it's not worth the tears you'll cry. Focus on the kids. Focus on yourself." That is the cruelty of time, no? We're blocked from changing the action of the past. As old Kierkegaard said, "Life must be lived forward and understood backwards."

I tried at that moment to regret what had brought me there, or what I had understood the reason to be: my illicit affair. My thoughts were there, yes, that's it. *I regret the affair. If I regret the affair, this will all be over like a bad dream.*

But the pit in my stomach betrayed what my mind was rehearsing. The body knew: I regretted trusting my husband. I regretted each of the little self-abandonments that snowballed over the years. Many would hate me after this moment when the news came to light, but none more than I had hated myself for so long. I regretted every time I had stayed quiet, bit my tongue in the face of another's cruelty; I regret every shrug of my shoulders and clicking sound I make with my tongue when asked if something was okay or wrong. I regret the times I was too quick to forgive the middle of the night rape.

Our most profound moments require context to be understood in their depth. We tell ourselves stories to help us gulp down truths, but if the story is wrong, it distorts our perception of reality from that point forward. The story I'd been telling myself was that I was a bad wife and a good wife wouldn't have cheated on her adoring husband. Who was I then to hurt him like I had?

But there's more to the story than that. It's easy to point the finger at the obvious villain. If you've watched even one episode of NCIS, you know, the obvious villain is rarely the true culprit.

There was a waiter at a local bar, Ray, a fabulously gay black man and recovering addict. He used to say non-chalantly while setting down a glass of wine, "Hey, when you look up and see that plantation gate open, you don't think, you just start running." The affair had been my plantation gate, and now I could finally look up and see the clear blue sky.

My first marriage cost me something; it was an unjust and unwinnable war that almost destroyed me. Although my sacrifices were scorned rather than celebrated, the affair taught me about my own survival and what I would do to be free, to live under clear blue skies, with quiet coffee mornings, and without the shadows in my intimate spaces.

There is a quiet war going on in our homes, a war that costs women their lives every day. We've come to recognize domestic violence as visible through scars and bruises, but our ability to sense the patterns that result in this quiet stamping out of light has a long way to go. There is a power grab behind every heterosexual home's doors. "But not all men…" I can hear the rebuttal beginning and I can say as a woman now married to another man, who makes me feel safe and loved, that yes, all men. All men grow up in a world that teaches them they are owed everything, that all things exist for their pleasure. It is only in living willingly in discomfort that they come to know a fraction of what it is to be a woman. And willingly living in discomfort is not sustainable long-term. Men despise other men who give up their power. Men resent women unwilling to give up their power or who step into power they believe is not a woman's to possess. Our history classes taught us that absolute power corrupts absolutely and that the divine right of kings led to some treacherous outcomes; but our teachers did not point the arrow back at themselves or at our own homes. Men have become little domestic kings, corrupted by the power the world tells them from birth that they are owed, just for being born male.

What do we call a man whose wife (property) has taken back her own sovereignty? A cuckold. It comes from the cuckoo bird, who lays its eggs in other birds' nests.

What was X, the cuckold, supposed to do? Just let it go by? He seemed so easygoing, but I did not pick up on what brewed beneath the surface. I had given him kids, I had moved where he wanted to live, I had shrunk to fit and reshaped my wishes into his and endured vacations and holidays centered around his family and his search for belonging in the world. I was idolized and amused while he squirreled away power: the career he wanted, the kids in his image, and then what? Wealth? Power? What was next for him? For us? I had given him everything he wanted.

When women get everything we want, we pay it forward. We make a way for other women to thrive, for marginalized groups to make their way. When entitled men get what they want, they want more of it. It's never enough. Look at the oligarchs running the United States right now and you'll see, it isn't enough to amass more money than you can spend in a lifetime. It isn't enough to control an industry or have a monopoly on it. Nothing will fill the void that their conditioning has taught them must be satisfied.

It's easy to sum up the end of the marriage as "growing apart," "irreconcilable differences," or that it was a typical experience of infidelity, but what I've learned is that there are no typical experiences, and "growing apart" is not reason enough to destroy a covenant without something else at play.

I couldn't sense it yet, in my salty, silent tears and wannabe-stiff-upper lip, buried in my sister's couch self that my new life was beginning without the person I had built it with the first time around.

Caterpillars and butterflies are the same life form. One strand of DNA runs through them, from little tiny egg to caterpillar, to pupa, and winged adult. The untrained eye might not recognize from its beginning what the creature will become. A scientist told me once that regardless of its outcome, every caterpillar carries in it "imaginable discs"—all the equipment for wings, and the kind of body and antennae it needs to fly. Does it know that all this stuff is inside? Perhaps the same ways that baby girls are born with ovaries that started in their grandmothers' bodies—of course we don't know how much, how vast the potential within us is. And even if we did, would such knowledge be "too wonderful for us"[1] most times in our lives to be truly rooted in?

My sister will say she was puzzled by my out-of-the-blue phone call that afternoon. We weren't really on speaking terms. She was six months pregnant, shuffling around in compression socks, anticipating a quiet weekend with her nine-year-old and the German Shepherd while my brother-in-law was on a long-term out of town assignment.

A few months prior she and our oldest sister had concluded I really didn't have an interest in relating to them. I was always preoccupied with work and sort of a miserable bitch to be around. Emily says "Remove the 'sort of' and you nailed it."

She picked up the phone, half-heartedly agreed for me to come and then hung up with bewilderment. The confusion only grew when the shadow arrived with an overnight bag, mumbling some shady line about "needing to get out of town" and "spending some time with my sister." My niece even asked quietly, "What's wrong with Aunt Elaine?"

If only Elaine knew. Swirling. I'm gonna be sick. If this is a roller

---

1. Psalm 139:6

coaster, get me off. I was on Willy Wonka's boat and there were no sweets in sight.

Like a shadow, I accompanied them to dinner. Thai food. My sister always backs into her parking spaces. Is this a military thing? Like a tactical strategy for if shit goes down and you need to make a quick exit? I shuffled Pad Se Jew noodles on my plate, tried to fake some conversation, but my eyes were dry and wide. Thinking about the kids. What were they having for dinner? Did they miss me? I went to the bathroom—was there anything left of me?

I imagined us piling in the car, peeling out of the parking lot in a high-speed exit, like they were getting me out of a war zone. Yet I hadn't even said a word to them about it. Instead, Emily quietly picked up the check and home we went to watch a movie.

I'd sent a few desperate texts to X that night. I felt like the Whiskey Priest in Graham Greene's *The Power and the Glory*; on the run from and towards something I didn't understand. I crumpled my body into Em's oversized chair, writing feverishly in my journal, googling things like "How to apologize for cheating;" "What are the odds for a couple to make it through infidelity."

Nothing at all about divorce or my rights. I didn't have the language yet for what was happening. All I knew was how shitty I felt about myself and that I wanted to surround myself with people who affirmed that shitty belief and I couldn't face those who couldn't or wouldn't affirm it.

If Viktor Nabokov was right and "The awakening of consciousness is a series of spaced flashes"[2] I was in an agonizingly long, slow blink.

My confidant, C, would engage me via text, critiquing every draft of an apology, reminding me what scum of the earth I was and that what I truly deserved was to be pushed off a cliff, which didn't sound like a half bad idea. I could feel every delight, everything I loved slipping away like sand. Could I take hold of any of it?

---

2. *Speak, Memory: An Autobiography Revisited*

Dark nights of the soul do end. Morning does come, even if through fits and starts of yearning. And when the morning dawns, what does one eat after getting kicked out of her home?

The answer is a sour cream old fashioned and donut shop coffee, black. I dunk the sugary globs in like its communion, still nursing that faraway look in my eyes in the shadow of shock. I combat the feelings of shame by insisting on being overly helpful. I play fetch with the giant German Shepherd, I pack up my things as to take up as little space as possible, breathe as little air as possible. My bowels have completely emptied; there's hardly anything of substance left in me.

While helping Emily change the sheets, I break. In monotone panic, I say, "X wants a divorce. That's why I'm here. I'm scared and I don't know what to do. I can't tell you why he wants a divorce but he does."

Rain drops pelting on the inside. Had I made it inside an ark, or was I losing my home in this flood?

The truth and clarity Emily had longed for in the last 24 hours landed with a thud at the foot of her king-sized bed. I don't even remember what she said, but there was a hug to cover the sack of bones I was walking around in. I knew the clock was ticking until X had agreed to meet and talk again.

I called Laura, the one person outside of us who knew the truth. She'd been an attorney in a former life and was quick to advise, "Don't leave the house. He can't make you leave the house." In that moment we became sisters. It's a gift to be seen by a person in the mess of consequences to your own actions. She was an angel waiting on me. She also told me the hardest truth I'd had to stomach yet, "Your ministry at the church is over."

The sun shone through the car windshield, warming my knuckles. The rays beat down on me with an empowering whisper. I am sixteen again; carefree. I can sing every word of the pop music coming over my speakers, no matter where I'm going. This solar-powered energy propels me down the road, back to the dark wood laminate floor of our broken home where I am prepared to grovel for a second chance. I've written an amazing apology and rehearse it in the back of my mind even as my lips are moving to that sunshine summer song on the radio.

I surmise there's about a 30% chance of success with this attempt which I'm willing to bet on. At this point in my 32 years, I'm accustomed to being surprised by grace. Often we think of grace as getting what we want. But grace is a deeper wisdom than the limitations of our desires. Grace today was not synonymous with what I wanted. The season I was entering would teach me to trust a wiser force at work than what the moment offered.

While the sunshine made me feel strong, I was only strong enough to submit, to cower in the face of malice.

The house was quiet, holding the trauma and secrets. X had taken the kids to a friend's house so that we could talk more. When he got back to meet me, I was ready. I knelt on the floor, crying before him, while he sat in my dad's hand-me-down leather recliner like a king on a throne, unmoved.

I tried two fronts:

One was the begging apology, regret, action-steps for amending the hurt; the other was flimsy certitude that there was no way he could kick me out and take the kids. He was mostly silent, and advised me to get a lawyer.

He also said it wasn't worth me fighting him on this. "If this is a chess game, Elaine, I hold all the kings, queens, and bishops, and all you have is a pawn. You should be afraid."

I was terrified.

This moment was a clear break for me. I offered to quit my job, to move, to do anything if we could reinvent our marriage together. The conversation lasted about twenty minutes and X left with the understanding that I would get a few more things and leave before he returned. This time I had to face my parents, not knowing where else to go.

Later this statement would come back to me while playing chess with my son. I may not be the best at the endgame, but only someone who doesn't know the game of chess well would offer the metaphor of losing with a pawn. You can win with a pawn, but you must have two other pieces that are not on the board: patience and foresight.

I didn't plan to take my kids away from him; I didn't plan to get a divorce. But over time they would come to see and know the covert cruelty of their father—the overpromising and underdelivering. The weaponized incompetence of failing to prepare nourishing meals or failing to protect them from harm and injury. It was painful to watch. Sharing custody made me feel like I was betraying them, even more than the affair did. At least during the affair, I still oversaw the home. So many times I wanted to pay the legal fees, restart the court proceedings, and sue for more custody, but that's not how the long game or the court system works. We had to make do with an imperfect arrangement that took 24+ hours of mediation to arrive at.

None of the terms that became part of my daily parlance during the flood sounded real to me. Mediation, custody schedule, temporary orders, Attorney Ad Lightem, Division of Assets, 3-4-3, 2-2-5— these were the vocabulary of divorce. I was learning a new language, all while being frozen by shame.

The loudest voices about infidelity in our culture scream about how it justifies violence—scorn justifies destroying property, stealing assets, even murder. Passion leads us to justify all kinds of awfulness. Some of you reading this may feel like a fantasy is coming true—"Yeah! Kick her ass out!" you might cheer internally. You might wish you'd have done that when you discovered your partner's infidelity. No pain seems like too much to inflict. Some might wonder, "Well Elaine, what did you expect him to do?" and look on him with justification and pity. But to take either perspective is to sit in a seat that did not exist in that living room on that particular Saturday. To take either of those perspectives would be to sit on a judge's bench. While the halls of justice exist in our culture, and many believe are waiting for us at the end of our lives, in this place, a judge's bench did not belong. You were either in the chair, or on the floor. That was it. And if you were in the chair, you have to watch the strongest person you know at her lowest, broken before you, begging to not have to live the consequences of her actions. And that too is a terrible place to be.

Okay, now that we're clear that I do realize what I did was really, really shitty, you want to hear how I did it, or what we learned from it, or how I got what I deserved and was never happy again so that it can preserve the order of things in the universal karmic justice system, right?

First let's pause a moment and hear the most honest and beautiful words my mother has ever said to me, uttered upon entering her home with a metaphorical tail between my legs, "Elaine, when you fuck up, you fuck up big."

What do you need when you're going through a flood? An ark. A place where you can batten down the hatches and wait out the storm. My ark was my sister; it was my friend Laura who was honest with me. It was my mom who welcomed me in and told me that I'd really messed up, but that I could stay there while we cleaned it up. It wasn't the community I thought I'd had, but it was love from near and far, bridges I thought I might have burned, but who still had arms big enough to hug me back into life from the sad sack of bones I had become.

In the flood narrative of Genesis, God gives Noah instructions for building it and for what creatures to put inside of it. Not everyone is welcome in the ark. When the flood waters rise, you learn that there are some whose presence on your ship will sink it, or invariably and perhaps without malice, poke holes in it. Those aren't your people and they don't get a place on your boat.

Wayfinding Practice: Build Your Ark

When the floods came, Noah was not unprepared. He'd done the work of building an ark, a safe haven to shelter not only himself, but his family and the animals in his care also. It's not "if" calamity strikes in your life, but a matter of when. This practice isn't about building an emergency fund or a fallout shelter in the backyard, but it's about getting your spiritual ark together. Start with your two hands: who are the people and what are the places where you feel safe, brave, and loved? Trace your hands on a piece of paper and write a person, place, or thing for each finger, trusting that when the storms come, you have hands that will catch you.

Guan Yin and Jesus

We got no food, we got no jobs, our pets' heads are falling off!

— *Lloyd Christmas,* Dumb and Dumber

ACCESSING JOY IS A WHOLE LOT LESS DAUNTING WHEN YOU FEEL SEEN. There is a sense of safety, of ground beneath you, when you come to the realization that you are not alone in the struggle. Not only are you seen, but seen up close, intimately. Not just some bystander or stalker from far away, but a companion, a co-conspirator. The reality of someone rooting for you to find your way out of the muck and the mire makes even the lowest and dirtiest of realities withstandable.

Some situations seem awfully lonesome. People may have lost their jobs, but they haven't lost *your* job. People may go through divorces, but they haven't been married to *your* spouse or been in *your* situation or endured the specific details that make you and your terrible thing The Most Terrible Thing.

We read headlines and news alerts about scandalous figures— people in high positions caught with their pants down or with a little secret on display to the world. Even as I write this, such scandalous behavior is becoming acceptable, normalized even in the Trump 2024 cabinet confirmation hearings. But there was a time, in which I wondered, what it was like for a Paula Broadwell, the accomplished author, academic, and former military officer who was caught in an affair with General David Petraeus, then CIA Director. What was it like for her to go home after turning in her credentials and falling so fabulously far in the public eye? Did she cower in shame or sit in her pajamas and wonder what was next?

Even those of us without the public profile or high security clearance see ourselves as main characters of our own worlds. "Is everyone watching me?" is an anxiety I have carried through every small community I've lived in, both as a community pastor and before that as the child of the local hospital's CEO. When we lived in a little town in Lower Alabama (LA, as the locals fondly call it), my sisters were told they couldn't date non-white boys for fear of a burning cross on the front lawn of the town's largest employer, where Daddy worked.

In the battery of psychological tests an aspiring Presbyterian minister takes, one of them is the Minnesota Multiphasic Personality Inventory (MMPI), a 500 question true/false test that examines the subject on ten clinical scales, including depression, hysteria, schizophrenia, and paranoia, among others. My test results were yawningly normal, except for a few stand-out responses on the paranoia scale. I answered "true" to the statement, "I know people are talking about me." and something to the effect of "People know who I am." My car was recognizeable in our small town of less than 20,000 people. If I were pulled over for a traffic violation, my mom would know before I reached my destination, with a report on what I was wearing too. Once someone looked in my grocery cart and said, "Good job. I'll tell your folks you're eating healthy." It was understandable that I thought others were watching me or talking about me.

But there is a difference between being observed and being seen.

Observation is more scientific, more clinical, and far less empathetic. In observation, distance from the subject is desireable. We don't want to be rooting for the success of the bird we study or the cells we watch under the microscope in a lab. In seeing, a connection between experiences is desireable; we look for overlap and identification. We can go through seasons of life where we are observed and evaluated by many and seen by very few. It's like the difference between being alone and lonely. We can be alone and feel quite the sense of belonging and connection even if physically apart from others. We can feel lonely in a big family or a crowded room when it seems like no one really sees or connects to our experience.

Loneliness is an epidemic, ironically in the most digitally connected period of history. It seems the more tools and platforms we have for building connection, the more effort it takes to be seen and the harder it is to empathize with another through keyboards and anonymous identities.

I know what it is to feel lonely, when outsiders see your "perfect" marriage and fulfilling career, and everything "just so" in its proper place...everything except you. Breaking this world up, made me feel both less a stranger to myself and more alone than I could even fathom. Now I didn't even have my precious illusion of belonging. I had to learn to see myself, even amid the shards of a broken life.

When you move back into your childhood bedroom at thirty-two and resign from your job with benefits, you all of the sudden have a lot of free time and a swamp of emotions to wade through. A lot of free time and strong emotions with no income meant one thing: a trip to the library.

I brought home a stack of books whose covers looked intriguing and whose titles sounded medicinal: *Commonwealth* by Ann Patchett with the lovely oranges all over the cover; *Start Where You Are: The Art of Compassionate Living* by Pema Chödrön were two that I remember. I plopped down to read and soon discovered I wasn't ready for *Commonwealth*. An affair plays prominently in the first chapter and how it unravels for the children in the story wasn't particularly inspiring for one so close to ground zero. But *Start Where You Are* was a reasonable invitation. In those pages, I learned how to meditate. I learned to see myself and feel the rough edges of being suddenly torn off of everything I had bound myself to in the former life. My lonely marriage was ironically to an academic whose expertise was in mindfulness, and yet, I had never really learned to meditate until now. Many people will testify about how their lives changed once they mastered the art of meditation and started drinking green smoothies. I wasn't looking for a new life just yet, only trying to get out of my head for a second, by being deeply in it. I sat cross-legged on my childhood bed, with the sun coming through the blinds. I closed my eyes and breathed. In and out, the choppy air went in and out of my nose and mouth. In my head, I said "Breathe. Breathe!" with desperation, like one closely following a recipe. Then, as per instruction, I would say aloud, "Thinking" every time a thought came into my head that wasn't an inhale or exhale. I did that forever, or approximately three minutes before getting all fidgety. It's common for beginner meditation students to say they wrote it off as a crock of shit at first, but I really didn't. I longed to be good at something and to believe, especially in a time when the messages coming in were "You're terrible at just about everything."

It was hard giving myself permission to be mindful; I'd connected it so closely with my former partner. "He was the expert," I told myself, and I couldn't possibly know enough about this to measure up. The more present I became with myself and my breath, even as slow tears trickled down my cheeks as I uttered, "Thinking, thinking, thinking" because the thoughts rolling in were echoes of the last conversation he and I had—"Every season with you is a hard season, Elaine." "It's not that you had an affair, but that you lied." "You are untrustworthy." Eventually my meditation practice grew, even through the hard pavement of these traumatic memories.

So much of the gooey soup season was defined by fleeing— fleeing to escape people who wanted to peek in and observe me, poke me, prod me, or find out the scoop. Fleeing from my own anxiety about the future or accountability for my past. But meditation made me stop and be present, even when the moment was one I wanted to be anywhere but in. Cookie Monster's mindfulness wisdom came into play, "Today me will be in the moment, unless it is unpleasant, in which case me will eat a cookie."

There in the quiet breath I experienced a person who was not chaos. In the quiet breath, I met myself, a truly peaceful person, dealing with a lot of bullshit, mostly of my own making. But if I could cling to her, to the peace within, we would weather this storm.

Pema Chödrön was a compassionate teacher—making me laugh and encouraging me through those pages that I could do this. She also was a divorcee before moving to Tibet and becoming a Buddhist monk. I could envision possibilities beyond the present misery, giving me just a glimpse of life beyond divorce and heartbreak. We can't all be Elizabeth Gilbert in *Eat, Pray, Love*, traveling the world to find ourselves; our inner depths contain riches aplenty. Before I could envision what a new chapter would hold, I had to accept that the old one was ending. That took a lot of breathing and a lot of "thinking."

The concept of Jesus, for me, was too scary at this point. I could feel those judgy eyes inside me, touching the sinful spots that were never far away from my awareness. I felt so broken and like I had created a funhouse of distorted mirrors that were my public faith. I wasn't a professional Christian anymore, which left me time and space to tend the private faith lost somewhere in that steaming bowl of chaotic soup I swam in. When we celebrate the birth of Christ, we call him "Emmanuel"—which means "God with us." But often the messages we receive about the presence of Christ are more like a divinely run National Security Agency—God is spying on us, knowing us more deeply than we could possibly know ourselves. It's especially disturbing when you know you've done something wrong. And you know that God knows, because X knows, who is definitely not God.

Finding the true peace of Christ meant dismantling the divinely run NSA theology, and meeting Christ's peace as breath. I imagined myself sitting around the table of disciples on the third day after Jesus' death. His body is missing. The authorities are on the loose. There's rumor of a resurrection, but where are they? Behind a locked door, afraid for their lives. Jesus doesn't just wave a hand and say, "The hell with you guys for not believing what I said!" But he went through the dang door. He breathed on them and said,

"Peace I leave with you; my peace I give you. I give to you not as the world gives. Do not be troubled or afraid."[1]

In my breathing and thinking time, I got the courage to leave the locked room and meet Jesus on the shores of my meditation practice. My breath became the waves and I pictured myself walking in silence next to the Palestinian Jewish guy of those stories. Not confessing, not asking, just basking in the presence of that peace. Without words, I felt seen. It wasn't that what I did was okay and Christ was patting me on the head. But we kept walking, he with me, and I with him, breathing.

I encountered actual waves on a trip to San Diego to visit family. It was over the weekend that would have been my tenth wedding anniversary and the occasion was my cousin Larayne's wedding. My cousins and aunts and I made a pilgrimage to the Self-Realization Fellowship Meditation Gardens in Encinitas. It is a gorgeous sanctuary of lush tropical gardens planted on a cliff overlooking the Pacific Ocean. Visitors are encouraged to move slowly and silently through the flora, taking advantage of the many quiet spots for sitting and meditating. The only sounds are the crunch of sandy gravel beneath soft footsteps and the in and out "breaths" of the ocean waves.

After a few hours there, we made our way to a new agey crystal shop nearby, where the bride to be loved to shop. I was delicate then, like newly blistered skin that didn't like too much close contact and benefitted from lots of space and air. On a random

---

1. John 14:27

bookshelf in the crystal shop, through the haze of incense and patchouli, I stumbled on Dr. Judith Orloff's *Empath's Survival Guide*. After flipping through a few pages, I came to the exciting realization that many people going through something do, that there was a name for who I was and why this was so hard: I was an empath.

Some call it a "Highly Sensitive Person" (HSP) or Dr. Becky Kennedy calls us "Deepy Feeling Kids." It isn't a clinical diagnosis, but an acknowledgement that a lot of things hit different for us HSPs—too much noise or crowds, the pang of people's careless words, and the ability to pick up on subtle changes in our environment and people's non-verbal cues. As I flipped through the pages of Dr. Orloff's book, I felt seen in a way I never had before. Here I was learning that there wasn't something wrong with me, but that I hadn't known how to care for this critical piece of my personhood. I didn't know that baths and soaking in the water was not just a "nice to have" but a must for clearing all the energy and emotion I absorb from others—that's why I craved the ocean! I no longer had to be confused by my extroverted tendencies and my need for alone time—those were understandable contradictions as an HSP.

One of the characters Dr. Orloff introduced me to in this newfound identity was the bodhisattva of compassion and mercy, Guan Yin. A bodhisattva is an enlightened person, who though she could enter into the pantheon of Nirvana, chooses to remain human in order to guide and be in solidarity with those of us finding our way through suffering. Guan Yin is akin to the Virgin Mary in Western Christianity—a divinely feminine image. Her full name in Chinese is Guanshiyin, which means "Observing the sounds of the world."[2] She is depicted seated in a lotus position, with a serene look, almost like the Mona Lisa whose eyes appear to follow you— Guan Yin looks like she is listening actively to whatever burdens you carry. She is the patron saint of us Highly Sensitive People, especially those who feel lonely and unseen by the world around

---

2. Soka Gakkai Nichiren Buddhism Library (https://www.nichirenlibrary.org/en/dic/Content/P/39)

us. Breathing while holding on to her image gave me a sense of being seen especially on the days I struggled to see myself.

As my meditation practice grew, I clung to a set of jade beads with a Guan Yin pendant on them. The beads helped me count my breaths and affirm whatever mantra I used. Here are a few that guided me on my way:

I am worthy of being loved.
Within me is everything that I need.
I can do hard shit.
I belong in this world.
Joy is within reach.
My peace I give to you, not as the world gives.
I am unafraid.
I am safe, I am loved, I am at peace.

The beads and pendant sit on my nightstand, and sometimes I use them to go to sleep. More than flowers or gifts, the assurance that I am seen for everything I am, not just what I accomplish, draws me back to the peace that Christ breathed on his disciples. Folks raised in a religious tradition are often taught to be afraid or distant from others' belief systems. In evangelical Christianity, Eastern practices are often all lumped together as "pagan" or "satanic" or as a distraction from the ultimate allegiance to Christ. But my experience has been one of expansion and drawing together the tools from wherever they arrive from to lead us towards oneness with God. I feel the peace of Christ, walking on the beach, and seen by Guan Yin in her limitless compassionate serenity. We don't have to choose.

Even if my prayer beads were to become lost or disappear, seeing myself has taught me to trust that I am never left in sadness or desperation alone. Access to joy cannot depend on something outside of us. External forces can always be stripped away, but we never fully lose ourselves. Our minds have the ability to craft worlds and stories. Our senses can take in what's outside of us and then we make sense of it by practicing internal observation and presence. When we see and understand our experiences with compassion, we are able to observe them with more distance—it doesn't hurt as much anymore.

Wayfinding Practice: Meditation

We don't do guilt and shame when we're trying out a new practice. Meditation, like prayer, can come with a lot of baggage when people start thinking of it as a *discipline* rather than a tool. You don't feel guilty that you eat some meals with forks and others with spoons or with your hands, do you? Then as you begin learning to meditate, to be present and clear your mind, you are going to treat this like picking up a spoon. Start small, just close your eyes for a minute. You can set a timer at first, but the key is to be in a comfortable position. I find sitting up rather than lying down keeps me from accidentally falling asleep in the quiet. Get comfortable, shut your mouth and soften your eyes. Close your eyes if it helps you not fixate on your surroundings. Close you eyes and just count your thoughts to begin with. Then start clearing them away. The goal is to sit with an empty mind for as long as you can. You can imagine your thoughts like browser tabs that are open and you mentally click the little "x" in the corner to make them disappear. Or one of my favorite visualizations is to imagine me sitting next to a stream, where each thought is a little paper boat, floating past me and off over the horizon. Play around with these images and as you do, let the time extend. Notice how clear and rested you feel when it's time for your meditation to end.

If There Is a Fall, There Is a Rising

The most dangerous stories we make up are the narratives that diminish our inherent worthiness. We must reclaim the truth about our lovability, divinity, and creativity.

— *Brené Brown*, Rising Strong

BURN IT ALL DOWN AND REBUILD.

When the whole thing burns down and there are smoldering ashes and ruble before you of what former days had been, the timeline of how far in advance we can live and plan shrinks suddenly. What was a five-year or twenty-year plan is now ten seconds at a time. **This is normal**. Everything we thought was stable and predictable is no longer that way and we must be *agile* in our adaptation. Eventually the ten seconds becomes ten minutes and then thirty minutes at a time. Soon the minutes will stretch into days, and then you find yourself staring down a week with some reliable expectations for what stops it will include.

Insecurity prompts us to look up and out, beyond ourselves for some outside force or source to save us, to pluck us out of the rubble and set us right again. Sometimes the outside help comes in a handout or a job, or a place to rest our heads for the night. But most often, the source of our rising comes not from above or outside, but from within.

When you fall, friend, know that for every fall, there will come another rise. You cannot stay down forever. What is the force that will lift you back up again? Many have struggled to name or describe it: God, Source, Spirit, Universe, Divine Love. The name is not as important as our access and relationship to it.

Affirmations were the path that led me down into the debris of what was in order to find the true foundation, this Source/Spirit/Truth, as opposed to the false floor I had built everything on before.

Affirmations can seem kind of "woo woo" to the more institutionally religious, but even mainline Christians have experience with them. In my tradition, we stand and affirm our faith every week saying aloud what we believe to be true about God. We can practice individual affirmatons too; when something isn't true, it won't feel right passing through our lips. We are taught from a young age to criticize and berate ourselves in negative/false affirmations,, often from a caregiver or authority figure who received the same messaging in their upbringing. "I'm so stupid. I'll never make it."

It takes **five** repetitions of the opposite positive truth for our brains to begin to pivot from negative messaging. Five out loud repetitions.

One time my 8-year-old went on a tear of negative self-talk after making a mistake. I sat with eyes the size of golf balls while he went on—before yelling "STOP!" I couldn't bear the thought of him, or anyone, saying such awful things about such a lovely person. We sat down and wrote them all down—eleven things. And then we made a list of fifty-five unique and wonderful affirming truths about him. His punishment was that he had to stand in front of the mirror and repeat the list to himself three times per day. I could physically spot how his shoulders that were once slumped, straightened with every declaration from his laminated list. He did not strut out of affirmation time, but it was some thin glaze of protection from the harshness the world is ready to spew at us.

We know we need a rising when the words "too" and "always" and "never" pop up in our self-talk, such as:

You're *too* sensitive.

You'll *never* be this way.

You'll *always* be that way.

It's no wonder you *feel* this way, because you *are* this way.

And before you know it, what might have started as a wondering that sputtered aloud sounds like a declaration, becomes cemented in your mind as factual truth: you are an actual a-hole.

Affirmations help undo the knots of our own cognitive making. We must speak the truth out loud, not just write it down or think it silently. Have you said "I'm too sensitive" aloud? It tastes like falsehood, like poison on the tongue. You cannot keep up that lie forever.

But to proclaim its inverse: *my tender heart is a strength*, rings true. Here's a way that affirmations led me back into the truth of who I am:

This is too hard became

This is really hard, which turned into:

Hard things do end.

This load is too heavy for me morphed into

This hard thing is making me stronger which then meant:

I can do hard things, and expanded into:

I can do hard things because I am a strong person.

I am strong enough to get to the other side of this.

This will get better. I am getting stronger.

Saying affirmations aloud is keeping promises to yourself, promises to be kind and hopeful. When we keep promises to ourselves, our confidence grows.

"Behold, I am doing a new thing. Do you not perceive it?"[1] the

---

1. Isaiah 43:19

prophet Isaiah said, as God's mouthpiece, calling the people who had been struggling and downtrodden, oppressed by their enemies and told all kind of untruths, to pay attention. God promises to change their name, from wounded and defeated to "My Delight Is In Them."[2] This promise is reliable for all people who have been in trouble, who feel far from joy.

You have inherent worth.

You are worthy of belonging.

You are going through an incredibly painful process and doing so with courage, strength and grace, kindness even towards those who need it.

When life can only be living in ten minute increments, I had to make lists like this one:

The list of those who need kindness today:

1. Me
2. Ollie
3. Isaiah

It was too much of a stretch to add X to that list, and now, when life is being lived in 10 minute increments, is not the time to start. That energy is needed for other things. Things like taking showers and brushing teeth, and out-yelling the internal monologue of worthlessness. What outsiders often don't realize about those who have been caught doing a Very Bad Thing, is that outsider judgment really *doesn't* help. It's not like I didn't know that what I did was Very Bad. In fact, I just used the guilt from the Very Bad Thing to prove the point I was trying to make to myself that of course I did a Very Bad Thing. Because I am a Very Bad Person. We don't need anyone else's help in the shame. Thank you.

If there is a fall, there is a rising.

I rose by saying affirmations out loud.

---

2. Isaiah 62:4

I am deserving of love.
Nothing I have done makes me less deserving of love.
There is life on the other side of this hard thing.

The gospel of Luke tells a story of Jesus' friends going through a hard thing, even before he is arrested and crucified. His friend Lazarus gets sick and dies while Jesus is off ministering somewhere else. When he comes back to them, Lazarus has been dead long enough for his body to stink and it seems as if Jesus has lost his moment to shine. He weeps with the mourners. The death of Lazarus was real. And yet, even in his sorrow, Jesus also saw another truth, that he spoke aloud to those mourning with him. "Lazarus will rise again." He said. And then he called to Lazarus, "Rise! Lazarus, get up!"[3] and then he told them to unbind him, get him out of the graveclothes so he could walk and live and move freely again.

Affirmations are a way of welcoming life that has not yet arrived.

Jesus saw the truth, that Lazarus would rise again.

He said it out loud.

And then he said it, even to Lazarus, calling him into the true thing that Jesus knew. And it was true.

Visions of life outside the tomb keep me moving forward.

"Rise! Lazarus, get up!" Jesus said.

"Rise! Elaine, get up!" I heard.

Unbind yourself from what has been and walk into what will be.

The call to rise is from the Divine. God does not want us to stay at rock bottom. God is invested in the true thing that is us rising to our full potential, becoming who God calls and affirms us to be. The first time God introduces themselves in scripture, they call themselves "I am who I am" or also translated "I will be who I will

---

3. John 11:43

be."[4] Our ability to rise comes from the heart of God's own identity, that God too is becoming what will come to pass.

"Let me live, God. Let me live through this awful thing," I prayed.

When X kicked me out of our home, he added, "I'm worried for you." I want to and perhaps do believe he meant it more confessionally, projecting, "I'm worried for me." I carried that worry for him, for me, until it was too heavy to bear. Worry got in the way of my journey to rising.

I am rising.

People sometimes ask how I keep going, or how I became pretty much unflappable in the face of scary things or shocking news. I smile and admit, it's because I had no other choice. Owning up when you've done somethiing wrong and hurtful is really hard. But it's not as exhausting as running from it and hiding it. I lament how twisted and broken our world is becoming—we are living as every generation has before us, in an era in which lies are accepted as truth, when the things we once trusted as sure are crumbling. It is said that "the strong survive," but I don't want to be the kind of strong that is made rigid in the face of uncertainties and tribulation. There is a Polish proverb that says it's the same boiling water that *softens* the potato, *hardens* the egg, and *distills* the tea leaves. In our rising from the ashes of tragedy, we have the option of letting it make us softer, harder, or wiser. Soft and wise are the affirmative choices I go back to.

I am allowing this hard thing to make me wise and kind.

---

4. Exodus 3:14

Wayfinding Practice: Affirmations

Give yourself a minute to do a little freewrite of all the beliefs running like ticker tape through your mind in any given moment. In hard times, are you beating yourself up? What are the voices from your past that tear you down? Just write a few down, don't go nuts at first. Then for each negative thought, write down **five** positive affirmations you can tell yourself. These aren't lies to inflate your ego. These are truths about the incredible, amazing, growing human being you are and that you are becoming. Feel free to take some of the affirmations I've listed in this chapter for yourself. Once you have your list of positive affirmations, read them to yourself, making eye contact in the mirror three times each day. Watch how your posture changes. It's okay if you feel silly at first. Watch how your life changes and your heart heals.

The Little Broken Bits

Our hearts are restless until they find their rest in thee.

— *Augustine of Hippo, who by the way was a total sex*
addict and we still love him

ONE OF THE TENSE DAYS IN THE FIRST WEEKS AFTER I WAS KICKED OUT
of our home and removed from my children, my still-husband-but-
on-the-way-out and I sat at the table on my parents' lovely backyard patio. Feeling brave and tender, I asked the clinical psychologist whom I still, after everything, trusted as a child does, "Am I a
narcissist?" I was so genuinely confused by all that had taken place
that I couldn't trust my own self-perception. The internet is full of
articles and comment forums where people rage against those who
cheat on their spouses. We are sinister, despicable, unloveable,
broken, disgusting people. So I thought perhaps the person I hurt,
but who I still believed was really smart, could tell me if it was true
or not.

It was like I was recovering from a blunt head trauma—I no
longer had my wits about me and wandered around in a daze,
unable to plan more than ten minutes at a time. I did not manipu-

late this. I could not have orchestrated this. This was not part of some master plan to devastate anyone. And if it were, I was a much worse planner than I thought.

He responded, "Well you act like one."

Thud.

Okay. There's my answer. Adding "I'm a narcissist" to the pile of things to dump on my therapist's couch. When I marched to therapy a few days later, I huffed and I puffed before even starting with the pleasantries, "Am I a narcissist? Because I think X, who is certified to diagnose people as that, just did."

Friends, you must know, and especially my perfectionist lovelies out there, that there really is no such thing as a permanent record. In school you grow up scared of not passing the state-mandated standardized tests or missing too many school days because (menacing voice implied), "It will go on your PERMA-NENT RECORD."

There isn't one. It does not exist. I mean, perhaps the NSA has one on you with a few questionable texts that you sent in college, joking about staging a coups, but no one is keeping actual records of things you've said, done, created, or been diagnosed with. Your therapists and medical professionals do not talk about you or pass secret notes behind your back. There is no filing cabinet of atrocities in the after life either.

If meditation or COVID-19 has taught us anything, can it be the truth that literally nothing is permanent? Tattoos fade, nipples sag, and nothing in this world lasts forever. But to the 32-year-old devastated homewrecker on my parents' porch that day, I want to contextualize and soften the response of the man she trusted to answer the question she asked in earnest. I want to remind her, "Sis, you've been married to a mental health worker. You know they're all hot messes and couldn't possibly get their shit together enough for something resembling a 'permanent record' on anyone." Their words are not magic, though they have the power to hurt and to heal. So the therapist whose couch I just collapsed on let out a sigh and a long outstretched, "Ooooookaaaay" and reached for her DSM-V.

It's like a spellbook for therapists, but way less sexy.

I grew up in a healthcare house, but not a mental healthcare house. We had *The Physician's Desk Reference* on the same shelf as our encyclopedias where we could look up minor ailments and save a trip to the emergency room. Other healthcare kids know, unless you have chest pain, don't ever go to the emergency room, and even then, think twice. It was fun to see latin words for things and read long multi-syllabic words that made us kids think "Wow, doctors must be some kinda special stupid if this is the language they speak," but the PDR never turned us into hypochondriacs.

If I had grown up with a *Diagnostic and Statistical Manual* though. Wow, could I have exposure-therapied myself out of ever having anxiety? Would I have a mental illness of the week? Could I have made it through the teens without diagnosing everyone around me with an Axis Two disorder? Axis Two is common psycho-parlance for personality disorders, like bipolar, hystrionic personality disorder, borderline personality disorder, etc.

Here in the therapist's office, the DSM was a controlled substance. I have **never** seen a therapist pull one out mid-session, especially not right at the start! But she did what my soul needed and craved. She didn't answer my anxious musing with her thoughts. She read aloud. It was like going to the Rabbi and having them pull a scroll directly out of the holy ark mid-session. I sat at rapt attention on her couch, ready to hear, "A reading from the Prophet Isaiah…" except it was the list of five or more traits of Narcissistic Personality Disorder (NPD). She listed them as questions. "Do you feel a grandiose sense of self-importance? Are you preoccupied with fantasies of unlimited success, power, brilliance, beauty, or ideal love? Do you believe that you are special, unique, and higher status than everyone else? Do you lack empathy? Are you envious of others' success or beauty?"

I sat and took it all in. "No," I said, with a far away look in my eye, quietly, reflectively. I am not those things. In addition to affirming the truth of who we are, accessing joy means releasing the identities that no longer fit us. We would not wear clothes that are too tight, or tattered and worn out. Nor is it good for us to haul around the hurts that others have lobbed at us that have no grounding in reality.

I don't doubt that X perceived my behavior towards him as narcissistic. And yet the perception of others is not absolute truth.

My memories of sharing a life in that house were colored by anger, more than grandiosity. I was angry when we couldn't work together on things. I was angry about the mental load I carried.

Anger is often the emotion women access first when we are overwhelmed and cannot identify that something is off. "Mommy rage" is how I expressed my overwhelm at all the touching, all the administrative household management of parenting two kids under two. It took time and space and a lot of therapy to realize that I am not an angry person.

Anger is a messenger—telling you that something is not right. Often we look at the outcomes of one's emotional expression or dysregulation before we examine the *inputs* of the machine. What goes on behind the scenes that makes anger the byproduct?

Our society has developed elaborate means of isolating women from their emotions, or protecting society from feminine "feelings." We burned the women as witches in Salem, but now we discredit them, gaslight them, attack them as mothers, cutting them off from the very responsibilities we entrust to them.

It's so much easier and more rewarding to punish and mistrust women than it is to be curious about our experiences and perceptions. The best pastoral care and friendship I've been on the receiving end of has asked, "What's that like?" instead of "What were you thinking?!"

Sometimes there are no words to say when someone is going through *a thing*, but there is only presence.

The light of hope shone only very thinly for me when so much was in flux. I kept probing, "Am I as narcissistic as the internet tells me I am?" while at the same time securing a therapist who took my insurance and making sure my kids had air mattresses to sleep on when it was my day to pick them up from school and also getting my lawyer all the documents I didn't know I needed or had access to and also searching for a job and crying into my wine at night, and trying to furnish the house I was going to rent.

A friend came with me to help empty the old house of my things as I started out on this new journey.

They helped me package up the nativity set with all the camels and wise men and Mary and Joseph—we wrapped them not in swaddling cloths but in newsprint and packed them away for a Christmas I could not yet envision.

There was one piece we forgot. It was a lone shepherd girl and in the move she ended up on my nightstand, away from the manger.

On the outside, she looked perfect, pristine. Gently holding her lamb in a posture for adoring the son of God. But on the inside, if you gave her a little shake, you could hear something was broken. Perhaps it was a broken heart. Perhaps it was a broken spirit.

Perhaps it was a deep-seated belief that she did not have what it took to belong at the manger or in God's house. Many of us ache and long for the place of belonging, the kind of grace that will heal those broken pieces within us and between us.

Paul wrote a letter to Titus, during a time when he was sent to minister to people who were in upheaval. Paul wrote, "The Grace of God has appeared bringing salvation to all people."[1] The grace of God has appeared even to those not present around the manger to those of us who would come later and much later and even to those who are still making their way, the grace of God has appeared bringing salvation to all.

This grace forms and shapes us to live sensibly, ethically, and godly lives. This grace—it even runs deep enough to that little broken part inside that the outsider's eye cannot see but that we know. This grace born in vulnerability, born in a world cloaked in

---

1. Titus 2:11

darkness and confusion worked on it to heal it, to call it to a new way of life.

Accessing joy is about welcoming a gift that heals, even when we may not be eager to receive it. "Grace" is a fancy word that make for a great middle name for pastors' kids, but which truly means "something we didn't have to earn." Grace heals us. Grace is powerful, but humble too—humble enough that it is there waiting for us even when we aren't ready to receive it.

This gift is a God who loves us humans, not from far away, but up close, and deeply, and personally. But also collectively and big and writ large. This gift is for the long haul, much longer than you can imagine. The grace of God is God never giving up on us. The grace of God does not read the comments section, so it doesn't care that everyone else thinks you are scum of the earth. The grace of God is always making new, changing forever the ways of "tit for tat" and "an eye for an eye" justice into new life and forgiveness that never expires. God had this Word, this grace from the beginning, even when times were chaotic and soupy. Long before humanity was a twinkle and it was thousands of years before that grace appeared on the silent night in Bethlehem with glories streaming and angels singing.

God has had a new beginning at work since the first beginning. A light that would shine and not be overcome by darkness—it's name would be Emmanuel, God with us. Grace came to my house and wrapped my nativity set in newsprint. Grace showed up in the cab of the truck my brother-in-law rolled in on like the Cajun Navy driving into a hurricane and asked, "Ok, what needs to be moved next?" Anne Lamott describes grace as that force that "Meets us where we are but does not leave us where it found us." For me that has come through people. I believe in people. I believe God acts through people and God's most miraculous acts are changed human hearts: the hardening and softening and kneading of Pharaoh's heart was Spirit's long way towards liberation—far more miraculous than any of those plagues in Exodus. Even the resurrection was a miracle of belief more than quickening pulse.

Miracles are not relics of the past, but things we get to experience with our hearts, minds, and souls every day. "You are the potter, I am the clay,"[2] the prophet Jeremiah prayed. Spiritual practice then is nothing more than managing our own elasticity and pliability—strengthening ourselves to remain moldable, while also attending to the integrity of the artist's work until we are formed for a new purpose.

There are broken little bits inside of you, just like inside of me. Grace gives us the power and the humility to ask the hard questions of ourselves. My process of self-inquiry started with, "Am I a narcissist?" but even beneath that was, "Is what others say about me true?" But it led to me asking, "What's making me feel so angry?" and, "How can I live differently in this chapter?" Self-inquiry is one of the ways we access our joy, and we do it with the grace of witnesses and friends, near enough to help us pack up the nativity, or even respond to our questions like my now husband did, "I don't know if you're a narcissist, but if you are, you're my narcissist."

---

2. Jeremiah 18:1-11

Wayfinding Practice: Get it OUT

Get out of your own head. Get it on a page, in a voice memo, on a post-it note that you throw in the trash.

X started each morning with three in a row super loud sneezes, which one, was the most terrifying way to wake up each morning if you're in the bed beside him, but two, taught me something about what first thing in the morning is for (and a bonus three: we're not married anymore). Start your day with clearing stuff out! Out of your nasal passages, your bladder, and your heart.

"I'm not a journaler" you might protest. That's okay. I'm not asking you to be. You don't have to pick methods other people pick in order to care for your soul. But everybody has stuff they need to get out.

If YOU don't get it out, it will come out at an awkward moment like oversharing with your Uber driver or unloading to a coworker —it comes out like a bad fart when you didn't take the time for a bathroom break!

So how do you get it out?

You can type it into the notes app of your phone, you can write it on a piece of paper, or you can say it out loud into a voice memo.

Here are the keys for successfully "outing" your stuff: It has to exist somewhere outside of your body. You can't do this part in your head. The point is for it to get OUT of your head. It needs to go somewhere safe, where no one else will see it or judge it. This part is really important and why I advise being very careful with digital tools. If you write it down, make sure what you write gets put in an inconspicuous place so that you can really be honest. This step won't work if you are writing for someone else's eyes.

It doesn't matter WHAT you write/say, as long as it is HONEST.

If you're just starting out, aim for writing or saying ONE true thing out loud. If that true thing is "I'm tired," then you need to write or say TWO true things, or go deeper.

What are you tired from/of?

Where do you feel the exhaustion?

What is its source?

The goal in step one is to take something OFF the load you are carrying.

You might be surprised by what comes out in this practice. The truth you express may seem totally out of nowhere and then come up again and again repeatedly. Sometimes this step reveals truths and directions for us that we don't make time to listen to at any other time of the day.

The Trinity of Pats

I summon spirit to protect me today from poison and burning,
  from drowning and wounding,
so that there may come to me an abundance of true reward.
Spirit when I lie down, Spirit when I sit, Spirit when I stand.
Spirit before me, behind me, and through me.
Spirit to my right, on my left, and within me.
Spirit beneath me, above me, and around me.
Spirit in every eye that sees me, in every ear that hears me, in
  every mouth that speaks of me.

*— Orna Ross, "My Mantle" —a version of Saint
Patrick's Breastplate*

I'M THE YOUNGEST DAUGHTER OF A YOUNGEST SON, WHOSE THREE brothers got a kick out of calling him, "Patricia" until he insisted on going by his first name, James. After a little family discipline and discussion on the merits of famous "Pats" throughout history, he's been "Pat" ever since.

Albert, my attorney, also goes by Pat, as well as Patricia, the therapist who is getting me through this.

How did three people come together and position themselves at such necessary posts as I make my way through crisis? When you're riding the murky, confusing, violent waves of trauma, that's when nothing is accidental, and every coincidence can be a message.

When Adam and Eve were confronted by God and kicked out of Eden, the writer of Genesis says cherubim and seraphim were placed at the entrance to keep the humans from returning. Cherubim and Seraphim art not little fat babies with wings—they are tough, strong, impenetrable armed guards—messengers of the Holy that say, "Thou shall not pass."

Next time you hear someone exclaim, "Oh, what an ANGEL?!" I'd watch out if I were you. The three Pats have been my angels—guarding me from returning to an old life, sealing the entrance with legal expertise, a father's broken heart, and a firm set of boundaries.

This chapter of my story is how I came to believe in the power of synchronicity—the idea that events that seem to be related but have no clear cause are meaningful coincidences.

It is said that significant things come in threes—deaths, illnesses, bouts of luck, or deities. It's hard to tell where the line was crossed between the old life ending in shards and the new life starting to knit itself together, but I know The Pats were major guideposts in the transition from there to here. In Tarot, the Major Arcana are the guidepost cards, indicative of big things afoot—cards like "The Sun," "The Moon" or "Wheel of Fortune" as opposed to the numbered suits of Minor Arcana, which usually speak to day to day activities. The Pats were Major Arcana of my Fool's Journey Tarot, angels in disguise.

There was Daddy Pat, who stood in his living room, while I cried on the couch and told him that X kicked me out because I was having an affair with Rob. He would sit many evenings in his chair (all Southern Dads have a "chair"—usually that reclines and that no one else in the house sits in, either because it's covered in dad fart or out of reverence or both), while I wept on the floor with a glass of wine and recounted what drama had unfolded and what my next steps were. Daddy Pat taught me not to text after the second drink, and how to set up a LinkedIn profile. Daddy Pat held my arm while we walked down the aisle at my first wedding, telling me that it wasn't too late if I wanted to turn back. He held the same arm as we walked down the hall to my first divorce attorney consultation. I can't say he refrained from judgment, but I know he held back and bit his tongue as much as possible.

Daddy Pat introduced me to Attorney Pat, who gave me my orientation to both the American legal system and the finer points of family law. I wept in Attorney Pat's office as I walked this good Baptist man through my infidelity, careful to preserve the identity of the afflicted, and how I didn't know what to do now that X had my journals and was using them as "collateral" to get me to agree to what he wanted.

"What's in these journals, Elaine?" Attorney Pat asked.

"Well * sob * a lot of things about how I resent my kids, how I sometimes hate the sound of their little feet when I'm trying to have a spiritual moment, about how many times and places I met up with my lover…"

"Let me stop you right there," Attorney Pat interrupted. "The state of Texas has very low standards for what good parenting is, which I think in this case should come as good news. Unless your journals have recorded instances of you engaging with hookers while doing blow, and even then, *only* in front of your kids, then any reasonable judge would dismiss this as hearsay and the ramblings of a very human and emotionally intelligent mother of young children."

I lived on these words. Hookers and blow!? They were like morsels to me in the wilderness of self-loathing. No matter what anyone convinces you of, the truth will set you free. I am a good mom, and not just according to the profoundly low parenting standards of the state of Texas. The more time goes by, the more I see both how naive and gullible I was then, and also how deeply X wanted to hurt me in my most vulnerable place. That is the hell of divorce.

About the time that I was so desperate for a roof over my head and immediate legal representation, I was also clamoring for a therapist. Thank God for employee assistance programs and for the saints who sign up to receive insurance companies' abysmal reimbursements. You got my sorry ass to the crumpled couch of the third member of the trinity, Therapist Pat.

Therapist Pat is a short, round, latina former Roman Catholic nun turned therapist who by day works with the criminally insane at the state hospital and moonlights to "The walking wounded" in her private practice, "In God's Hands Christian Counseling." Disclaimer: "Christian Counseling" is often a misnomer, being neither Christian, nor counseling. Most people who set out to practice are neither all that knowledgeable or committed to the Christian faith, nor too well-versed in the standards of professional counseling. Reader beware when "Christian" and "Counseling" are paired together. It is a **grace** that I stumbled into the safe place of Therapist Pat's backyard bungalow office to spill the pieces of my heart.

Therapy intake sessions are utterly exhausting. How do you know what to share?

"Where do I start?" I asked through tears, just after my butt hit the couch. Tears came overwhelmingly easy to me in those ten-minute-at-a-time days.

"Let's start at the very beginning," Therapist Pat invited, like Fräulein Maria teaching the Von Trapp children to sing. I spilled it all. Honesty has never been a problem for me in therapy and as I have learned, in writing either. She nodded, asked some clarifying questions, and let my tears guide me towards my truth. Towards the end, she closed her notepad and said, "Ok, this is a God thing, that we have been led together. There are many parallels in your story to my own. I won't get into them, but know that you can trust me to hold this as sacred. Your peace has been shattered, but God does not disturb our peace, except to lead us to a deeper peace," the angel spoke.

From September to May, the Trinity of Pats held my battered boat together to withstand the flood. Daddy Pat got me into a little rent house, which I named "The Healing Hygge Home." Not what every newly retired parent wants to do with their funds and free time, but he did anyway. Attorney Pat got me through two full-day mediations and managed to not lose much hair while fiercely advocating for me. He inspired the working title for this book as he railed across the table at the opposing lawyer, "My client is owning her shit!" Eventually he passed off my case to Attorney Amy, who is a whole enchanting chapter to herself, so he could take a spot on the judge's bench. Now *Judge* Pat's signature on our divorce decree is frameable, tattooable, or at least cheers-able in gratitude for all he taught me about accountability, lifting one's head high, and knowing how to negotiate.

Therapist Pat worked with me for five years, helping me to reclaim my deeper peace, grieve my marriage, show up for my kids and myself, question, test, and ultimately choose my new marriage, and never let go of my vocation as a minister of God in the process.

Daddy Pat, I'm fortunate to say, still comes to dinner and helps me with less terrifying life problems like how to replace the electrical socket the former owners painted blue.

What I'm saying about these three wonderful people is that when you are going through hard things, reinforcements come from unexpected places. Delight in them. Take stock of what they are saying to you, even when it is a hard truth. Synchronicity leads us to the aquifer of joy, even if we have to pass through a bit of thorny bramble to find it. A friend of mine whose husband died from a long journey with cancer kept finding dimes everywhere after he was gone. Constant reminders of his presence and little breadcrumbs to show her she was on the right track. Look after these messages from the universe. They are not accidents, but messengers.

Wayfinding Practice: Name Your Saints

 You may have already listed a few folks in your ark-building exercise a few chapters back, but naming your saints focuses specifically on the angels in disguise who have come into your life. Maybe they've just come in for a specific season. They don't have to be with you "through thick and thin." Make a list of these people. Who are they? How did they come into your life? If you feel so moved, write a short note of gratitude to them or express a hope for the unique role you see them playing in the world. Send it if you're feeling brave.

Naming Loss and Not Living There

Everybody Grieves

The way we conceive the future sculpts the present, gives contour and tone to nearly every action and thought throughout the day.

— Eugene Peterson

KNOWING HOW TO ACCESS JOY IS A MOMENTOUS STEP TOWARDS A NEW beginning when you've been through a hard thing. But joy alone will not save us. We have to believe, no matter where we are in the foundational repair process that loss will not always be our truth. Some speak of grief as a thing to be "metabolized," which is a process that happens physically as much as spiritually, mentally, or emotionally. Metabolism is the process of converting one material (like food or drink) into energy to keep you alive and functioning. Naming loss is the beginning of that process. Metabolizing will come, but first, we must dare to name it out loud. Perhaps you can only write it on a piece of paper or in the notes section of your phone. Soon you'll move from metabolizing to *alchemizing* your grief, but first you name it, claim it, own it.

It took me months to be able to say, "I'm going through a divorce," without a quiver in my lip. The "D" word—divorce, made my lips tremble for months, and I remember shaking my head as if that would make the reality go away. No! Divorce wasn't in my life plan! Divorce had so much baggage I didn't want to carry into *my* lived experience. Before I could afford to gloss over those sections of the Bible where divorce was discussed, as if those applied to someone *else*, not me. But for now it felt so heavy.

And yet, when we name a reality, it loses its power over us. Before family gatherings, I would practice in the mirror, watching my lips move, saying, "I'm going through a divorce." "What's my marital status? Divorced." like Dory in *Finding Nemo,* repeating the address until "P. Sherman 42 Wallaby Way, Sydney" became my new relationship address.

When we name loss, we neutralize its staying power. As soon as a reality is spoken into being, it is fleeting. When we grieve, grief persists when it is held without being named. Like a monster in the basement, the unspoken but deeply felt emptiness keeps getting bigger and bigger. Nothing stays the same forever, but denial only makes the monster under the bed grow larger and scarier. Naming it turns on the light and helps you to see that while some life changes are quite permanent, they don't have the ability to steal our joy or prevent us from experiencing transformation. In fact, naming these realities is how we make it *through* to transformation.

In a flurry of words and directives, the big loss arrived on August 30th, 2019, but the little losses kept compounding from there. Naming each one was part of the untangling and restringing a new life together. I lost my home. I lost my job. I lost access to my children. I lost a husband. I lost my sense of safety. I lost money. I lost dignity. I lost face. I lost friends. I lost a vision for the future to which I had clung quite deeply. These are serious risks for a nervous breakdown according to some list put out by psychologists. When the hits just keep coming, one must wonder, "At a certain point, will I just waste away? Will I have anything left to sustain all these losses?" There is. By some miraculous divine accounting, there is more of you than you think.

We have been conditioned to believe that you give and you give and you give until something is gone. But *hope* is regenerative. You hope and you hope, and hope persists. Hope is often depicted as an anchor; it grounds us, unmoved by the storms of life. Some losses may seem like acid, eating away at what our anchor of hope is made of, but our hope exists even beyond the waves of feeling.

Our most superficial experiences of hope are often tied to concert tickets and lottery chances. But even beneath the desire to get a good parking space or into your dream college, is a hope for a good life, a joyful experience, redemption, belonging, safety—a basic need. I hoped that X would see that I was worth working through our crappy marriage to build something better. It broke my heart when that hope was dashed. But the anchor of hope is tied, not to the whims of others, but to the very foundation of the earth itself. "My hope is built on nothing less than Jesus' blood and right-eousness" go the old hymn lyrics, which speak to a reality that our hope for the things we need: belonging, safety, redemption, joy comes from a source deeper and stronger than any force on earth, to the mystical body of a man who taught alignment with God's desires and that all material is temporal.

It took me even longer to be able to say what happened: I had a relationship with someone before my marriage was over, and it caused my spouse to lash out in anger, and he hurt me deeply with that unchecked rage. Instead those losses came out in a flurry, "He stole my journals!" To which the 95% of the world who does not write in a journal every day would raise a quizzical brow as if to say, "Um, okay, so what?" And the grief would compound.

The best companions to naming loss are those who will sit in the heavy pauses with you, nodding or saying in a text, "That is so hard to hold, my friend."

What's the difference between naming loss and fixating on it?

Dr. Suess writes in his infinite wisdom, *Oh! The Places You'll Go* that you are the hero of your own narrative,

"You can get so confused
that you'll start in to race
down long wiggled roads at a break-necking pace
and grind on for miles cross weirdish wild space,
headed, I fear, toward a most useless place.
The Waiting Place...
...for people just waiting.
Waiting for a train to go
or a bus to come, or a plane to go
or the mail to come, or the rain to go
or the phone to ring, or the snow to snow
or the waiting around for a Yes or No
or waiting for their hair to grow.
Everyone is just waiting."

There comes a point in the transformation of struggle when we feel stuck. The lines all sound the same. The pain still makes our lips quiver. The situation hasn't been resolved, or at least not to our satisfaction, and the bus/plane/mail/rain has not come. I do not believe we will remain stuck there without choosing to stay there as long as we need to. There was a time after many hours on Therapist Pat's couch when all my stories began to repeat, and nothing was shifting regarding my court case, and I was stuck. I had coping skills and was no longer in therapy triage. I knew how to yell at the ducks to relieve my tension and to set boundaries when whatever X said made my eyebrows shoot up to the sky. But progress was stalled and we both knew it.

She gave me a small terracotta pot. with the instruction to write every terrible, awful thing. All the losses. "All the hurtful things that were said to you. I want you to write it all in permanent marker all over this pot. Carry it around with you and when a memory comes to you, add it to the pot."

Oh, I could not wait. Yes! I needed a listening ear, which I could not exhaust! I turned to my terracotta pot and said, "Did you know he did this?!" And then I would say to her, "And did you know my so-called friend said *that*?" I carried the little pot around with me for a month or two. I took pictures of her. I was instructed not to put anything inside of *"Terry"* but words, and keep my eyes out for a wide-mouthed vase to bring when I was ready.

Writing by hand is one of the physical ways we name loss. On the full moon, my cousin encouraged me to write down the things I was ready to let go of, light them on fire in the moonlight, and flush their ashes down the toilet. Deep cleaning with a broom, blowing the leaves, kneading bread, punching a pillow—these were all physical ways to process the grief, the sadness, the anger my body held.

The days grew farther between when I would write things on my little terracotta pot. It sat on my desk like a centurion, observing the pencils and me while it bore reminders of the mire I was stuck in. Finally, I took the pot back to Pat and brought the blue thrift store vase, too. She asked if I was ready, and I said yes. We stepped outside on an early spring day, and she showed me where the pieces of other people's pots were buried in the earth outside her office. She said this place has borne a lot of pain. We tossed the pot back and forth to each other across the parking lot. At first, I was careful, but gradually, we moved further and further from each other, and the pot flew in the air, its orange color contrasting with the cerulean sky.

A Brand New Day

The sky was a piercing blue backdrop
for the terra cotta pot that flew in the air up against it
with unrecognizable Sharpie inscriptions all over it.
The therapist and I played a game of catch;
we stood farther and farther apart, and I released all the
    feelings
about all the things written inside and outside the pot.
"I don't want to be angry anymore."

I don't want to carry them in my heart or let them haunt me
    in my bedroom.
I no longer want to apologize for the things I allowed him to
    do to me.
"Then throw it up," she said.
I flung it there against the blue November sky
and heard the cracking, blasting sounds of freedom.
The shards scattered, but there were still big chunks of
    discernable words I was ready to forget.
Memories lingered on the pavement that were no longer
    welcome in my psyche.
Those chunks went flying, again and again.
Splat. Crack. Crumble.
I put the rest into pieces with the toe of my leopard loafers,
like putting out a cigarette whose light no longer tars my
    lungs.
What now?
We put the small ones in a vase.
Those broken pieces will always be with me, but I'm
    wiser now.
You can grow things on top of the broken pieces.
They aerate the soil and keep the roots from rotting.
But the big ones we buried.
She and I, digging in the earth, let the pieces go.
"Be gone," I said in my head.
You've troubled me long enough here.
It's an old trope that divorce helps women get in touch with
    their anger.
No, anger boxed me in and trapped me.
Now, in between the cracks, the joy and the light get in.
I can see the colors,
like how adobe cuts through clouds and cerulean
to open up a brand new day.

Silence came over me. There was all my pain and all my loss.

164

All I had carried with me was now broken on the ground. I couldn't carry it anymore.

We split up the pieces—none of the words were recognizable anymore. Half of them I buried in the dirt next to other people's unmarked terracotta graves of pain. The other half I used to fill my bright blue vase. I took it home and added water and an ivy clipping. Roots grew around the painful mementos. You never leave your pain fully behind. It goes with you. In naming it, you will not lose it, but it will lose its power over you. *Name your losses.*

The best example I can think of and why you should believe me when I tell you that you will not live in loss forever is from the classic children's book: *Everybody Poops*. The cheeky title is more than just a biological explanation for young readers about different animals' excrement practices, but has been a comfort as I embarked on my first experience of unwanted grief™. Everybody grieves, and there is always, even in the most expected and anticipated changes, some part that is necessarily unpleasant and unwanted. Perhaps grief's subtitle should be "Expect the unexpected!"

Grief surprises us.

We might feel laughter and glee where we thought we'd be heartbroken. Not all surprising reactions can be attributed to shock either. I have met with many a family over their beloved's funeral plans who could not hide a grin or broke into an uncomfortable fit of giggles, not out of happiness, but because grief is powerful and brings out emotional expression, sometimes with little regard to what kind.

I saw a neighbor whose father's obituary was in the local paper recently. I said, "Steve, I'm so sorry to hear about your dad" and he nodded and gave me a look like, "I don't know how to say this but I'm *not*?" And then right there, while I leaned off my bicycle and he watered his front yard he explained the surprising bite of guilt that followed him around while the primary emotion he felt at the loss of a "great man and a great dad" was *relief*. Sometimes change can be welcome and letting ourselves feel the full range of what a loss brings—more free time, less of a certain food you ate together, for example, can help us name the fullness of the loss, and not set up shop there forever.

Some might call these "silver linings" as in the cliché, "Every cloud has a silver lining!" said with an air of upswing and hopefulness when the reality of a situation just sucks. I resist "silver linings." Some clouds are just full of acid rain and you ought to take cover as quickly as possible without looking up. I chose to call the upsides of my grief the "King-size bedisms" of our divorce.

X was very tall and couldn't fit in a bed shorter than a king; footboards were out of the question. When I changed the sheets of our marriage bed, I'd get all huffy and out of breath tucking in the corners and smoothing them across. Also, king-sized comforters require an industrial size washing machine to clean. Now that we weren't together, I could sleep in whatever size bed I wanted! In all the sad and hard, I clung to the satisfying joy of never having to make a king-size bed again in my entire life if I didn't want to.

Why is naming what was lost important and even claiming the little joyful subterfuge that came with it? The voices of those who have not sat with their own pain or losses will tell us to "Get over it," "Let it go," or "Quit being a victim." But we cannot possibly walk across the bridge into something new without saying goodbye to what was and naming the pain of losing it.

You will find your way through loss. You will find it through practicing it in the mirror, writing it down on a piece of paper that you burn, or sweeping it out the door (but not under the rug!). You will plant it in the ground, or metabolize it in the way that fits you, or do lots of these things over and over again, until you can say it out loud at the DMV or in a church meeting, or from a pulpit with pride, "I'm divorced" or whatever your big thing is like a badge of honor, as someone who has gone through something and not only survived but rebuilt and thrived.

Wayfinding Practice: Exformation

We go through a world filled with information and messages from the moment we wake up until the lights go out and we nod off to sleep. Advertising, news, communication —there is information flying back and forth into and out of our brains, not to mention all the messages still in there from days and years prior.

We have plenty of information. But imagine trying to breathe and go through life *purely on inhalations*? You wouldn't make it a minute. Your body needs oxygen, but it also needs to release carbon dioxide. So what *is* exformation? Exformation is a physical act of moving energy and information out of your body. You probably do some exformation without even noticing. But if you've ever had a case of "the mean reds" or anxiety welled up within you with no place to go, pick up a broom. Grab a dusting cloth, put your feet to the pavement, or move your body in a way that contacts physically with something else. This is not a practice limited to the fully-abled body either. Sweeping a floor, washing a dish, making something beautiful, cleaning, or pumping something from one place to another is a way we allow the information we absorb to metabolize into energy that can be stored or used elsewhere.

When The One Who Inspires
Others Falls Apart

God will not disturb your peace, except to lead you to a deeper peace.

— *Therapist Pat*

ON MY LAST SUNDAY AT THE CHURCH I SERVED BEFORE EVERYTHING fell apart, the children of the church followed me around the sanctuary. Our tall, arched ceiling lights were being replaced, which involved an electric lift and removing the bolted down pews while the construction crew completed the project. The sanctuary was in almost as much disarray as my heart. The kids and I took a "field trip," looking at all the equipment in our holy space and marveling at how something that is often so put together looks really messy, but that it was on its way to a brighter future, with the power of all its lights to shine. Our prayer that day was an acknowledgement that with God and each other, "We can do hard things" —a lesson I clung to from Glennon Doyle. Those words became a part of me over the months that followed. Five simple words got me through a surprise divorce, resignation from a job I thought was my one true calling, and the strength to leave behind a community and discover myself.

There were moments when I didn't believe that these hard things were possible. After each crushing blow, one wonders if the lungs are strong enough to keep breathing— will the wind one day just get completely knocked out of them and never return?

How does the one who is counted on to inspire others, pick themselves up to keep going? It seemed cruel to go through a hard thing that I had walked with others through, only to find there were no companions for me. Even my mentor in ministry, who had met his beloved through an affair, had died the year prior—oh I would have given anything to summon the voice of the dead to coach me through this!

As we established in prior chapters, there is no one coming to rescue you, and even if they were, you wouldn't follow them the whole way anyway, because you are the only one who can write your story and live your new life.

At the same time, it is a lonely road when there is no one to turn to who has shared your unique tragedy, or been dealt the complications you are now holding. I cannot give you the path out, but I can hold the map. I can pat you on the back and when you're in need of a pep talk or a swift kick to get you going but have no one to call. Here's how you show up for yourself: find a space.

Protect a space in which to breathe, to cry, to fall apart and lick your wounds. Is it a big comfy chair in the corner of your room? Is it a quiet spot under a tree that no one knows about? Find a place that is yours—a space where you can set down all the heavy things and you don't have to perform for anyone. Carve that space out, carve that time out, the one in which you do not have to be the strong one or the one thinking ahead of every little thing. It can't be that way in all the spaces, or every hour of the day, but you really need to know there is at least one. This space is your weeping place —where the psalmist says, "Weeping may last through the night, but joy comes in the morning." (Psalm 30:5)

Then, protect your space.

When you feel it's been a while since you've laid those burdens down in this consecrated place, or the forces of life keep getting in the way, preying on your generosity, protect it. Don't let your safe space slip away.

It's okay to be scared, to be afraid to reclaim your space and return to it after its been neglected or you've let things get in the way of you tending to yourself there. It is a brave thing to claim your space in the world; it takes courage to admit when you have avoided rest for whatever reason, and that your soul now needs a place to exhale again.

One of the strangest realities of going through a hard thing is that time doesn't stop when your world does. There are still kids to pick up from school, dinners to make, tasks to complete, jobs to do. Going through all of these motions while your **emotions** are all over the place is double or triple exhausting. Your mind has too many tabs open at once and at least one of them is sucking all of the oxygen out of the room.

Cue safe space.

You make it through the days and the hours by counting down until the kids go to bed, and you can cry and ask yourself what the freaking frack about the latest in your healing process. This space will be a workshop for you—you may write, talk or meditate. You may numb out there some times, but you won't every time. Safe space is a good place for affirmations, to remind yourself that you are strong. You have strong people in your life who know all about you and love you anyway. You don't have to know all the answers today or how it will all turn out because that is not in your control. This safe space is your spiritual gym—where you start strengthening and repairing your hope muscle.

Wait, hope is a muscle? Hope is a skill. It's not something you are born with or born without. It is not a chemical balance your brain has to strike. Hope is something within us that longs to be nurtured. You will have hope outside of this safe space you've carved out, but in the same way you use your muscles all day long, not just when you are intentionally exercising them, you will especially focus on building up hope in this space you've set aside in which to fall apart and also to heal.

Hope is the vision to see that things will not always stay this way; they will get better. You will learn to have hope in the morning when you wake up; you will learn to lay down exhausted and fearful but with that tiny "Thing with feathers that perches in the soul—and sings the tune without the words—and never stops —at all."[1] We may find ourselves on top of the world at times— what need for hope do we have then? But until there is space on that mountaintop for everyone else to be there with us, we hope. The vision of the world getting better that God speaks of in the Bible references mountains brought low and valleys raised up. When it seems like one side is always is on top and another always on the losing end, the good news has simply not arrived *yet*, the transition is incomplete. Hold on to hope.

About six weeks after moving in with my parents and quitting my job, I got the courage to "own my shit" as Attorney Pat declared. I made an appointment with the Presbyterian version of a bishop, and confessed that Rob and I had an affair, that X intended to share this with the community, and that I was ready to own up to the truth and work with the regional governing body to mitigate the harm a communications crisis could cause. A flurry of next steps began—starting with a couple of pastors assigned to my case to suss out what sort of disciplinary and legal risk this confession opened the church up to. I shared my story with a quivering lip and many tears, and as I did so, the man across the table from me responded: "This'll knock you down a peg or two."

"No shit" I thought. His response led me to wonder if my sin was adultery or if it was existing as an ambitious woman with a calling. As I sat in the chair inside an empty Sunday School room at a country church, I grieved. I wasn't grieving my marriage then, but I mourned the loss of the cheerful, vibrant, radiant, enthusias-tic, wild-eyed, encouraging 32-year-old pastor I had been. I grieved

---

1. Emily Dickinson "'Hope' is the thing with feathers"

that she was gone and the church hadn't realized it yet. We faced my **sin** together, but they couldn't point to the *grace*.

The person I had been was gone, but I couldn't see who was coming next. My dad summed up my condition: "Your skin's been peeled off and you're pretty raw," which brought to mind an image on posters around my high school. There was a beautiful girl in the prime of her adolescence who had been hit by a drunk driver, requiring several plastic surgeries to heal her severe facial burns. The person on the poster was an unrecognizable version of the young, beautiful coed she'd been before the accident. Will I be that damaged? I wondered. Will I become the poster child for the importance of boundaries and the damage of clerical sexual misconduct?

I decided that "poster child for infidelity" was not on the menu. Giving myself permission to choose that was empowering. Naming what I wasn't going to be, helped me to see what I could choose to become: a force for reconciliation. It wasn't up to me to make the church grant or believe in grace, that undeserved gift that calls out from within us to heal and forgive and start anew. But *I* could claim grace from God. Grace enables us to lay down the bricks we hurl at one another and see that in every interaction there is a scared child between us waiting to hear that they are loved, that they are safe, that they will be okay.

Change is impossible without a sense of safety. From serving churches all over Texas and especially in rural communities, I've learned our sense of safety is the difference between hearing one another and not. In these spaces, church often represents an insulated safe space—away from the big, wide, scary "liberalism" out there in the world. Preaching must be gentle, curious, and come across as a soothing invitation, like bathwater that is "just right"— not too hot or cold to ease the hearers into the healing waters of grace and growth. We make many assumptions when trying to change others, when trying to change ourselves; the best assumption is a generous one—assume that everyone is doing the very best they can, and then bring your best self to the pulpit, to the negotiating table; even drag your best, crying, broken self to your therapy appointment.

The internet told me that it takes 18 months to heal from divorce and I am counting each of those 547 days with tears. I kept a countdown going and would often google, "How many days since August 30th, 2019?" and then, "What is 547 minus that many days?" Deep breath. Only 400 more days to go. A shame-rinsed journey to vulnerability and authenticity is the theme of my one-third life crisis. I'm tired of pretending to be someone I am no longer, or perhaps ever was. I am drinking more calories from alcohol than I am eating from food, and running, lifting weights, HIIT workouts are the things I think are keeping my life from decaying under a pile of blankets.

I have a file of memes saved on my phone that remind me about the important truths of a growth mindset and incrementality, but I gotta remind myself that it's ok if some days I can't bring myself to believe any of that crap. I don't believe I'm any crazier than the rest of humanity walking around. I do believe I've been cursed with slightly more self-awareness about my feelings and proclivity for articulating them as often as possible. I'm learning that feelings are like storms; they pass, occasionally blowing a roof or two off in the process, but they do end. Storms are indications though, of bigger weather patterns. The swirling way the earth spins and the high pressure and low-pressure systems crash into one another, or narrowly miss, allowing a warm-front or artic blast to slip by— human emotions are like that too. Weather patterns are not a system to solve or fix. The patterns are an indication that life goes on. If I keep going at the rate I am 147 days into this process, my climate will kill me. I'm looking for miracles.

Lessons I'm learning from the crappiest season of my life to date:

- The challenge of naming 10 things I thank God for at the beginning and end of each day is the miry wet clay that keeps it all from crumbling.
- Friends come from surprising underbellies and shadows of the places you thought you knew.
- The edge of society is not just reserved for sinners and wrongdoers, but also for witches, prophets, and some of Christ's dearest followers.
- I'm surviving.

In the gospel of Mark, one of Jesus' first miracles occurs at an encounter with the Gerasene Demoniac- a crazy man running around naked who flabbergasts the poor townspeople of Gerasea.

Jesus sees him, yes, *sees him* in his nakedness and calls out the demons (a multitude!) who call themselves "Legion." Jesus then casts them into a herd of pigs who throw themselves off a nearby cliff.

Jesus sees someone in his scorned vulnerability. This is the kind of miracle we need right now, when we are naming our losses and not living in them.

Jesus sees someone in his scorned vulnerability and calls out what in him is good and kind and faithful by culling out the legion of things that are not. None of us has a simple existence or one small pockmark of sin, but we are all "Legion" with complex abnormalities, generational trauma, and systemic realities that no one size fits all solution could fix.

As I work through my own grief, motherhood, divorce, vocational wilderness, encounters with patriarchy in the institution and so on, I wonder where my herd of pigs is? Where is the thing that will take on these burdensome curses?

Don't wait for someone to tell you you're crazy. You will waste your life away holding your breath, looking over your shoulder, listening like a thief for the voice of your abuser, the voice of imposter syndrome to catch you by the coattails on the way to destiny.

The best gift of going through something tragic before 35 is that I am listening to and trusting myself on a level I didn't know was possible. I used to marvel at my mother, 37 years old with three kids in tow and braces—getting carded for buying box wine at the IGA in our one-horse Alabama town. I used to be in awe of her strength and tenacity, do-no-harm-but-take-no-shit attitude, but now I see: that posture is forged out of going through some crap you'll never tell anyone.

I got caught doing something I desperately wanted to be honest about with X. I walked in the house so many times with the words just dangling on my lips: *I'm screwing another man and I feel totally justified because you left me as a priority a million years ago.*

Did the feeling of abandonment make it okay? No.

It was unethical. It was a lie. But who has the power to determine the consequences for that?

The judgment belongs to our wronged spouses, to ourselves. Our trustworthiness or value and place in society, friendships, and neighborhood are in our hands, but it doesn't feel that way at all. I longed for the **_church_** to be the meeting place for reconciliation, the place where grace would forge us back to ourselves, to our God. But church became the instrument of our shunning, punishment, and withdrawal.

I encountered a church that made an idol of integrity. Does any politician or statesman/woman have a shred of dignity left? "Is there one righteous, not even one?"[2] It seems God has been on the lookout for a worthy companion for eons and we've all failed. William J. Bennet, arguably the Father of American Virtues and morality was caught up in an excessive gambling scandal. Other names are too many to count. We're all hedging our bets too high that the people and institutions upon whom we are dependent will be without blemish.

---

2. Romans 3:10

From this side of moral failure, I want to warn everyone else, especially the ones who claim or project an image of being more moral than the status quo, that everyone gets their day and their thing. It may not be sex or money, but whatever it is it will tempt you to beg the Lord God to open up the ground beneath your feet so you can fall into the abyss you have created. And yet, even then and there, no pit we can dig runs deeper than the love of God that goes on and on, catching us even in our shame.

We witness and identify the unsustainable patterns impacting climate change, and in the same way our own self-destructive patterns call out to us to heed and pay attention. Humans cannot withstand chronic tsunamis and annual devastating hurricanes. Our bodies cannot repair on too much booze or exercise without nourishment and rest.

We live in a time when salvaging things that seem past their prime is out of fashion. We want when the computer battery stops charging, to chuck the whole thing in the trash and get a new one on sale. But there is a character lesson to be gleaned from tinkering with the broken things long enough to make them right again. My *marriage* was chucked in the trash by X, but *I* was not. Just because someone gives up on a relationship with you does not mean *you* were given up on, nor does it mean that you are unlovable or worthy of abandonment in a trash heap.

Consider our ancestors who would save every scrap, who did not have weekly (or sometimes twice weekly!) trash service. The landfill wasn't a thing in 1850. Pioneers were frugal, treasured the simple, small things, knowing one couldn't just buy a new one if this was lost or broken. How are we extending that into our patterns of daily living? It isn't just waiting a year to buy a new phone, but what about doing what it takes to fix the phone, building phones that don't give out every two years, and so on? Frugality is not just an individual practice, but one that companies, inventors, entrepreneurs can aspire to and work towards as well. Our relationships to one another are all part of how we relate to the things in our world too.

Practicing frugality in our relationships is a different form of **generosity**. Instead of creating something new, let us repair what has gone bad, breathe new life into sad sacks of friendship that are stale or damaged. The Presbyterians have a term in our rules of discipline, "Voluntary Acts of Repentance" to show that one is truly remorseful and turning in a new direction after you have sinned. In our friendships, have we been too hasty to toss aside when we are hurt or offended? It can seem like too much to consider how much we have harmed or been harmed, but one number that has kept me going is this: 30%. Thirty percent is the number of times an infant and their caregiver "repair" ruptures in order for the infant to still trust the adult.[3] That's seven out of ten times failing and still being a "good enough" parent (no hookers and blow, okay?)! The relationship needs to repair from harm and conflict at minimum three out of ten times in order for the bond to keep growing. That's it! That means seven out of ten arguments can technically be left unsolved and you will still grow. Toss aside perfection and aim for 30% reparation.

---

3. Tronick, E. Z., & Gianino, A. (1986). Interactive mismatch and repair: Challenges to the coping infant. Zero to Three, 6(3), 1—6.

Wayfinding Practice: Living Amends/Tikkun Olam

Sometimes repair isn't possible with the person we've harmed, but we can learn to practice a "living amends." This doesn't keep you from doing that self-inquiry to reflect on how you caused harm or were harmed. But after you do this, you vow to live differently, in a way that honors the change you've made in your life, even if they can't see it. Making amends is more powerful than an apology, because all an apology does is express sorrow that something happened, but without much focus on how the future will be shaped by lessons learned. In the Jewish tradition, *tikkun olam* is a Hebrew phrase that means "the healing of the world." When we repair with one another, even if the other person is not alive or around to receive it, we participate in a larger collective healing. In my own practice, choosing to parent the way that I do in my divorced family has been healing for friends who are children of divorce and say, "I couldn't get this kind of parenting from my parents' divorce, but I'm glad your kids are getting it."

On Safe Spaces

You do not have to be good.
You do not have to walk on your knees
for a hundred miles through the desert repenting.
You only have to let the soft animal of your body
love what it loves.

— *Mary Oliver*, "Wild Geese"

OCCASIONALLY A RURAL TEXAN WILL HEAR THE SOUND OF PITTER-patter feet in their attic, or go out to their shed to look for the Christmas decorations and discover animal droppings. My first encounter with this was a ring tail cat who took up residence in the little storage shed next to our carport. We never saw "Ringo" but we found his evidence in the way of excrement all over the box of old school files my parents had saved from my childhood. The exterminator spotted the poop and immediately recognized its producer. From the evidence left behind, we determined that Ringo had found his way inside seeking protection from something and then realized once he got inside that he was stuck, panicked, and then proceeded to shit everywhere. What a metaphor, right?!

Elaine Murray

There is a wildness in all of us, seeking shelter from the storms of life. When we seek protection from the wrong place or a place not meant for us, our panic can make a real mess of things. We long for sanctuary—and not for the whole world to be that way, but for a small enclave that we can duck into and reconstitute ourselves from the brashness of the outside world. In the last section, I encourage you to find and make a safe space, but sometimes we camp out in places that are not safe. Especially if we've become accustomed to choosing people and places invested in our harm, you can expect to mess up the first few times you hunt for safety. Experiencing harm in your quest for safe space is not a sign that you have failed, or that you are undeserving of protection.

One of the most powerful images we have from scripture is of God as a shelter:

- God is our refuge and strength, a very present help in trouble —Psalm 46:1
- In you, Lord, I have taken refuge; let me never be put to shame —Psalm 71:1
- The Lord is good, a stronghold in the day of trouble; He knows those who take refuge in him. —Nahum 1:7
- My God, my rock, in whom I take refuge, My shield and the horn of my salvation, my stronghold, and my refuge; My savior, You save me from violence. —2 Samuel 22:3
- In the shadow of your wings will I take refuge. — Psalm 57

God provided a cave for David when he was on the run;[1] God made Joseph into a relational shelter for Mary when she was called upon to bear Jesus into the world.[2] Safe spaces are necessary for the vulnerable among us: victims of abuse, groups targeted by authorities, immigrants, and marginalized populations.

---

1. 1 Samuel 24
2. Matthew 1:18-25

October 11th is National Coming Out Day (also National Vegetarian Day?) Where do they come up with these days? On National Coming Out Day, many folks feel the need to express that they are a "safe space" for someone to come out to—they won't judge someone for the sexual or gender identities that are part of their personhood on that journey of self-discovery. But being a safe space isn't something *you* get to announce. It's something you live into, that the people around you who long for a safe space to exhale identify in you through the way you live. You become a safe space when you speak up for those who are not in the room to witness it. You become a safe space when you ask yourself, "How would this sound to someone who is gay, lesbian, bi, transgender, queer, intersex, or asexual?"

To truly be a "safe space" for any person needing cover from the storms of life, the expectations are higher than simply voicing,"No judgment." Can you imagine if you were literally out in a storm, trying to find a soft place to shelter? Hearing someone yell, "Hey, no judgment, for finding yourself unexpectedly caught in a downpour" from the comfort of their warm, dry home is the last kind of noise we need when trying to strategize. What would it look like to be *hospitable* to those in crisis? How could we celebrate the unexpected visitor in our midst, camping out until the storm has passed? One of the most welcoming responses I got was from an angel named "Patrick" (of all names—I should have known it was a wink from God!). Patrick managed a wine bar my mom and I dropped in on during the season of upheaval—finding a place to live, making a legal strategy, and starting out in a new career. Mom asked for a table for us and said, "This is my daughter. She's going through a divorce" to which Patrick immediately replied, "Congratulations! You can sit here." It was the first "Congratulations" I had received. It was disarming and unsettling at the same time. There are people who *delight* at a marriage ending? I found safety that day, but like a mouse who was so accustomed to having wet fur and shivering ears, I didn't know what to do in this dry, warm place.

Safe spaces, even when named as such aren't always that. Sometimes the louder someone proclaims to be safe, the further they are from living that way. Like churches that say "All are welcome" usually possess a sinister unwelcomeness that is yet to be discovered, like a jack-in-the-box waiting to be cranked only to pop up and surprise you in the worst way.

How do you spot a safe space?

Safe spaces are where you see other people getting free. Like that infamous scene in *When Harry Met Sally*, when the woman in the restaurant sees Sally's exclamation and says, "I'll have what *she's* having!" We know a safe space by the look and feel of others in it. Our intuition knows. We have become so accustomed to denying and gaslighting ourselves that it takes practice to recognize that gut knowing again. I learned through being hurt by places I thought were safe to listen to myself when something seems off.

Sometimes life requires us to step beyond the safe space, into a riskier place in order to grow. When I gird up my loins to enter a church pulpit, I know it is a risky place. It is not a place where I can be myself, no holds barred. There are indeed holds that are indeed barred. There are rules and ethics, some explicit, but most dependent on the audience. A faithful preacher is not surrounded only by friends and "yes-people." But she must be able to rely on them and be honest with them about the unsafe people in her midst. She needs prayers, support, knowing glances, and advocacy of her friends and confidants when the gospel calls her to push the envelope.

One of the "Great Ends of the Church"—a foundational statement in the Presbyterian Church USA's constitution about who we claim to be is a promise to provide for "The shelter, nurture, and spiritual fellowship of the children of God." This is my favorite thing about being a minister of the gospel—that even when the communities I appear before on Sunday mornings are not entirely living into the call to be safe shelter, *I can*. I can create and commit to being part of the shelter, nurture, and spiritual fellowship of all God's children. This has led me to officiate same-gender weddings before it was legal from my living room; it's led me to talk others through their questions, their wrestling, their searching for a way of relating to Spirit beyond the bounds of their fundamentalist upbringing.

Safety is a minimum for belonging. In some ways, being a pastor means I am called to the edges of belonging—to the unsafe arenas in order to teach, to protect, to call forth the voices long silenced by the human reality of harm.

Like the character *Ant Man*, I can say for a while I went "sub-atomic"—that is, beyond the limits of which I could return to safety —to an area of being that I needed time and prayer and space to reconstitute myself into belonging to God, to myself, and where the bounds of safety could be found again.

Wayfinding Practice: Building Safety in Ourselves

If you have suffered abuse or neglect, or trauma, so basically if you are a human being, you may struggle to feel safe in many environments. Start with yourself, with your own body. Grounding with a rock in your palm or with your bare feet on green space like a lawn is a good way to start. Breathe. No one can violate your personhood. Your thoughts, beliefs, meaning, and ideas belong to you. Hold this truth. Affirm this reality and you will never lose your safe space again.

The more I learned to trust myself, the more I could be around my family, my children's father, in the pew of a church, even before a hostile committee, or in tense meetings because I knew no matter what was said, no matter what occurred, I would be safe in my own skin. We build trust with ourselves by listening to what we like, what our soul wants. We build trust with ourselves by making promises and keeping them, such as "I will move my body today" and following through.

I'm Glad to be Divorced

I sing because I'm happy;
I sing because I'm free
His eye is on the sparrow and I know he watches me

— *Civilla D. Martin, "His Eye Is on the Sparrow"*

"Divorce is a sin...except for..."

When abuse is involved

Or adultery...

Or you're running for office.

I don't know the rules of divorce but I do know that once I found myself in it, it was essentially like someone finding Rose Dawson floating on a board at the end of *Titanic* saying, "I'll never let go" while dead, frozen Jack slips off the board where there was plenty of room for him all along, if she'd been a little less self-absorbed. "Frozen Jack" was my commitment to being committed —which is what I believed was the secret to a long-term relationship. If you *just* stay committed, then no matter what, your marriage *won't* fail. "You can work through infidelity and toxic in-laws and gaslighting and conflicting goals, if you just BELIEVE in the commitment you made!" I told myself, through tears. But the frozen waters of all our relationship had borne sucked the commitment right out from under me.

Before this, I thought being a person of integrity meant living without regrets. It's hard to think of "no regrets" without the image of that classic tattoo typo, "No Ragrets" (oops!). It is just as silly to think that living without regret is morally more valuable than living in a way that does include regret. There's no avoiding regret. Experiencing regret is arguably a sign that we are restorable—able to learn from our mistakes. We can be glad something terrible happened or that we went through something; we can not want to repeat it, wish it had gone differently and be more loyal to ourselves and the Divine within us, yet remain chock full of regret. I was not a great first wife, or a great friend for a time. I can't say I was a terrible person, but I made some selfish choices in my twenties and early thirties. It takes courage to admit those things and not leave my humanity and dignity on the chopping block as well.

I'm so glad to be divorced. Even though I've remarried, sometimes when I'm filling out demographic surveys, I want to check "Divorced" on the marital status question just as a testimony that it was the best thing that ever happened to me. Instead of parenting my children in the overwhelm and misery of the emotional labor most U.S. American moms carry, I split that shit in half with my kids' father. I learned to stop apologizing for not overfunctioning in divorce and start apologizing and repairing the mistakes that matter like losing my temper on my kids.

After Glennon Doyle wrote *Untamed*, an accusation went around that she was convincing good, well-behaved women to divorce their husbands and become lesbians. Doyle's rebuttal was, "I am not saying that every woman should divorce her husband and marry a female Olympian. Although most of you should."[1] While cheeky, this response proclaims the secret we all know: when another woman gets free of a broken marriage and the cage that

---

1. Glennon Doyle's Instagram Post: 13 April 2020

tamed her to gulp her needs down and become invisible, pleasing, and agreeable burns to be considered worthy, the angels in heaven rejoice. Those of us who know and who hear the shaky voice of truth that speaks out loud for the first time to say, "Actually, I want *this* instead of that" want to clap and sing and start a parade through town for one who hears and heeds her own voice rather than the voices of those who have dominated her.

So what about this regret piece then? To become wise is to live with regret of some kind or another and to make peace with it. I do not regret divorce. It was the best worst thing that ever happened to me. I am a happier person, and a better mother and partner and contributing member of society because I freed myself from a relationship I committed to before my pre-frontal cortex was fully formed. Do I regret having married in the first place? I don't regret everything I learned from being with X, and I don't regret the children that came from it. **I regret the timing**. I regret that I limited myself *before I even knew* what I was limiting myself from by choosing life **together** before life on my own had even begun. I live with this regret, and yet there beside it exists the healing that comes from forgiving one's own regrets.

How do we forgive? How do we move from a posture of shame and beat-down to celebration and delight in the places we've been and the wrong turns we've made?

You might think it takes an astronomically out-sized ego, but it's the opposite of ego. Our egos are so desperate for affirmation that we will appear to the world as larger than life, more deserving than anyone else of attention, admiration, love, and loyalty. But forgiveness means shrinking, lowering ourselves down to the size in which our decisions can be understood, contextualized, empathized with. Forgiveness involves self-inquiry and wonder, not judgment. *What need was I trying to meet by making the choice I made?*

Some time on the other side of this storm, I was invited to preach at a church's "Women's Day" Sunday—dedicated to celebrating the gifts of women. We talked about the absurdity of the

189

call to be "One body" of Christ, how hard it is to get along and work together when so much of our energy is dedicated to tearing each other apart with judgment and isolation. We told the inalienable truth—that we belong to one another, and to God. That even when the body is awkward and tense and struggling, grace knits us together again. After the service and when most of the congregation had moved on, one woman pulled me into the nearby "Cry room"—the one for babies during a solemn time of worship. There in the shadows, she tugged down the strap of her dress and said with exhuberance, "Feel!" Guiding my hand, she continued, "That's where my tumor is! *That's* what breast cancer feels like!" Here was a person holding their hurt, their physical sign of a trauma in their body with wonder, and sharing it with me. If that's what a laying on of hands is, I don't know who was blessing whom. I may have inadvertently felt up this woman (with her consent and invitation!) but in that moment, the awkwardness of grace moved me. She had a testimony. She wasn't glad or grateful for the invasive ductal carcinoma, but even with kids and life and all the things that folks who aren't going through something are doing, she carried this heavy load, this sense of doubt and wonder tightly enough to be precious, and loosely enough to be shared. Do I believe it was God's will for this mother of three young kids to have invasive ductal carcinoma? No. And yet in the flow of disease, even there, "Even if I make my bed in Sheol, even there your right hand shall hold me fast."[2]

None of us get out of this life alive, and we will carry with us many sad and hard experiences—the sharp left turns that we didn't see coming. A sense of humor and humility, awe at our place in the order of things, wonder at the will of God moving us through the ups and downs with lessons upon lessons to learn—these are the things that will move us to receive hard news with gladness, or at least the possibility of it.

In some ways my story is an old and familiar one—of lonely

---

2. Psalm 139:8

wife gets fulfillment from her work, benefits from the attention of her colleague who is also lonely in his home life. They experience passion and fire and excitement together—feel seen and heard and voila! An affair is born. But the affair was only a symptom of the deep longing for meaning, the deep loneliness and sadness that comes from abandonment of the self. I credit God with getting my attention through heartbreak and scandal, long enough to peer deep into my own soul to see how I had neglected and lied to her. One of my dearest friends got so mad at me for suggesting that this extramarital relationship was God's plan, and while I felt for her, her anger did nothing to change my conviction. God's plan (if indeed there is one) was much bigger than our marriages. God's action often encompasses loss, betrayal, and heartbreak. I have to believe God's action involves the reconciliation of big, big offenses, and healing of major, deep, multi-generational wounds.

I say "If indeed there is one" with regard to "God's plan" as a caveat, because one of the guiding feminine images for God is as a Mother Hen, sheltering her brood with the cover of her wing. I, too, have been a mother, and I know that what others may perceive as some thoughtfully executed long-range strategy, is sometimes the result of a brilliant woman at the helm with no more ideas left besides "Let's try this one, kids!" I thank God for every turn that brought my beloved and I together in the time that they did. I thank God for the years I had with X to learn how to value my own needs and express them.

One of my mentors once said about his prayer life, "When you get to a certain age, it is just 'thanks.' Thanks! That's all I can say anymore! What a gift!" While every social media influencer will try to make some new spin on gratitude, I do wonder if that is the only word left. In the meantime, I'm still glad to be divorced.

Elaine Murray

Wayfinding Practice: A Gratitude List and Sacred Stones

 When I was way deep in the middle of loss, a package arrived as if on Angel's wings, but it was really through Amazon Prime. It contained a single pink heart stone: a rose quartz. My cousin said "Call me when you get it" and proceeded to explain how I should hold this rock heart until my real heart came back together again. And then she said, "Start your day writing down ten things you're grateful for. It's going to be hard. And then at the end of the day, write another ten things you are grateful for. This will stitch your heart back together." Dear Wayfinder, I invite you to this practice of gratitude. Your items can be as simple and mundane as the cup of coffee bringing you to life on a weary morning, or the fact that you have shoelaces to tie instead of the alternative. Ten items may seem like a lot, but it will transform your vision into one that sees possibilities instead of lack around every corner. If there's a sacred stone that has meaning to you, I encourage you to take on the practice of carrying it with you in your bag, your pocket, or your cupholder. A tiger's eye for confidence, a citrine for joy, rose quartz for love, labradorite for intuition and connection, amethyst for inner peace and healing…the possibilities are endless.

Ways to Process Grief

Give me instead
The blessing
Of sitting with me
When you cannot think
Of what to say.

— *Jan Richardson*, "The Blessing You Should Not
Tell Me"

WHEN MY FIRST BABY WAS STILL A BABY, A FORMER PARISHIONER HAD her first child. We oohed and ahhed over the internet about their cute smiles and all the exhaustion and "WHAT NOW?!" of new motherhood. And then one day while cooking dinner, her partner went in the backyard and unalived himself with a gun, all while their cute baby was trying her first foods in the kitchen.

My friend was outrageously honest and out loud in her grief. In addition to postpartum hormones and the adjustment to mother-hood, she found her spouse's desperation so failingly selfish. Single parenting and widowhood was not part of the picture for what she expected about becoming a mother and bringing life into the world.

I carry her with me as I write about the pain of my divorce. She would be quick to say it is "not the same" and she is right. One of the ways her grief came out was in anger at other moms—moms who joked about "solo parenting" being the same as the situation into which she was suddenly and traumatically dropped. She expressed envy for us divorced parents. Even if the other parent was a trainwreck, at least he was *alive*.

Grief is not an olympic sport. It's not a game at all. It sucks. From the dead goldfish you woke up to at age four to the crushing loss of a job, a marriage, a life—grief sucks. Gently and humbly I whisper into this painful season, grief will **bless** you too.

Grief has a clarifying flash to it—you see immediately in a new way who you can trust and who you can't. Priorities will rise to the surface and with stunning clarity, grief will make you forget the things that just don't matter right now in this heartbreak. While grief never goes away, it does soften. At first it yells loudly and blocks whatever direction you thought you were going, but eventually it learns to take up its place beside you, even as small as a crumb in your pocket and whisper softly and only at appropriate moments. But before it becomes the tiny companion, it must be heard and processed. Great grief is a sign of great love.

Practically speaking though, how do you help grief on its way to shrinking from the outsized giant life-disruptor to the small, loveable pocket companion? By exercising it, processing it, metabolizing your grief. Grief is love that demands to be heard and caressed. It has complex edges to it—we can both love *and* despise someone. We can be resentful towards their parting and relieved at it too. Grief insists on not fitting into a standard shape, size, or experience. My childhood was shaped by the teachings of Dr. Elizabeth Kübler-Ross, the "Queen of dying" or grandmother of grief, a Swiss psychologist who coined the Kübler-Ross model, naming so many stages of grief we use in common parlance today: denial, anger, bargaining, depression, and acceptance. My mother was a hospice bereavement coordinator and directed grief camps for kids. Grief has been a dinner table companion to us for many years. As a teen I heard tear-filled tales of sitting with the dying, witnessing "a good death," or lamenting how someone was stuck in a particular stage of the grief cycle. I learned that grief doesn't follow directions and hardly goes in order. The "stages" Kübler-Ross describes are not linear and can often overlap. Grief is a chaotic monster at first, like the Wild Things in Maurice Sendak's *Where The Wild Things Are*. You will not tame your grief, but you will befriend it.

Healing is not linear, so this chapter will not include step-by-step instructions, but some ways and strategies for how you exercise that big grief monster down to a reasonable size. First it will take time. But when something takes time it does not mean we must passively wait for time to pass. It is working time, a time with tasks. We must listen to our grief. We must say it out loud: I am divorced. My pet died. My marriage ended. My child is gone. My job was terminated. In the process of moving towards new, joyful realities, we must say out loud and release the really real ones that have come to pass.

Grief needs physicality. The words physically must be formed by our tongues and the vibrations sensed through our ears. Movement helps. Pounding the pavement, punching a pillow, screaming/guteral vocalizations, throwing rocks into a stream or a ditch, lifting something heavy are ways the heavy energy of grief has an outlet. If you write about your grief, do it by hand if you can. The hand to pen to paper heals. You are literally making strength from the ashes and tears of what has been—a special kind of spiritual alchemy.

Grief needs space. Fresh air, open windows, wide, open spaces. When a traumatic thing happens to us, our bodies tend to clamp up and seize. Space helps us to expand and open our lungs again, allowing our nervous system to release, our pupils to contract and everything to become clearer. At first we will want to hole up and shut the world out because the thing that has changed has caused harm to us, so we perceive everything as a threat. But living this way will exhaust your muscles and make it more difficult to open up and relax. You will become more brittle and rigid in your thoughts, words, and actions.

Grief needs grounding. Often our thoughts are manic and swirling during a healing time. We can think and write and fire off texts and emails to try to make the world right, but it is all noise. Grieving can be such an isolating experience; we often don't feel fit for polite society, but the earth is a solid place to start. Remove your shoes and step outside. Feel the soft earth beneath your feet. Is it hot? Is it cold? Hard? Bumpy? Crunchy? Sandy? Let the earth hold you. If you close your eyes and remain still, you can sense the force of gravity, and almost feel the slow rate at which the earth keeps spinning as you remain upright. The earth is holding you and gently reminding you in its grasp that life goes on.

Grief needs to be fed and watered. Comfort foods, like mashed potatoes, mac and cheese, ice cream, are the kind full of fat, salt, and sugar, and they feed us. They stick to our bones when we have become "skin and bones," but they also feed our souls. Grief takes energy and is not the time to engage in any other kind of life change or weight loss attempt. Your body shape will change as you befriend grief. You may add extra pounds or lose them. I have done both. Grief is a time to "let the soft animal of your body love what it loves[1]" and if that is an extra serving of carbs, say yes. That said, "eating your feelings" will not dig you out of grief's hole. Remember that grief is a wild monster. You cannot starve it, nor can you force feed it into not existing. It must be nourished with plenty of rest, plenty of protein and fiber, and water. Too much caffeine, sugar, or alcohol will only make things worse. Put the kettle on, steep a cup of tea and settle in for the winter. It will not always be this way.

"Go outside and yell at the ducks" was a special piece of grief advice Therapist Pat gave me. I raised one eyebrow her direction. It combined a few things—fresh air, wide open space, grounding my feet in the earth, and physically making noise, saying my grief out

---

1. "Wild Geese" by Mary Oliver

loud. No ducks were harmed in this activity. At one of my mother's grief camps for kids, they made drums out of coffee cans, decorated them with feathers and beads and photos of their loved ones and marched around through the wild texas hill country, literally to their own beat. Your grief journey will not follow a template, but your grief will be heard and attended to, or it will **make** itself heard.

One day you will be in a meeting or at lunch with a friend and a familiar scent or sound or memory will enter your mind, and you might cry or feel overwhelmedy at the memory that jumped in your path and completely derailed things. But one day, the memory will come with its scent and sound, but it will come as a whisper that even makes you smile, grinning at how big you are and how small that grief monster is, just a little breadcrumb or action figure in your pocket, reminding you that once you loved someone or something and now you have grown. And no ducks were harmed in the process.

Wayfinding Practice: A Grieving Reset Walk

"Go for a walk" is good advice for lots of things—your heartrate, your blood pressure, your metabolism. But a grieving walk is different. This practice varies in pace, but is more for your emotions than your cardio-vascular system. Sometimes the grief monster is so big that it needs all four things I described in this chapter: physicality, space, grounding, and to be fed and watered. Grab your emotional support water bottle, step outside and feel the earth beneath your toes, walk as fast or as slow as you need to and let the tears come, let the primal scream out, and breathe. You may walk fast and hard, almost like a stomp if anger is coming to the surface. You may move slowly and reflectively, just letting the memories wash over you. You can raise your eyes to the horizon and imagine what it will feel like a year from now, a month from now, or even just how you want to feel when you get back from this walk.

This is not limited to the able-bodied either. The time outside in fresh air does wonders for your emotions, like letting them out of the crate to move around and dissipate. If you're not able to touch the earth with your feet, hold a handful of earth, as a reminder that from dust you came, to dust you will return, and through the many mountains and valleys between, you are beloved.

How to Recognize When You Are Stuck in Grief

You can get so confused
that you'll start in to race
down long wiggled rocks at a break-necking pace
and grind on for miles across weirdish wild space,
headed, I fear, toward a most useless place.
The Waiting Place...
...for people just waiting.

— *Dr. Suess*, Oh! The Places You'll Go

At sixteen, my dad taught me how to drive a manual transmission. No one, regardless of gender, sits in the driver's seat of a stick shift and immediately coordinates the release of the clutch with the pressing of the gas pedal in a smooth manner while their right hand glides the shifter into the next gear. No one. In fact the sound most associated with learning to drive this kind of vehicle is an awful grinding accompanied by the smell of burning transmission fluid. The first day I learned to drive on a loaner Honda Accord I did pretty well until I got to a traffic light at the top of a hill in the center of town. The light turned green and instead of gliding into gear, I panicked and stalled out, started to slide backwards down the hill before stomping on the brake in a cold sweat. Honks from the cars around me filled my ears as I turned to the passenger seat, red-faced and sweating to get instruction on what to do next. For the moment, I was stuck.

Getting stuck at this place, on my very first day with this borrowed car was expected. We re-started the car, tuned out the noise, and got it into gear. Wouldn't it be nice if we could so easily restart and move on from the situations we find ourselves stuck in?

We've established that healing is not linear and that you might go through all the stages of grief in one five minute span and also for years and years and over and over again, but I hate to tell you that occasionally you may find you have gotten **stuck** in the same rut and cycle, replaying the same memories or triggered by the same old wounds with seemingly no progress. Those around you may honk or move on in frustration while you are there, stalled out on the same loop. Befriending our grief can be as tedious as washing the same clothes over and over again without recognizing all the places those clothes have been with us in between.

It had been several months since I'd started seeing Therapist Pat. In that time, I'd moved into the Healing Hygge Home, started a new job, been through a couple of rounds of mediation towards a legalized divorce, and while nothing felt complete yet, progress towards new life was moving. I was fighting towards healing on many fronts. Every therapy session would circle back to me rehashing the feel of the sun, baking my sandaled feet in the gravel driveway; the smell of our living room and leftover pork abandoned on the stove; the echoing sound of X's voice, "I want you out of the house and I'm taking the kids. Every season with you is a hard season. You're the most selfish person I know." As I relived this memory over and over again, eyes narrowing into a tunnel, another nauseating sensation began in the pit of my stomach. I was stuck. Therapist Pat had heard this before. All my friends had heard this before. My family, though they loved me and would stick by me through anything, couldn't hide the truth that they were as tired as I was of rehashing the scene, analyzing it from every angle and coming to the conclusion that X was horrible and I was to be pitied. Or that *I* was horrible and deserved every terrible and true thing he'd said. Before, telling it over and over again had power to it; each time I could mine some new truth, observation, or meaningful angle that would help me come to terms with myself and my new reality. But now there was nothing left to glean. The mining part was over, and only the hollowed-out story remained.

I needed a reframe—not only permission to tell the story, but to tell it in a new way. In the sermon preparation process, a preacher will wrestle with the text to get a truth out of it. If you just read it over and over again, the words become rote and you miss some of the valuable nuance the sacred has to offer. Some strategies for hearing an old story in a new way is to read it by mixing up the syllable emphasis or pronunciation, or to try and tell the story in your own words instead of what's on the page. Preachers sometimes practice telling the story from a different character's perspective, such as the story of Jesus turning water into wine—how would the bridegroom tell it? Or the head waiter? I needed a perspective shift on my own sacred story.

Instead of remaining the victim, and going over each detail like picking through an old boneyard for any meat left on it, Therapist Pat invited me to tell that story again, but this time as if it were a **birth story** instead of the beginning of loss. The hot sun and the pea gravel were the dust, not of my ashes, but of my formation. When the door to our home closed behind me, I was not being shut out, but being ushered into a new world. Now I go over that story with reverence—I was being knit together for the first time in that driveway. The mistakes I made, the motions I went through to get from death into the next ten minutes were as precious and critical as the first hours of a new baby's life. I could forgive myself for stumbling —because stumbling is part of the process. Us bipedal human beings learn to walk through a series of falls; could it not also be so with other kinds of mastery? August 30th, 2019 is the day I was born, a new me, who was never known intimately by the person I had journeyed with up to that point. I had to get to know this new me and give her the freedom to become without the burden of what had been before.

How do you know if you're stuck? Supreme Court Justice Potter Stewart famously said, "I know it when I see it" in 1964 with regard to obscenity, and I believe we know it too. Your traumas and losses are precious and dear, delicate things, but if we spend our lives guarding and peering into them, we miss out on the beauty and new life unfolding before us. You don't have to let go or forget or stop saying their name or speaking your truth, but sometimes we must meet what has happened to us in a new way. This is what forgiveness is—not forgetting, but remembering in a new way.[1]

How do you remember in a new way? Tell the story you are rehashing from a new perspective. How would your child self tell the story? Or imagine yourself at 80 years old, remembering this hard thing that happened. Listen to your best friend (or imagine how your best friend would) tell it. What details are different? Where is the emphasis? What can you see about this story that you have glossed over in *your* stuckness? When you retell it or remember it, what are the big "rocks" of the plot that you are sure to say with intention or wonder if others really understand the magnitude of? In my story, I kept coming back to this line, "...and he stole my journals!" expecting the hearer to gasp at how significant and precious these extensions of my soul are to me. But over time it said more about how caught up *I was* in that—no one else could be sufficiently outraged or damaged by that act as I was, and it was up to me to soothe and heal and forgive. Telling it again and again, and even putting it in a book, is no substitute for getting unstuck. A way that hard "rock" of my traumatic plot eroded was by continuing to journal; in daring to put pen to page, I took back some of what was taken from me. It isn't easy to admit when you are stuck, but you won't always be. Your healing timeline may take longer than others' or go by more quickly. The time it takes is not a

---

1. Paraphrase of Henri Nouwen

measure of your worth. You are progressing every day. Every moment is teaching you something. You are a student of life and what has threatened to end you is only your beginning.

Wayfinding Practice: Remember an Old Story in a New Way

Now it's your turn to practice. What's one of your old scripts that you've been hanging on to—a story that tells you something about why you are the way you are? You can pick a childhood memory or an interesting or sad event tied to a major milestone in your life. Try to pick a particular event or incident or a day. Now imagine the same thing in a new way. Maybe you tell the story but emphasize different parts of the plot. You could try telling it with a really different mood than it normally strikes—turn a funeral into a celebration. It's just practice. You aren't changing the truth, but you are *playing* with the story, which helps us to hold ourselves more lightly, take life a little less seriously, and imagine new possibilities even with old histories.

Wilderness

Knowing how to be solitary is central to the art of loving. When we can be alone, we can be with others without using them as a means of escape.

— bell hooks

ON WHAT WOULD HAVE BEEN OUR TENTH WEDDING ANNIVERSARY, I found myself in a Zen monastery on a cliff overlooking the Pacific Ocean. My tears sheltered beneath my sunglasses, I appeared stoic, all in my head, swirling about what went wrong. It was a rare moment in those days that I wasn't drinking my way through depression.

I went to California for a wedding. Someone I loved, my sweet cousin, Larayne, had found her person after her own wilderness and wandering through abusive relationships. She had spent the time and invested in herself and now we were celebrating new life, while I lingered at the tomb of my old one. I felt like a shell whose hermit crab had left for someplace bigger, but I would learn later that I was indeed not the shell, but the vulnerable crab itself, searching for a home that would fit my now huge, growing capacity. At the time, I just prayed to not get stepped on. The meditation garden was a sanctuary for an afternoon, and also the new age crystal shop, where I first learned the term, "Empath" and stumbled on Judith Orloff's work in this area. Since then, that word *empath* has sort of exploded, with many therapists opining that anyone who describes themselves as such is probably just a person who has been through trauma.

Trauma or not, reading *An Empath's Survival Guide* was like having my own soul read back to me. It was refreshing to realize I was born this way and that my highly sensitive nature was not a mistake. I often bore a sense of foreignness in my own family, as if I was missing a layer of enamel on my soul's "teeth;" being an empath meant being all too familiar with the accusation, "You're just too sensitive." Maybe, as Glennon Doyle writes, I'm "Just a person who is paying attention," but finally receiving a **word** for this sensation I'd experienced my entire life equipped me with confidence to claim that sensitivity and live into it. Picking up on energies and taking the harshness of the world "too personally" has been a part of me for as long as I can remember. Language is such a pragmatic creation, that if the term *empath* speaks to your experience, *use it.*

Living into this empath identity was like carrying a sacred stone that helped me to forgive myself for all the harshness I'd been processing over the last several months. I was not a monster; I had taken on years and years of others' too muchness myself. Having an affair didn't make me a predator; it was an expression of my self-preservation in the journey towards love. Embracing this newfound empath identity didn't excuse me from the work I needed to accomplish on the path towards wholeness either. Empaths, while possessing heightened sensitivities to energy and almost a sixth sense of intuition whether related to the feelings of others, plants, animals, spirituality, or all of the above—require _serious_ reinforcements to their boundaries. It was as if a door had been open in me my whole life, and so much energy had been expended trying to regulate my internal temperature, without me realizing I'd been trying to "air condition" the whole neigh-borhood!

Sometimes when I'm out in public, I joke that I seem to "attract the crazies," as if I give off a vibe that says, "Please come talk to me, come! Over-share!" Like Emma Lazarus' words on the Statue of Liberty, my outward vibe seems to convey, "Give me your tired, your poor, your huddled masses yearning to be free..." except mine attracted dysfunctional family dynamics, addiction, and psychosis. The thrill of interacting with cross-sections of humanity energizes me while at the same time, my witness of others' pain, sorrow, unsolveable problems, or the overwhelm of systemic brutalities saps me. Whether introvert or extrovert, I don't know. I'm told that it's "all about where you recharge your energy" but what is it called when the exhausting nature of being human seems to chase after you? If you've ever been to therapy, you're probably reading this part muttering, "Boundaries. It's boundaries. The answer is bound-aries" and what began as an off-hand whisper is now building into a shout back to me through the void.

"Boundaries" is another self-help word thrown about, but what does it mean? Prentiss Hemphill in *What it Takes to Heal* defines boundaries as "The distance at which I can love you and me at the same time." Boundaries are not brick walls we erect to keep others out or ourselves protected, but more like cell walls, sometimes porous, intended to discern where we end and another begins. The wilderness is a season, a place in which we investigate and nurture our own boundaries. Who am I? What do I like? What do I not like? What are the behaviors I will allow into my life? What feels good to me? What am I not willing to include or abide?

When I was learning to drive, before we even put the car in gear, we had to do a mental exercise of noticing where the front, back, and sides of the car stopped and started. We had to develop a sense for how much space we took up on the road. This spiritual inventory is part of nurturing boundaries too. I must know where I start and stop, and where the rest of the world begins. Time alone is the only way to discover this. Part of my self-care *must* involve time alone to fortify my boundaries, like checking the locks in the evening to make sure the house is secure.

The best example of wilderness put to good use was where the Israelites were led after fleeing their enslavers in Egypt. They crossed over the Red Sea on miraculously dry land, while seeing their captors drown in it behind them. Then they wandered for a good long time, just them and God, learning new ways of being, able to listen closely to the things God likes and the things God didn't think were good for them, and learning to trust again a new way of being in the world.

It takes a while to recognize that you, in some ways, *were* part of the problem. Any time you are navigating an ending or a season of loss, there is an opportunity to reflect on what role you played in how it went south. The term "reactive abuse" is one that's trendy as we talk about our "highly toxic" and "narcissistic" former partners or bosses or parents. Everyone is highly toxic to some degree, and all of us carry within a degree of narcissism. Not to relativize abuse at all—abuse is far more common than any of us thinks because abuse is a way of showing up in the world. Abuse seeks to build and maintain power and control. Many of us are unlearning it from prior generations. When faced with an overwhelming situation, who wouldn't want to feel empowered and in control? And yet unlearning abuse involves summoning up the courage to ask and answer the question, "Was my behavior problematic? If so, how did I cause harm?" In the investigation process, you may come to realize you behaved in ways that were hard to recognize as yourself, or stayed in relationships with people who are now unrecognizeable to you.

I was unrecognizable for many who had once been in my inner circle. Rob and I built a community but kept our truest selves hidden from it. This is a common experience for pastors trying to build a spiritual haven of support and mutual growth, but feeling like they themselves cannot grow authentically within the community. We're told throughout our formation in seminary and within the faith communities who accompany us in listening to God's call that "Boundaries are important," without giving specifics on what those look like. Boundaries are not a set of do's or don'ts, but begin internally within ourselves. What kind of behavior will we tolerate? How will we self-soothe or assertively speak up when a boundary has been crossed?

The prophet Isaiah tells a story of a King who prays to God to be delivered from the conquering Assyrian Army. And miraculously, God delivers the King and the people from defeat. Later, another army sends officials with lavish gifts to visit the King, to "ooh" and "ahhh" and fawn over his palace. The King shows the visiting dignitaries every room, where all his treasures are stored up. The prophet Isaiah is in disbelief. Why would you show them that?! Would you roll out the red carpet for them to invade? Sure enough, the visiting dignitaries go back to their king and plot an invasion that is successful.[1] This is what boundaries are like. Who are we allowing to see our store rooms and treasures? Who gets access to our inner world? The wilderness taught me to recultivate my inner world, that not all of my journey had to be shared. Before this season of isolation, there were no lines between what was shared with others and what I kept inside. I posted about my marriage, my house, my children on the internet, projecting an image I wanted to be true, but that was wanting of peace, wholeness, and joy.

This is part of what made the collapse of everything so shocking for those who thought they were close. "What? You had a *perfect life*. How could you be getting divorced? How did we not see this?" like angry magic show audience members who could not understand the trick, but realized they'd been had.

An authority figure in the church hung up on me after concluding that I "hurt hundreds of people" and that she was one of them who had considered herself a friend but was deeply hurt by my duplicity. There was no grace for this kind of sin.

It was those closed doors and hang ups that hurt the worst in

---

1. Isaiah 36-39

the wilderness. As a pastor who often concealed my true reactions to people's behavior in order to love them, her honesty was painful and cruel.

"Speak the truth in love,"[2] Paul wrote to the Ephesians. It's truth and it's love. Too much truth without the love is brutal. Too much love without the truth is enabling. Often we trip the balance, relying more on the truth as brutality than as love, or sweep dangerous behaviors under the rug in the name of love while avoiding the truth.

Therapist Pat helped me understand the boundary-making like this: imagine you have your house and the store a short drive from your home. You go to the store every day. The road between the store and home is in bad shape—there are potholes, jagged edges, and shards of broken glass all along the way. But in the healing process, you built a new road, that's a little longer route, but it goes *around* all the craggly bits that tear your car and tires up. You LOVE the new road—it is smooth and good for your car. Learning the patterns of a healed life, respecting your car/yourself are like this: sometimes you forget on your way home from the store, and you go on autopilot, not remembering that there's a new way to get from point A to B, and you find yourself with a flat tire on the old, messed up road. You are not doomed! You can switch routes, even midway through! As soon as you become aware of where you are, switch to the new way of doing things in which you hold your boundaries, stop overfunctioning and denying your needs, quit choosing the path of victimization, and gently, lovingly, speak the truth.

---

2. 4:15

Old way: leads to
broken wheels,
danger, unreliable for
getting you home, but
familiar

New way:
safe, clean, maybe
takes a little longer
and harder to
remember at first

It sounds like a lot to switch from a path that has been comfortable for you to a path that helps you feel confident, whole, and like you can offer your best to the world, perhaps even giving you the courage to go more places beyond home to store—building more roads and expanding your world! The wilderness is a time of road construction. In the Bible it was called "a desert highway" where valleys are raised up and mountains are brought low. You are paving the way towards new life and it is your daily patterns that shape it most profoundly. The little things, like flossing, hydrating, moving our bodies, saying kind and true things to ourselves in the

mirror. These are the blessings that construct a new road out of potholes and squalor and into new life.

Wayfinding Practice: Practice Road Construction

We make the road by traveling it, but before we set out on our new road, let's imagine what it looks like. If you could design the perfect day, what would it include? Would you wake up early or late? How would you spend your morning? What would you eat? What kind of activities would you do? What would the "clumps" be to punctuate your time? How do you want to feel on your perfect day? What clothes do you wear? No, not every day can be a perfect day, but as we envision the possibilities for making the most of our time, the losses become smaller and we build a road we can enjoy traveling on.

On Getting a Divorce Dog in the Middle of a Pandemic

Dogs make us believe we can actually be as they see us.

— *The Monks of New Skete*

WHEN WE NAME LOSS AND COMMIT TO NOT STAYING THERE, WE'RE honest about how we ended up in the place we now find ourselves in. In the spirit of honesty, I'll admit this: the real reason I adopted a dog was because X told me that I couldn't take care of anything and I was far too selfish to parent or put any other creature's needs before my own. I adopted a dog to test the claim.

In 2020, I joined the ranks of so many Americans working remotely and sheltering in place who decided, "What the heck? Let's bring something cute and cuddly home to ease our sorrows." Five years later I can emphasize as all animal shelters do that HAVING A DOG IS A FREAKING COMMITMENT, Y'ALL.

But also as I grow, I am less afraid of doing what everyone else does and embrace that yes, during the pandemic, like everyone else, I adopted a dog, and yes, during my divorce, a new dog helped me through the sads, and yes, I sometimes want to send her back to the pound for being a holy terror.

There will never be a yard big enough for Ruthie. There will never be a creature nearby that she will not want to lunge at. Or a deer that she will not want to chase. Accepting this and behaving accordingly is the key to my dog-owning happiness.

"But you can train her can't you?" you ask. Why, of course. We did private obedience lessons in which she learned to sit, to lay down, to shake, and at least theoretically how to heel. The lessons trained me on how to cross my arms and not engage when she jumps or misbehaves. She will not come when called if there is a remotely more enticing offer. She reacts to other dogs, school buses, trucks with trailers, cattle, bicycles, and anything too loud, too flamboyant, or too closely resembling a fresh kitchen trash bag.

Ruthie has taught me to own my own shortcomings as well as hers.

People will accuse you of the things they are too ashamed to confess about themselves, and this accusation shaped my behavior more than I want to admit. I adopted a dog to prove to myself that I *am* loving and I *am* capable of caring for something besides myself.

Ruthie has tested that love.

In truth, she saved me, mostly by needing every single day, rain or shine, Covid or no Covid, at least a twenty minute walk and fresh food and water. Has Ruthie ever had a perfect day in which all her wants and needs are met? No, absolutely not. She can outwalk, outfetch, outsnuggle, out-Ruthie anyone. She is relentless. And she has taught me that being a LOT and taking up space and having NEEDS can be part of one's charm. Also that spending your whole day napping is a completely respectable use of time.

Heel: to walk directly next to, instead of behind or before. A learned patience and pacing to virtuous companions.

Heal: to become sound or healthy again.

Ruthie has taught me to observe my surroundings. To pay attention to behavior patterns. There are some snooty ladies who gab and use hand weights on their morning stroll. There's Bo, the Standard Schnauzer who takes his owner on a long leash along the creek to peer at the neighboring golf course twice a day. And Bud, the aging Shih-Tzu who parades his owner out a few times daily, careful to avoid Hudson, the uppity Poochon who runs with the family of six down the street.

These characters were peripheral, mild annoyances and distractions out my bungalow window, that is, until Ruthie.

The decision was mine, but Therapist Pat's hearty endorsement came in what I can only imagine sounded like this in her head, "Jesus lady, get a damn dog if it means you're going to stop believing this dude's nonsense projections!"

The search was underway, and a sweet so-called "terrier mix" emerged as a frontrunner. "Helga" was her shelter name—an awfully ill-fitting name for a creature with such irresistibly charming and deep eyes. Her mis-identified breed swiftly surfaced — she was an Australian Cattle Dog, also known as a Heeler.

ACDs are on the larger side of medium dog breeds, love activity, are super smart, eager to please and great with kids (especially after said children realize this dog is not another sibling, but a bonus parent, herding them to bed and off to school). Intellectual stimulation keeps Heelers from terrorizing your home. The name "Heeler" though different in spelling than healer, seemed to carry some magnitude. This dog has been part of my healing, and I hers. Ruthie was found with her litter in a dumpster with Parvo Virus, a pernicious puppy disease that is difficult to survive. At just two months old, she was rescued and treated, nursed back to health and put in a foster home.

The day we met her, we were immediately smitten. Those deep green eyes, copper eye-patch, and red speckles down her white coat and gregarious demeanor sucked us in just seconds after laying eyes on her. But the name "Helga" had to go.

The kids and I wanted to enter into this thoughtfully and in earnest. Many names were tossed about: Coco, Spot, LuLu, Dora, nothing quite fit the feelings we had for this new addition to our lives.

Just months before meeting her, our country mourned the death of Supreme Court Justice Ruth Bader Ginsburg — who many felt was the last vestige of 87-year-old glue holding us together at the end of Donald Trump's first presidency.

Additionally, Biblical names have been important in the naming of my children:

Olive—the first sign of hope and new life after the Flood.

Isaiah — a prophet who envisioned desert highways and new dawns.

Ruth is a short book, jammed between the chaotic time of the Judges when "Everyone did what was right in their own eyes" (Yikes) and Israel's saga with a monarchy. Ruth is a young widow, no stranger to suffering, who comes into the Hebrew family tree by persistent companionship to Naomi, her grieving mother-in-law.

In the tradition of the Notorious RBG and my biblical super-hero, this new addition had a name. Heelers tend to pick their "person" and stick to them wherever they go—living up to the term "velcro dogs." "Where you go, I will go," Ruth said to Naomi. "Your people shall be my people and your God, my God."

"Ruth" is also pretty close to "Woof" and has a certain solemnity to it — unbefitting the cuteness of this particular pup, so Ruthie she became.

Puppies need to be walked several times daily, and Ruthie was the talk of the block when she first arrived. Her lovable curiosity towards every person, dog, or deer; her unique coloring and expressive face drew the neighbors of every age with infatuation and intrigue.

With Ruthie, I finally had something to say to Bud's human and Bo's leash-lead. My neighbor, also named Elaine and I chatted about the latest with her pup, Benji. I learned this is a common thing with dog people, connecting on a deep level about the special pooches in our lives. We talk about age and breed, the last trip to the Vet or the Groomer, things to watch out for, how beautiful and charming each one is, and regale stories of dogs past and puppy park adventures.

On a few occasions, Ruthie has slipped through the door with kids coming and going, and the Dog People have been there to catch her. Even the non-dog owners have taken a liking to this girl. A puppy incites people to visit their grief and hope — stories of dog loss and out loud wondering, "Maybe it's time to look for a new one."

A common rhetorical question in pet circles said with a gleam in our eyes is, "Who rescued who?"

I wonder that to myself regularly. Ruthie's needs give my day punctuation and camaraderie. She's there to hear whatever eye-rolling absurdity comes up during a Zoom call and we process it on our walks.

At first, I speculated if she was my "Emotional Support Animal" — a concept I thought was Grade-A foolishness until becoming an enamored pet parent. In a conversation with my cousin about Ruthie's keen sense for knowing when I need a cuddle, walk in the sunshine, or to just go to bed, the term "Wisdom Dog" bubbled up.

I call her my Wisdom Dog instead of my emotional support dog, because if anything she has been a teacher more than a thera-pist. She has taught me how to apologize to my neighbors, how to let go of the fantasy of taking iced coffee to the dog park for a chill Saturday morning. Ruthie teaches me that a walk and a little food and water is a great way to start every day.

Wisdom has built her house;
she has hewn her seven pillars.
She has slaughtered her animals; she has mixed her wine;
she has also set her table.
She has sent out her female servants; she calls
from the highest places in the town,
"You who are simple, turn in here!"
To those without sense she says,

Elaine Murray

"Come, eat of my bread
and drink of the wine I have mixed.
Lay aside immaturity and live,
and walk in the way of insight."

— *Proverbs 9:1-6*

Ruthie is the accompaniment to this wilderness walk towards Woman Wisdom's house (see Proverbs 8-9) as I learn to set the table and mix the wine, to prioritize the self-care and rhythms that keep me healthy and growing.

When I moved into this house, broken and shell-shocked from an abusive marriage, I suspected that this place was special. The "Healing Hygge Home" I began to call it. Strong bones, surrounded by trees on a private street where I could fall apart and be stitched back together. Ruthie is the perfect companion to fit in here.

We're both learning to trust again, in ourselves and in others. Now I've become one of "The Dog People" who I see as fellow pilgrims, both rescued and rescuing, walking our way into heaven at least three times a day.

To someone else going through the goo, naming their losses and trying to get up again, I would not advise getting a dog, or anything that needs care, not even a goldfish. Your needs are so big right now. But I do believe dog-walking, or even walking yourself in such a way that you commit to it, rain or shine might stitch your weary soul back together again. A dog has helped me connect with other humans again in a period of isolation. Your wayfinding tool to name your loss and not get stuck there is to cling to something that brings you out of yourself. Is it a coloring book or a nice set of pastels? Is it joining a quilting group or a clay studio? Is it walking other people's dogs? Or bird-watching? Whatever it is, commit to it. Even just once a week to start. Don't let yourself miss more than twice in a row. It will stitch the pieces of you back together again.

Wayfinding Practice: The Art of Doing Something Poorly

No, you don't need to get a dog to heal (or heel). But when we're naming loss, there can be so much fear—fear that we will mess up again or break something irreparably. Here is an invitation to do something that you know you won't do well the first time. For most folks, any form of art will do. Try your hand at poetry or pastels! Don't take a class, just get the basic materials and start doing something you know you won't do well. Why? It loosens us up. It brings playfulness back into our lives. We experience forgiveness and appreciation and humility when we try our hand at something we aren't skilled at. It makes us appreciate the folks for whom that kind of art/hobby/activity comes easily or well too. It recenters our world: we are not the most amazing at every single thing and we do actually need other people to get along well in the world. Sucking at something helps us see the things we are really quite good at by contrast. After you do something that is a big challenge for you and messy, it's good and right to give your soul a break and engage in something soothing that comes easily and well to you.

Pizza Night Will Save Us

Baruch ata Adonai, Eloheinu Melech ha-olam, hamotzi lechem min ha'aretz
Blessed are you, Lord, our God, King of the Universe, who has brought forth bread from the earth

— *Sabbath blessing for the bread*

WE KNOW THE BODY KEEPS THE SCORE WHEN IT COMES TO PROCESSING trauma and grief. Even when our minds and emotions have gone through the steps, the body will feel the anniversary, the cyclical nature of the thing that happened washing away from us and lessening little by little. I got kicked out of my home on a Friday afternoon, and every Friday after that was like a mini rerun of the experience. Eventually I would forget that it was Friday but my body would just know. As afternoon faded into evening at the end of the week, instead of feeling that free sense of anticipation for the freedom of a weekend, dread and irritability would take hold of me.

In the process of crafting our custody agreement, the negotiations landed on kids spending every Friday with me. My attorney

221

sold it to me as "Such a win. Any of my clients with kids would love to get Friday afternoons with their kids and never have to get them out of bed on Mondays!" Picking them up from school on Friday afternoons was a little salve to my broken spirit. It gave us time to build new traditions as the three of us and didn't leave me alone with the weighty dread Fridays brought. I unearthed a memory of my childhood best friend whose parents were divorced. We often spent Fridays sleeping over at her house, which included a stop at the grocery store for frozen pizza and snacks, a movie rental for the weekend, and a drive through the car wash during which her super cool mom played the *Titanic* soundtrack while we pretended to profess our love to each other on a sinking ship. Fridays wouldn't be all bad.

I could count on Friday being pizza night. You don't have to *think* about pizza. It has enough structure to be a guardrail and enough freedom to make it whatever you want it to be. Pizza is the perfect recovery food, whether from heartbreak or a long run.

I made the dough from scratch because I could and because it was cheaper and tastier that way. I learned to make dough from a friend in seminary a decade prior—little did I know all these pieces were parts I would use in discovering a new me.

My company had a 3 pm All Hands Meeting over Zoom every Friday afternoon (UGH!), so kneading the dough while watching slide presentations became part of my weekly rhythm, while kids created chaos around the house. After making the pizzas, we could all relax and decompress from the week with a movie of their choosing. So many skills were being built during this ritual of designing one's pizza and picking out a movie. The siblings learned how to negotiate and plan together. One could only veto another's suggestions so many times before there was no discussion to be had. Mom could come in at any time and for any reason and decide we were watching something else, but I couldn't play that card too many times before chancing the magic of the relationship and their interest in spending time together. Isaiah loves pineapple and prosciutto and will eat it in any form as long as it has those two elements on it, every single week, without fail. Ollie wants a piece of what everyone else is having and there is no ingredient that will keep him away.

Pizza night taught me emotional regulation. This isn't a skill I learned as a child. Whenever my mom's emotions would get out of control, she would rage clean or go away; Dad would storm off or go for a walk. But I never saw them work through discomfort. Even when I would get upset, the instruction was "Go to your room until you quit acting like a two year old" which bred years and layers of emotional avoidance.

On Friday nights, everyone is tired. All the women in us, to paraphrase Nayyirah Waheed[1], and all the big feelings our kids have been learning to regulate are exhausted. The energy we don't know how to contain is on the loose and bent out of shape. Friday night is not the night for big emotional discussions. It is not a night for guests. It is miracle enough to be sitting together in front of the same screen and sharing a similar meal together. It is a night for stretchy pants and processed sugar and all the soft things.

Inevitably for maybe the first year of Pizza Fridays, I would lose my shit and raise my voice and cuss in the kitchen while the pizza was inevitably not doing what I wanted it to or the sausage had gone bad or, or, or any realm of calamity had overtaken my tired body. We learned to love each other, and I learned to receive the love of my children in these imperfect moments. I learned to apologize to them and commit to managing my emotions better. They learned that I could be counted on to repair with them if they were scared. I learned that adults yelling and cussing even if kids rationally and logically know isn't about them is still scary. And I learned I didn't want to be a scary parent. I wanted to be their safe place, their rock, their center that they could come back to when the world was scary and chaotic. The really good flavors of pizza helped.

Pizza Fridays were punctuated by the scent and sticky feel of

---

1. "all the women. in me. are tired." Nayirrah Waheed, *Nejma*

223

sweat and flour while I prepped and baked from four to six pm and then the glorious exhale of propping my feet up with a beer while the familiar sound of Disney's classic Cinderella's castle began before one of the films from the vault. This sacred weekly tradition held our precious three together and protected us into the future. The sense of holiness that came with Pizza Fridays must be akin to the nostalgia Shabbat-observing Jews feel about the lighting of the candles, as familiar blessings are chanted over bread and wine, *Baruch ata adonai, Eloheinu Melech ha olam* (Blessed are you, Lord God of the Universe). The Sabbath meal is one full of sensory experiences—Jewish people light two candles, break a loaf of bread, pour a glass of wine (or other fruit from the vine) and spend time with family and friends letting one week end and holding together until a new one begins. Sabbath starts on Friday nights, ushered in by candle light, and concludes at sundown on Saturday—a day for rest and remembering that it is holy to rest and delight in the presence of one another. Sabbath is a meeting place; it is poetry, "a momentary stay against confusion,"[2] a place to orient ourselves again to the things that are most important.

Loss can leave us stunned and bereft. Even if it is a mess of our own making, no one deserves to be stuck there forever. One pizza won't pull you out of the muck. But making rituals that remind you that you are human, that you deserve love and belonging and to experience joy—over and over again? That will save you. That will resurrect you, one Friday at a time.

---

2. Robert Frost, "The Figure a Poem Makes"

Wayfinding Practice: A Recipe for Ritual

Super Simple Pizza Sauce & Dough Recipe:

Let the water run from your faucet on warm until your pinky finger feels the warmth, but isn't scorched by the warmth. Then measure out **1 and ⅓ cups (320 ml) water**. Dump a packet or **2 and ¼ tsp of yeast** into the warm water. Put **a squirt of honey** or a sprinkle of sugar into it.

Then in a big bowl, measure out **450g of flour** (can be bread flour or all purpose) and a **teaspoon of salt**. Drizzle in a **tablespoon or two of Olive Oil** and mix either by hand or with a stand mixer. After the yeasty water mixture has shown you that it's all puffy and alive, pour that into your flour mixture and stir/knead for 5-10 minutes, until it really feels like dough instead of just crumbly flour. You can meditate on your enemies while you give that sucker a beating or envision that each push and turn of the dough is making you a happier, kinder person in the meantime. The dough should feel soft when it's ready to be left alone for a bit. You should feel softer too. Cover the dough with a damp towel and let it rise for 60-90 minutes while you get your toppings ready and preheat the oven with a pizza stone in it to 500 degrees.

After the dough has roughly doubled in size, rip off chunks of it to stretch and roll out into flat pizzas. You'll want **parchment paper** to avoid cussing at the dough and some **cornmeal** to help with the stickiness. You will likely get three personal size pizzas from this amount of dough. After you roll one out, top it with your sauce and cheese and fixin's. Then bake it for 10 to 12 minutes. While one pizza is baking, you can top the next one.

The Sauce

Take **a can of diced or whole tomatoes** and pour them in a blender with **a tablespoon of oregano**, as much **garlic** as your heart desires and a **tablespoon of olive oil**, some **salt and pepper**. Blend that sucker until it's smooth. Use liberally all over your pizza dough.

Favorite Topping Combos from the Healing Hygge Home:

Isaiah's fav: pineapple and prosciutto; Pastor pizza: kalamata olives, hot italian sausage, and spinach. Traditional with a kick: pepperoni and jalapeño slices.

Embracing New Life

Embrace the Sweetness: The Journey From Broken to Abundant Life

To be fully alive, fully human, and completely awake is to be continually thrown out of the nest. To live fully is to be always in no-man's-land, to experience each moment as completely new and fresh. To live is to be willing to die over and over again.

— *Pema Chödrön*, When Things Fall Apart: Heart Advice for Living Through Difficult Times

SO OFTEN WHEN WE ARE TRYING SOMETHING NEW OR EXPERIENCING personal growth—whether that looks like a faster mile pace or an advanced degree, the advice out there for us can be summarized as "Embrace the suck." There is of course an element of pain and sweat associated with being human and experiencing growth, but there's also joy and pleasure and goodness there too. Why else would we grow? This section of finding your new beginning is about *embracing*—not shying away from, the sweetness that is **rightfully yours** in a new season.

Embracing new life after the storm is the sweet juice of making it through a whole lot of hardship to the other side. But if you haven't let go of what has been, it's hard to usher in what's coming.

229

The chrysalis image that has been such an emblem for me in this season comes in clutch, yet again. Once the caterpillar has turned to goo and their wing buds have now taken shape and become actual wings—the thing that was once worm-like is now lighter and a different creature entirely, but still has one more task: busting out of that cocoon. Embracing new life is the sweet and sticky task of transitioning to what comes after the storm.

I cried over lunch (I cry less often, but with more generosity these days) when I told my pastor that "I didn't know it could be this good." She looked at me with a mix of sadness and happiness and said, "I hate that it was that bad for you to not know it could be this good."

A memory rushes over me: I am in the kitchen at our old house on a January day. I am baking a cake and frosting it with glitter in the shape of the number seven. It is an anniversary cake for our little busy bustling family to enjoy. Because "It's really a day for all of us, right?" and in my mind I am going over the mantra I have chosen for this year of marriage, *marriage is a bitch, but you're not.*

I blink and am back again in the present. Marriage is not a bitch. It is not the ball and chain or something to hold your breath and get through so that all your remaining friends in old age can look at you with awe and say, "Wow! FIFTY years? That's incredible." No, marriage isn't worth it if the payout is adoration for sticking together that long.

You deserve relationships that help you access that river of joy that runs beneath you and between you. When you've been losing for so long or had so much bad stuff happen that you come to expect it, new life can feel foreign and unreal. Good things can come not just one at a time, but snowballing into your life. This isn't a lottery-winning kind of luck, but a good, happy, stable, sun-rose-again, coffee-is-giving-life-again kind of goodness. New life is stick to your bones kind of good. The tiny trauma survivor in you can hardly believe it- when you find yourself laughing too hard around a dinner table with friends or crossing not just one, but multiple items off the to-do list with ease. Emotions flood, but not the scary kind. The kind of emotions the Psalmist wrote about, "Such knowledge is too wonderful for me."[1] New life is that orgasm that seizes you from head to toe and fries what feels like every nerve-ending in your body to the point where you are pinching yourself that this must be a dream. **I wish that kind of blessed good on you**. You, dear wayfinder, deserve it.

And if such a surprising blessing seizes us too often or too close together we might wonder, could a person die from this much pleasure? Can I burn out from too much good? Where is my other shoe that will drop? Wisdom softly shakes her head and says, "No. You can't squander abundance. You can't waste it."

One of the foundational stories of Christianity is the parable of the prodigal son in Luke 11. "A man had two sons..." the parable begins. The younger son who squandered a fortune, cut off his family and wasted it on the stuff of life, only to return empty-handed, begging for a job from his dad. On his way back to his father's estate, he rehearsed what he was going to say, telling the story of how he had messed up and how undeserving he was of good things. But the father, instead of turning him away or telling him "That's what you get!" with arms crossed, or even making him work off the fortune he took, the father welcomes the son back with open arms, puts on a feast, and rejoices that new life came from a place he thought only death and loss were. He greets him on the road, lavishes him with gifts of honor and celebration, and doesn't even let him finish his apology before welcoming him with grace: that undeserved abundance that shows up and changes things for the better. The son didn't squander the joy of his father's love that welcomed him back with reckless abandon. Grace does not run out or expire. It is never too late for something good and wonderful to land in your lap. Embracing new life is training your brain and senses to be ready for and open to new possibilities. When we've been losing for so long, like the son in this story, we tend to rehearse the same story of loss, of mess ups, of how undeserving

---

1. Psalm 139:6

we are of welcome and inclusion. **But new life tells a different story.**

In the Texas Hill Country, any time you go about beginning a landscaping project, like digging a garden or holes for fence posts, it doesn't take more than about three inches of "This is fun! Look at me doing things and making the world more beautiful!" before you hit solid rock. Limestone undergirds just about everything here. I think sometimes when we go through life, we expect that we haven't truly lived until you hit rock bottom. Take a lesson from the country folk though, who wouldn't still be here if they didn't believe the rock was worth pushing through. Beneath rock bottom is the soft, squishy marrow of joy, whose nutrients like collagen and glucosamine literally make our skin brighter, our joints less inflamed and surely grant our spirits a path of ease too.

New life sneaks up on us. I didn't immediately go from homeless, jobless, and single-parenting to married and thriving in safe housing again. There was a falling, a sinking, a death; and then a rising and rekindling and rebirth. If these pieces had all come together as immediately as they went out from under me, it would have been another trauma in the making. *Trauma is anything that happens too much and too soon.* Even wonderful things can be traumatic if we aren't ready for them. So we slowly and methodically welcome new life, grateful for the time it takes for positive changes to occur. When we hole up and protect ourselves from the bad that could come to us, we can also keep out the good. You don't have to embrace new life alone—in fact, you can't. New life comes with community and vulnerability. For this part of our new beginning, we're going to rely on each other, we're going to learn through mistakes and delight and whimsy and play. This book was never about self-help; it was about one beggar telling another where she found bread. Embracing new life is a journey more than a destination. New life will wash up on you like a sand dollar on the shore, sometimes in shards and pieces, but sometimes whole and alive. There is beauty in the brokenness and the promise is real that abundant life awaits even on the other side of suffering. Up until this point we've borrowed tools from hydrologists, children's literature, poetry, scripture, and Tarot. We will use all of these as we search the horizons of our lives for what we can welcome, and what we can filter out as "not for us" in this new season. For now, I encourage you to anticipate. Make yourself ready for what is to come. Sometimes this looks like decluttering or clearing things out. For some it is dreaming and brainstorming, allowing yourself the courage and imagination to envision possibilities you haven't thought of yet.

When my kids come in the kitchen, lured by the smells of what's cooking and their hunger pangs, they ask, "How can I help?" knowing the more they do to assist, the closer we are to eating. Setting the table and pouring the water is the most common task they're handed in anticipation of the feast.

We are now setting the table for the goodness yet to come. On a practical level, for me, that looks like setting out my tea cup and filling the kettle, making sure the candle and lighter are ready to go next to my journal and pen, so that as soon as I wake up, I can welcome the day and its goodness by writing and reflecting with a cup of tea. What does setting your table look like? Is it picking out your clothes the night before? Is it filling up your water bottle? Or packing a lunch? How can you anticipate what you hope to receive in this new season?

Wayfinding Practice: Set the Table

Your new life may not be here yet, or not in the way you want it. What's something you can do to "set the table" for it while it's on the way? Imagine what kind of style you will have and get a piece of clothing or accessory that is emblematic of that. Imagine new life in another country? Make a dish that's a regular staple of that culture's diet. Begin embodying the life you desire, even while you wait for it.

Sobriety And Me: All the Things I Never Set Out to Do

May you be tender to yourself, to your pain, to your humanity, to who and how you are in this moment. May you never stray from this tenderness, knowing it is the birthplace of caring for yourself differently. And may you — through this curiosity, compassion, and care — embrace the grace as you weather the frustration that comes along with it, such that you find peace in never being quite done, never quite settled, ever growing in the Spirit.

— *Erin Jean Warde,* Sober Spirituality

WHEN I SET OUT TO RECOVER FROM "THE HARD THING," I DIDN'T imagine sobriety from alcohol as part of it. Healing is a love story for one's self, and among the brave and radical acts of love we can put into practice, reducing the poison we ingest is one of them. We ingest poison in many forms: harmful beliefs about ourselves, toxic sources of news and gossip, anger and hatred towards one another, and harmful substances we take to numb out and escape from the pain in our lives. In the trenches of such pain, I found love for the tenderest parts of myself, that included asking myself what role alcohol played in my life and what role it should play in the future

I was dreaming of for myself and my children. I never set out to be sober, just like I never set out to be divorced. There are many realities we don't set out to embody, but life has other plans. I didn't have a big, dramatic moment in which I poured all my booze down the drain and started going to meetings. I picked up a book that a friend wrote about the spirituality of becoming sober (shout out to Erin Jean Warde and *Sober Spirituality*) and found that sobriety was a super reasonable offer of a lifestyle. Way led on to way as it so often does. Except this time instead of "If you give a mouse a cookie..." leading me from bike rides into the bed of a married man, investigating sobriety led me to be more curious..."sober curious" and to learn more about alcohol's effects on the body.

I read stories about moms who lived for the end of the day glass of wine, as I lived those stories. While shepherding my babies through a pandemic we leaned hard on respect and reverence for the holy time of Happy Hour, a time in which we would all cease from work, pull out a cutting board with pears, cheese, cashews, and crackers and I would begin my evening descent into alcoholic beverage after beverage. By the time bedtime came around I was reaching through a fog of bath time and pajamas and dishes, punctuated by glasses 1, 2, 3, and 4 of wine or bourbon. Then followed by an exhale, an unmaking of the bed, and tucking myself in for a night of restless sleep. Booze was a little solace, a nice cozy blanket to take shelter beneath while navigating the sea of loneliness, guilt, and regret. But I could sense light beginning to shine through as though a cover was lifting for me too, peeking in from a new future ahead of me.

When my son wakes up in the morning, he comes out to the living room, still in a stupor of sleep, grabs a blanket and curls up on the couch to continue sleeping. I laugh that he is a "couch-finished" kid, like a grass-finished cow, and that this extra dose of cozy must make him enter the day with his own level of refinement. Eventually, the day begins and he must emerge from beneath the blanket, get out of his cozy pajamas and into cold clothes that have been waiting for him in his dresser.

Eventually all of us must leave the places of safety in order to grow. This is what embracing new life is—the butterfly doing the squeaky, clumsy work of flapping its wings violently enough to break the hard fibers of its chrysalis and emerge as a new creation. While we may be reluctant to leave the shelter of wilderness, there is a promise waiting for us on the other side.

The wilderness taught me not to put my trust in substances to save me. The alcohol was a cloud, but a poisonous one. The more I noticed its effects, the less I could stand it. Becoming too dependent on alcohol makes good people into shallow versions of themselves. It destroys relationships. Alcohol lies. Alcohol creates poor intimacy and poor solace.

And yet, the *ritual* of drinking gave shape and punctuation to my day, especially when everything was not only upside down for me, but for the COVID-19 impacted world from which no substance could make us fully escape. We can lean into rituals *and transform* them at the same time. Five o'clock is still a holy time of day. Remember when the hard thing first happens, and we can only live ten minutes at a time? And then our capacity for life and healing and growth expands, but the full expanse of time is still too wide for us to see and plan and find ourselves within. Rituals punctuate time. The ritual of meeting together to worship early on the first day of the week (Sunday) began as a way of marking time after Jesus' death when the women went looking for his body and found it had been raised. Rituals before we eat allow us to take note of where our food comes from and set aside distractions to be present to the task of feeding ourselves and each other. Happy Hour became the ritual to mark the end of the traditional work day and the beginning of leisure time.

I found in seasons of embracing sobriety, that I cared more about what a drink symbolized than what it contained. Every day after five o'clock, I pour a non-alcoholic beer into a pint glass. I clink it with my husband and then I either start cooking dinner, playing with my dog, or wrapping up my work day. The bubbles from the beer make me less hangry, the act of pouring it into a glass and changing up my tasks is energizing. I feel like I am part of something bigger than myself that is going to make me more engaged with the people and tasks that are reflections of my values, rather than gradually more checked out from them. Then I get to choose—do I have a glass of wine with dinner? Do I pour an after dinner nightcap while Rob and I unwind from the day? Do I brew a comforting cup of tea, or treat the kids with a "Mommy mocktail" — which is a magical concoction of what I have on hand: a squirt of some kind of fruit juice, some sparkling water, a little grenadine and plenty of love and attention?

There are days when the world hits hard and I want to hit it back by pouring a glass and another glass in the company of my support system. But the days I drink are never the happiest ones. Sobriety taught me to expand my set of coping skills. Sobriety is more than abstention from alcohol—it's also a mindful swerve away from the tin of cookies or sleeve of crackers; it's a decision to face the fear instead of drowning it or numbing out. Before this journey, when I felt anxious, the solution was "to drink." Sad? Drink. Celebratory? Drink. Want to feel peace? I don't find it in the bottom of a glass anymore. I feel peace as I tie the laces of my running shoes. I feel peace when I hold my jade Guanyin beads, or take the sketch pad out on the patio. I feel peace when I write. The multitudes I contain stream down on the page into one single stream controlled by the logic of only one pen or crayon or bead in one hand.

But that single stream is not at all what my mind is like. Ramparts crumbling and being rebuilt simultaneously while ideas topple one on top of the other at once, beating down another section of the wall of sanity while she is being remastered.

The city of Jerusalem, in its checkered and challenging history, has been loved and fought for by many a holy people. So much so, over time, that the word "Zion"[1] became a word for what

---

1. Side note: this is one of many reasons identifying as a "Zionist" these days can be problematic—because it eschews that the only people deserving of home and respite

Jerusalem represented spiritually—the very presence of God. Even when the visible parts were in shambles, one could cling to the divine presence that can never be destroyed. One of the times that Jerusalem, the geographical place, was under siege a psalmist wrote a "song for Zion"—a song for finding God's presence when the walls are crumbling.

> *God is our refuge and strength,*
> *a help always near in times of great trouble.*
> *That's why we won't be afraid when the world falls apart,*
> *when the mountains crumble into the center of the sea,*
> *when its waters roar and rage,*
> *when the mountains shake because of its surging waves.*

> — Psalm 46:1-2

While not a city, my life has felt like a house with many rooms, a mansion on acres and acres of beautiful land, more than I could dream of discerning or occupying in one day, week, month, or year. But life with a mismatched person is living on all that great expanse while getting smaller and smaller, closing doors all around you until your space is one tiny room with no windows and no doors and it is locked from the outside. So it is no wonder that you feel trapped. Sobriety gave me the wisdom to understand that no one could kick me out of the mansion of life. That eviction tore open the doors of life's mansion and made the window fly open, let fresh air in so that I could fly, spin, twirl, dance, and take up space.

I had become so small, even my voice was pinched, disembodied from my self. If I had done energy work then, my throat chakra would be burning aglow, blocked and very nearly my heart as well. Wilderness helped me realize that it wasn't old life = bad and new life = good. It wasn't Rob good, X bad. But it was me, *all*

---

in Jerusalem are "God's people," as opposed to some people *not* being God's people. God loves all y'all and there's space for us to get along without hurting or hating.

good. And whoever I chose to be worthy of a place, even the smallest postage stamp size piece of *my estate*, had to be deserving of access to the all good I was discovering about this beautiful mansion of life I could now occupy.

Our words and our language matter. They shape our thoughts and feelings and actions.

> "God is within her, she will not fall."
>
> - Psalm 46:5

The song is a guarantee for neither protection nor success, but a true proclamation of inalienable blessedness. No institution or person can hold your blessedness for you. Sobriety has been a gateway to examine how I had placed my sense of safety and belonging in the hands of untrustworthy people. A turn of phrase used in 12-step circles is that one is never "recovered" from addiction, but one is always "in recovery"—sobriety is active and continuous, even if you've successfully been abstinent from the substance for a long time. Embracing new life means being in recovery from mistrust.

At one point I trusted the church with everything, putting my future, my finances, my wellness in her hands. But She failed to treat me with honor, she failed to hold sacred the truths I had to offer from broken hands. I put my whole trust in my ex-husband, I've put my safety and belonging in the hands of employers, and each time I am disappointed, I come back to the truth that God is within me, I will only fall as deep as the universe's palms are knit to catch me. New life begins with nurturing a connection to yourself and to what is divine within you, that then grows authentically to include connections to your community—friends, lovers, colleagues and co-conspirators.

The process of sobriety is a pruning of all that has not authentically grown out of your own values. It's a *process*—neither Rome nor any grand garden was built in a day. But little by little, as we shape our behavior by making it through a day without our vices and numb-out strategies, we begin to nourish the parts of ourselves that have been dormant.

Elaine Murray

Wayfinding Practice: Recipe for a Ritual

One way to start nourishing the parts of ourselves that have been dormant is with a ritual—here's how you make one:

- Pick the time of day—start off easy. Where is a natural break in your day? What needs shifting?
- Pick something small that brings you joy—Is it a big stretch and loud yawn when the alarm goes off in the morning? Is it the celebratory "pop" and fizz of a beverage going into a cup at five pm? Is it throwing the ball for your dog, or letting your pet bird nip at your shoulder?
- Commit to doing it for a week.
- Revisit, shift, don't be afraid to change it up. Rituals help us to punctuate our days, but are not the periods in the middle of a sentence that isn't done yet.

The Hardest Question to Answer

Our deepest fear is not that we are inadequate. Our deepest fear is that we are powerful beyond measure... As we are liberated from our own fear, our presence automatically liberates others.

— *Marriane Williamson*, A Return to Love: Reflections on the Principles of "A Course in Miracles"

MARIANNE WILLIAMSON'S NUDGING QUOTE WAS FRAMED IN THE pastor's study as a gift at my ordination. "Our deepest fear is not that we are inadequate..." yeah right, I thought. Crippling inadequacy is the context in which I have made many life decisions. Subconsciously, I allowed a deep-seated fear of my own not-enough-ness to drive me into an adolescent marriage, to surrender my livelihood at the feet of fickle institutions, and now to be on the precipice of choosing something new for myself.

Elaine Murray

The Power of Naming

A former employer uses technical documents with project headings and my favorite one is, "Non-Goals of This Project" because in my mind it says, "Here's what we're NOT gonna do." Sometimes, unless you say, "Ok, the sky's the limit, but not THAT" then THAT is precisely the briar patch you end up falling into and then you hate yourself and what you are doing because in your mind you thought, "God, anything but THIS" but you didn't say the THIS part out loud or let anyone in on the little secret conversation you were having with your inmost parts, so "Ope!" as the midwest-erners say—there you are, in the exact place you prayed **not** to be.

At no point in my journey did I say, "Ok, self, well here's what we're NOT gonna do." In fact, I pride myself on being pretty open to most things. And yet, openness is a failure to be specific. Mothering my oldest child, whose indecision is a badge of pride, has taught me that being "Open to most things" is not as wonderful as you might think. Imagine trying to order doughnuts at a bakery with someone who can't decide what they want. You're standing there, holding up the line, getting hungrier and more irritable by the minute. Being "Up for just about anything" is driven by fear of missing out on something.

Answering the question, "What do you want?" is the hardest question of new life. But when we actually do it, name what we want, or even what we don't want, we tap into the power of the divine within us.

When I was in college, I wanted to live in a one-bedroom apartment by myself, working, and living the single gal life. At the same time, I carried with me the model of my parents who found each other quickly, decided they were each other's "one" and sealed the deal for more than fifty years at the ripe ages of 20 and 22. In my twenty-year-old brain, holding these two desires felt at odds with the other and the more convincing one won out—I started looking for a life partner at the outset of college because I didn't want to miss out on the opportunity if Mr. Right was right there on my small university campus. But even then, scarcity—the fear of missing out—drove me into the arms of the first guy who seemed to check the boxes.

Now that I see my parents as the adults that they are, products of their childhoods, and it makes sense why in 1972, they ran towards the other for a sense of security, home, and excitement navigating the upheaval of the 1960s and 70s with only the tools they'd been given in their upbringings. I have a different set of tools. I'm not ashamed anymore of the process it took for me to learn what tools I do possess. For my parents, it was being raised by emotionally immature parents who had come out of World War II and raised children in a time of prosperity, but also huge cultural upheaval, that led their children (Mom and Dad) to want to hurry and settle down with someone with whom they could finish the job of parenting each other through adolescence. The completion of adolescence took more time for me—partially because I hid out from finishing it by playing house for a decade in my first marriage. On paper, both my parents and X and I hit all the life milestones of marriage, children, degrees, and home ownership around the same time, but the dynamics were totally different.

Growing up means choosing for yourself—deciding what you want and what you don't want.

There is power in naming not only what you choose, but also the negative choice, what you choose

> "When I was a child, I used to speak like a child, reason like a child, think like a child. But now that I have become a man, I've put an end to childish things."
> - 1 Corinthians 13:11

not to do. I choose never to cheat on my current husband. It hurts, it's awful, I wouldn't wish the pain of cheating on someone you love to anyone, even the long list of enemies I've cultivated over the years.

I'm also not going along with everything everyone else says I should do. It means committing to something and necessarily saying no to the things that are not that thing. All my life I have wanted to write a book—to write what I see. But first I had to see myself. What will come after these pages? If nothing at all, I saw my story for what it was and embraced it as whole. That in itself is a powerful thing. The power in these pages is that others benefit when a woman looks at herself and beholds who she really is for the first time. I am not a liar. I am not a slut. I am not two-faced. I am not weak. I am not a bitch. I am not ambitious. I am not an egomaniac. I am not a narcissist.

But who am I? What do I stand for? I stand for joy, for empowerment, for growth, for truth. I arrived at this statement of purpose, of choice:

I am a truth-teller who empowers, hopes, and makes room for others to find their purpose and place in the struggle.

I only could have arrived at this statement of purpose and desire for my life by facing the consequences of all the janky turns I took to get here.

Every Choice Has a Consequence

I still stand by my decision to marry at 22. It was the best I could do with the knowledge I had at the time, but I also admit that in doing so I denied my dream of the one bedroom apartment "Living on dreams and spaghetti-O's"[1] because one must choose. The work of embracing new life comes with understanding our choices and claiming even conflicting truths. Truth is a challenging thing to be *for* in an age in which lies sell better. The truth is I pursued the person I loved although he was married to someone else, and I allowed him to pursue me though it violated our professional and personal ethics. Is that kind of love doomed from the start? The image of a fire guides me through the consequences of facing these choices: fires are still beautiful, whether they exist in the safety of a ring of stones on a campout or engulf a building. It's the engulfing fire that brings the tears and heartbreak. A fire warms, yet destroys; a fire is utterly captivating and can squelch life out with its destructive smoke.

---

1. "This One's For the Girls" by Martina McBride

How does a person eventually stop punishing themselves for the choices they made? The forgiveness I needed most from myself was for relational arson. Forgiveness begins with curiosity—asking yourself why—what was the context of why you behaved in the way that you did? Context is the foundation for forgiveness. Context will ruin you though. If you *like* looking at the world in black and white and concrete extremes, block your ears from receiving more context or background on any of your pre-scripted stories and presumptions about what a good life is. Because eventually the context of everyone you want to blame or indemnify will start to make sense. You'll have a hard time forgiving and begin, well, you begin forgiving *yourself*.

My dad says, "If you have a choice between laughing and crying, choose laughing." And I am fortunate, often to have choices. Choices are often more accessible with money and privilege. We are not born on equal footing when it comes to financial well-being or health and abilities, and so much of generational wealth is not limited to our families' real estate holdings, but also their skills and ability to navigate conflict, dysfunction, addiction, and duress. But we do all have *some* choices. Our emotional expression is a choice; perhaps one of the most basic ones. We know the common axiom about the number of muscles it takes to smile (17) versus frown (43), and in prior seasons I was guilty of advocating for choosing to spiritually bypass the hard shit, grin and bear it, and it will get better. But my choice also came with a lot of tears and frowns and cussing and anger. And a few broken pots along the way, and several thousand dollars worth of talk therapy. All of those things led me to my choice—to choose to laugh at the absurdity of all that has happened—from a genetic mutation that "Surely there's such a slim chance that all THREE siblings could have" (8% to be exact), to the friendship that turned into a torrid affair that "Surely we wouldn't get caught, and if we did, I bet X wouldn't even be mad" to the slut-shaming response of the institutional church to my confession, the custody battle for a place in my children's lives. So many things all at once that eventually the tears run out—there are no more laments, there is only laughter.

"It's just that I've been losing for so long..." wrote Jackson Browne in "These Days." But the song's imperative is to keep moving on and to count the time. "Teach us to count our days, that we may gain a wise heart,"[2] wrote the Psalmist. The only way to get over it is through it. One word, one second, one moment at a time.

In the goodbye letter I wrote to my ex-best friend (the breakup that hurt the most), I said, "I pray you never have to forgive yourself for infidelity" and I mean it to this day. It is a long, painful, never fully finished journey. I still cry every time someone tells me they understand or that I'm forgiven, or that I don't have to keep being so hard on myself. I guess grace is like that. Tearworthy. Gut wrenching.

But there are some days that grace makes us brave enough to try again. To pick up the pen and write, to put on the ring and say "I do; I will" and trust that those promises will mean something this time. I used to think the people who got married a second time must be naïve or so dumb, but now I know they are the brave ones. They have watched their world go up in flames and still said, "Fire is beautiful and necessary" as they sharpen the flint and make one again.

The Sankofa. Mythical African Bird. Wikimedia Commons, public domain

---

2. Psalm 90:12

When Saul became Paul in the book of Acts, his transformation wasn't visible to the people he harmed the most. Life moved on. He received a new name, but also a new context for doing miracles.

The Adinkra image of "Sankofa" depicts a bird who flies in a forward direction, while its neck is craned looking back. We never truly leave those we love behind. We carry the lessons we have learned, but let go of the harm we have experienced. Answering the question "What do I want?" takes telling our stories over and over again to pull out the lessons and desires, and leave behind the hurt and dead ends.

Wayfinding Practice: A Permission Slip to Live

What do you need permission to want or to do? Listen to what you want. The you-est you inside knows it, even if they are afraid to say it out loud. I'm gently holding your hand and guiding you through. Here's how you do it:

Ask out loud, like SAY these words so that your ears can hear them:

"What do I want?"

Count to three like you are waiting to reveal it to yourself, then say the FIRST thing that comes to mind.

Honest thought.

If "World Peace" is your first thought, or something equally as broad, then ask again (out loud):

What do I really want? Right now, at this moment?

Say the first thing. And keep asking until it is a true and honest thing. And then give yourself permission to go and do the thing.

Things I am Learning about New Life Now

What's the greatest lesson a woman should learn? That since day one, she's already had everything she needs within herself. It's the world that convinced her she did not.

— Rupi Kaur

I don't have all the answers. But I do have belief.

We must tend to our spirits, like gardeners do their plants. Make sure we aren't rotting from the inside out. Tend to our roots, keep ourselves pliable, moldable, alive rather than brittle, dry, and breakable.

Sticking with something that isn't working in the hopes that it will is a recipe for disaster and burnout. We sometimes stay, because our minds favor the sunk cost fallacy. But it's better to cut and run.

Creativity is more like a candle than a cake.

Like many things, creativity does not deplete by being used up. It is a force to be cared for, nourished, nurtured, and groomed. Creativity contains endless possibilities. The wick never runs out.

We ~~can~~ must forgive ourselves.

I want to forgive and apologize to myself for feeling shame in hating kids' birthday parties. They were crushing, along with so many other forces, to my wild imagination. They didn't have to be, but I was running on fumes then, so summoning the creativity to engage on a level that wouldn't deplete me was out of reach. I am in a much more sustainable phase of life now. **And kids' birthday parties, still kind of suck.**

The best promises to keep are the ones to yourself.

"Do you promise to serve the people with energy, intelligence, imagination, and love?" is part of the ordination vows a Presbyterian pastor takes. It is a posture of relationship. Reworked as a vow to myself, I ask, "Do I promise (am I able to promise?) to tend to my own spirit in a way that is receptive to channeling God's energy, intelligence, imagination, and love for God's people?"

Pastoring is more folk art than task.

Pastors are much more "Mediums" than we were taught in seminary. It is more folk art than task to accompany a people as they listen and humble themselves to the Holy in their midst. Tending to the tools, to the receptors for God's presence within us is so much more important than how much knowledge can be stored up and meted out, Sunday by Sunday.

"Mommy, does God bless people who go to church and pray more than people who don't?" he asked at bedtime. Bedtime is when the best questions come—right when a parent is too exhausted to function and rest is just on the other side of that door. I want to rush to say "No! Of course God doesn't work like that!" But the first thing I know about God is that God is Their own being —They are sovereign and bless who They bless. Now I wish I'd said that. I stumbled through something about how going to church makes me feel better, uplifted, like I have something to think about as I go through the week. That's what I hope I give people as I enter the pulpit again. Sermons are powerful ways of interpreting the Word. And most of the time we pray and we hope that we're doing it right when we show up to speak a word—kind of like any other task you show up to with love—parenting, partnering, art, science, vocation.

Some good things happen after midnight, but it's rarely anything better than sleep.

The closer you dance around midnight, the nearer the demons of despair are to you, or the temptations of drink, or reckless activity. But also sometimes great sex and let-loose dance parties only occur to you around the midnight hour. Sure, you might feel it the next day, but don't let the rigidity of rules get in the way of an occasionally delightful late night orgasm. Don't get in a car after midnight if you can help it though.

Lots of things taste better than being skinny feels.

Healing from diet culture is a whip, no? Where are my 90s girls raised on Snackwells and 100 calorie packs at? Bodies are made for enjoying—enjoying the sun on my belly at the beach because every body is a bikini body if they want to be. Bodies are made for getting our heart rates up through the exercise that releases such good neurotransmissions to protect you from the spiral of despair or keep you from snapping at your family when the oven vent fan is so freaking overstimulating. Bodies are made for letting the juice from mid-summer bruschetta run down our chins and the sauce from pasta dripping in ragu slap us on the face in delight as we slurp the noodles in and laugh.

The more you see it, the more you will be it and believe it.

It's true that we need to see advertising with more black and brown and fat and queer bodies in it because those bodies exist in our real lives. I used to mumble "divorce" or happily skip over that term when describing my family or my experience, especially when talking in church. "Custody" and "They're with their dad" are not dirty words. Divorced people have been shamed out of showing their faces in God's house like they aren't also spiritual beings having human experiences and in need of nourishment. On the outside, it looks like I am married to a man and we have 2.5 kids and a dog. But shattering that veneer on purpose is part of my life's work now. We are partners and friends and lovers, who happen to be married to each other too. Our last names are different, and those last names are different from two of our kids. The point five kid is in college and has a strained relationship with us, but he's still part of the family. We're a divorced family. We're a repairing family who has nothing to hide. Being seen in our mistakes and with the scars of our past does not make the church weaker or less pure. But it shines a light on many ways of being family. There are grandparents raising their grandchildren who need to be seen and whose experiences need to be believed. There are single parents, there are childless people, and the more we see and hear these stories the more we can believe that yes, there is a holiness within each and all of us, waiting to shine.

Perfection was never the aim. Growth is.

Doing something perfectly is boring. Can you do it better the next time? Can you fail even more fabulously the next time? The latter question is not one I'm interested in trying out in my second marriage. Getting up is more profound than nailing it just right. In preaching, the two hardest Sundays to write sermons for are the ones immediately following a "Home run" sermon where you really hit the message out of the park, and the Sunday following one that you flubbed up so miserably that it's a struggle to show your face again in the church. Getting back up on the horse is what matters.

We can inspire ourselves.

We don't have to wait for someone outside of us to do it. When I set out to write this book, I wanted to write the book that I needed in 2019 when life as I knew it crumbled into pieces. I was helped by so many people, but it was my own waking up and rising, and going to the journal pages that pulled me out of this slump. You can inspire yourself too. Look at what all you've been through! Look at the thoughts you think, the experiences you've had! That is incredible! There is no one you-er than you. Take peace in this. Let it light a fire within you to keep going as your most authentic self.

Sometimes the worst thing is the best thing.

I'm not ready to include X in the acknowledgements, but I will say getting divorced was the best worst thing that happened to me. I came alive when everything ended. It forced me to look at all the other "worst things" that had ever happened in my life and to see that on the other side of them, I became more myself. Like when I didn't make the top band in middle school like all my friends did, I learned to practice harder, to really inquire—is playing an instrument my thing? I learned to walk a lonely road and to make friends with people I didn't expect, to delight with them when we succeeded, and to understand that success comes in many forms.

Wayfinding Practice: One True Thing Creates a Snowball of Truth

Speak something into being. I know your type—so many of us are "wait and see" folks—watching, observing, like the scared kid wanting to join in the Double Dutch game, but afraid the rope is going too fast. Here it is! Here's your invitation to JUMP IN to the game of life and express something out loud that's been lurking beneath your skin.

You can say it in the shower if you don't want anyone to hear it.

You can shout it from the socials—just say something! Often a fear of being wrong or fear of how others will receive our truth keeps us all clammed up. But there is a truth in you that someone needs to hear, maybe even your own self. We know the world is full of people sending out messages that maybe don't need to be said? But I can tell you right now yours is not one of those.

What's true for you today?

The big secret about truth and honesty is that the more you do them, like just about every other hard thing, the easier they get. The more truthful you are, the bigger your snowball of truth becomes.

What I'm Learning about Negativity & Abundance

Once you make a decision, the universe conspires to make it happen.

— *Ralph Waldo Emerson*

EVERY STRUGGLE WE FACE CARRIES A PIVOTAL QUESTION: HOW DO WE name our desires while we're in the middle of the hard thing, and how do we confront the negativity that tries to hold us back? Finding abundance and inviting transformation is how we live into and embrace new life. In every kind of struggle, the way we name our desires and confront negativity shapes our ability to find abundance and embrace new life. The journey through hardship teaches us that contrast can paralyze, but naming our hopes, even in whispers, can invite transformation. The adage in sports, negotiations, and overcoming challenges is true: it's mind over matter.

We laughed in college when *The Secret* was released and Oprah had it on her show. *Saturday Night Live* did a skit making fun of the Law of Attraction, scoffing at how silly people thought they could just "Put a message out into the universe" about what they wanted and it would come true. How ridiculous, right? That's what capitalism and struggle made us believe; that wanting something and naming it was silly and absurd.

The wilderness taught me to name what I want, even if just in a hushed whisper. I paced my parents front lawn through tears and said, just weeks after everything fell apart, "I want to be with Rob." It wasn't a prayer. It wasn't a manifestation, but it was a truth that longed to be said out loud. And behold, it did come true.

What we're going through on a personal or private level is not separate or disconnected from the collective. This private moment on the front steps of my parents' house was a faint whisper teaching me the importance of naming what it is I desire, and collectively what it is *we* desire. What was private for me is bigger than just one individual though— what I whispered there echoes a collective yearning for change, for justice, for connection in a world often clouded by negativity. Our individual desires weave into the larger tapestry of shared human experience, where what we name has power. This practice isn't just some trick to get your crush to like you back—we are collectively part of a conscience being tested and the desires we name in response to it matter.

It isn't just naming our desires that changes things either. It's also weeding out negativity. Naysaying voices have no room in a crisis. Negativity is not just an external force; it's internalized within us too. The doubts we harbor in silence, the inherited criticisms from our past, become the most insidious voices. These voices have shaped my journey, often stopping me before I even started. As I dared to voice my desires, I found myself weighed down by toxic words: "Every season with you is a hard season;" "You're the most selfish person I know." These voices, internal and external, take effort to silence, but only through that effort can we hear the truth of our **desires** clearly. It takes incredible resolve and a commitment to weeding out these voices inside of us to be able to hear loud enough the desire, the reality, the hope that is before us.

The United States is in the midst of a profound crisis, one that has been brewing and steeping even since our founding. The soul of our nation has again emerged on the chopping block since the tragic deaths of Michael Brown in Ferguson, Missouri, and Trayvon Martin in Sanford, Florida, followed by countless others around the US. But the crisis is not just one of police brutality or political division—it's a crisis of the stories we tell ourselves about who we are. The more dismissal dominates our conversations, the more we risk losing our dignity, our honesty, and our collective humanity.

I believe the more we allow under-rug sweeping to dominate the conversation, the more that force grows that robs us of our dignity and our honesty. Even good people do it, calling names or making references that continue to keep evil in circulation, attacking the evil forces on the level of body image or intellect instead of at thought, behavior, or action. We shouldn't ignore hard things or difficult emotions, but we cannot get stuck there either. Climb the mountain, and cross the desert, but take in the sunshine and shore on the other side. We cannot take on the fullness of this fight all at once. Otherwise, we will continue to stay down, to be under the thumb of this force. What was true for the fledgling community in Corinth in the first century still speaks to what we experience in the fight for our country and our sense of belonging to one another:

"We are experiencing all kinds of trouble, but we aren't crushed. We are confused, but we aren't depressed. We are harassed, but we aren't abandoned. We are knocked down, but we aren't knocked out."[1]

We can name the trouble and the confusion, but we cannot set up camp there. To get out of pits of despair, we must be able to set sights on or name or envision the place where we will arrive, to the power of the journey we are on, even if only in a whisper, and we must rest and delight along the way.

Rest and reward are necessary pieces of resisting the oppressive hold that white cis-hetero patriarchal supremacy has on us. Its demonic voice is always found in the urge to buy more, to conform, to not raise alarm, to obey. Resistance is heard in the loud chants of

---

1. 2 Corinthians 4:8-9

Occupy Wall Streeters, Black Lives Matter marches, Palestinian Liberation protests, and the surges of human thriving who will never cease to be quiet for long. While I celebrate the gift of advocacy and the power of unions (thanks, Labor Movement for giving us weekends, fair labor standards, and the 40-hour work week!), insisting on what we stand *for* rather than continually naming what we are *against* will take us further for longer and bring more people to the cause.

In Reformed Theology, we talk about salvation as an event that isn't just about being freed from something like hell or death, but as something we're being freed *for* as well. The prepositions matter. We are freed *for* a life full of abundance. This isn't just a future promise, but a present reality we can experience even amid hardship. The freedom to live with joy, creativity, and purpose isn't a passive state—it's a choice, and it requires active participation in a life of gratitude and resistance. We are not *only* freed *from* the bonds of sin and death but the emphasis on what we are freed *for* matters most: we are freed *into* abundant life, joy, gratitude, and empowerment.

Abundance isn't about wealth or success in the traditional sense. It's about richness in experience, community, and inner peace. When I named what I wanted in the wilderness, I didn't just wish for material things—I named a life of connection, clarity, and joy despite the struggles that surrounded me.

In the rules of Improv Comedy, you are never allowed to say "no" to a character you're on stage with. Imagine, you and Tina Fey are riffing about being on a safari and she says "Look at that hyena over there!" and you say, "There isn't a hyena there, this is Second City Comedy Club in Chicago, Illinois." Ugh. What a buzzkill! Ruins the scene and denies you, Tina, and your audience of what could have been an incredible experience. In Improv, you say "Yes" to everything, and you don't stop at "Yes." You say "Yes" *and* you add your riff to the scene. "Crikey, Tina, that's the biggest giraffe I've ever seen and it's about to eat that ostrich egg—we gotta watch that fat lump go down the tube!" Now that's a funny scene.

Scarcity is a mindset heaved on us by these forces of white supremacy and capitalist hustle culture. Pausing to rest, to celebrate, and to call in the abundant desires of your heart is part of thriving instead of just surviving. Can you imagine if every year on your birthday you refused to eat cake because birthdays are just progressions towards your inevitable death? Maybe this is why so many people struggle to celebrate their birthdays. You don't get cake when you die. **You have to eat it along the way.**

The wilderness opened the way out of perfectionism, toxicity, deceit, competition, betrayal and adultery into freedom, abundance, self-efficacy, hope, enjoyment, growth, vitality, and wisdom. Along the way are slips and surges—moments when it was too overwhelming and I wanted to quit. I thought back to the many times in my life when I witnessed my mother, passionately invested in her faith community, exclaim, "If this happens, I'm leaving organized religion!" Sometimes it was getting the community to endorse a project of the youth, or the church to call a specific senior pastor. Regardless of what it was, taking a week, a month, a year away was not enough; changing churches was not enough. For her, it was quitting the whole hog or nothing. Life's challenges and valleys teach us to hold our successes and failures loosely. She no longer sees anything as a big enough issue with which to quit the whole enchilada of organized religion, but her relationship with it has changed.

The desert changes us. It weathers our faces, it dries out our skin and bones. There is minimal feasting in the desert. But we are also stronger in it. Throughout the Israelites' 40 years of wilderness wandering out of Egypt and towards Canaan, they whined at times that in the past there were luxuries like cucumbers and melons (even though they were also slaves in Egypt—the land of cucumbers and melons). I too shared some whines and grief over defined pension benefits and homeownership in the prior life. Eventually, the whines become less as we set our sights on what is on the other side of wilderness. For the conquest narratives (Joshua, Judges), the other side was a land "Flowing with milk and honey" promised by

God at the beginning of this ordeal. But other people called that place home. Other people had to be displaced from it. The milk and honey were owned by someone else. Do you think God intended for them to share it? Was it anyone's milk or honey but God's? Was annihilation part of the holy plan?

The struggle for ownership, whether of land, wealth, or our destinies, is where the oppressive forces of power show themselves most starkly. But what if true abundance isn't about owning more, but about sharing what we have? Perhaps this is what the wilderness has taught me the most—true freedom comes not from clinging to what we think we own, but from sharing generously, building community, and honoring the dignity of all. Self-determination made me the richest of all—no longer being in places I didn't want to be or relationships that stifled me.

Wayfinding Practice: Naming Desire

Finding abundance in the face of adversity is a journey that begins with small steps. Often when navigating an ending, we cut ourselves off from desire in favor of getting our needs met. *If* we can make our needs as small and palatable as possible, *then* we will find a place to belong. But embracing new life, means letting that small, palatable version of you go. As we name our desires, challenge negativity, and move toward a life of generosity and community, we reclaim our power—not just as individuals, but as part of something greater. Earlier in this manual, you learned about writing down gratitude. That gratitude list can give us clues for desires that have materialized. What do you want to be grateful for a year from now? What kind of desire is percolating in you? Desire isn't just a wish list of wants; it is like a fruit growing on a tree. It takes time, sunshine, water, and cultivation.

A Blessing for the Ones Who Hurt You

Forgive others, not because they deserve forgiveness, but because you deserve peace.

— *Mark Twain*

I TOOK MY CHILD TO URGENT CARE TODAY. HE GOT HURT ICE SKATING at his dad's house. While filling out the paperwork, I had to check my phone for his Social Security Number. I used to keep it in the Notes App (don't do that, by the way). While searching for it, I came across a scanned copy of the entries X annotated from my private journals for the attorneys to read. It was like an old ghost popping up to say, "Hey! Remember when that trauma happened?"

After the appointment, I read through them again—they had headings like "Lack of Shame" and "Abandonment of the Marriage," accompanied by direct quotes from my diaries.

I laughed. Of course, I had no shame in my journal-it was my safe space! When these entries began circulating around our community, I felt so raw.

They (my then friends and X) warned me, hoping, "I'd be okay" and told me to re-read the words I had in those journals, and really

"Take them in" like they were telling a goblin to look in the mirror and take in his own ugliness, if he was brave enough.

Well. I did. I did it fearfully at first, but what I found was not a monster to be afraid of, but a version of me who needed to be understood. I found a Samaritan Woman at the well, trying to get some of Jesus' living water.[1] I found a silently imprisoned woman trying to break free but not knowing how.

The gift of perspective allows us to see our shortcomings again in a new way.

On a run, listening to The Counting Crows' album *This Desert Life*, a lyric came up:

I got some things I can't tell anyone
I got some things I just can't say
They're the kind of things no one knows about...
I'm thinking about leaving tomorrow
I'm thinking about being on my own
I think I been wasting my time
I'm thinking about getting out[2]

And it dawned on me. I was breaking free.

When a child is born into the world, they pass through a birth canal. The mother screams, perhaps, or silently squeezes—every part of her is breaking open for someone to be born. They literally have to cut the child from the mama. It's painful for the mom, it's terrifying for the baby. There are witnesses who see the blood, the shit, the tears.

The road to freedom and compassion is paved with suffering.

During our divorce, the final benediction from the mediator was,

"He's angry. And you're free. So go, live your life. Be happy."

While I stood over the stove and read over these entries again

---

1. John 4
2. "Speedway" by The Counting Crows

today, it brought a smile to my face. My favorite Bible story comes from the end of Genesis, when Joseph reunites with his brothers who have inflicted chapter upon chapter of pain on him. He says,

"Even though you intended to do harm to me, God intended it for good, in order to preserve a numerous people, as God is doing today."[3]

It may take years of quiet reflection, of accessing your joy from the pit of despair, naming and releasing your loses, and embracing new life as it flows to you for you to come to a place where you can see how much you have grown, how far you have come in your new beginning.

If you're going through hell and think, "Who or what have I become?"

Cling to that wisdom from Therapist Pat, "God does not disturb your peace except to lead you to a deeper peace." Let your grip around the poison bottle loosen enough for you to feel something besides white-hot rage buried beneath shame, wrapped up in resentment.

Brené Brown, explores the emotion "Resentment" in *Atlas of the Heart*. She finds resentment is rooted in envy rather than anger. We resent others who have or do something we wish could allow ourselves. I've started daring myself when that ugly little rat resentment pops into my head to get the thing. Grab the free time, the take-out, the indulgent latte. Don't let others' poison steal your peace.

Karma is "in" right now, as a pop spirituality concept. Who doesn't love a little rage-y revenge song about how those who hurt you have it coming? But the reality of karma is tied to cause and effect. The energy we bring to the party of life returns to us. Pain is not healed by exacting more pain. The more I hated and resented and lamented what others did or said about me, the more I fanned the flames of a soul-consuming fire.

Of course, Christianity has tons to teach about forgiveness, but

---

3. Genesis 50:20

not all of it I find helpful or accessible, especially for members of marginalized communities. Even though much of Jesus' audience in the New Testament were disabled, poor, conquered, immigrant, non-white audiences. What can I say? Bro could not have hacked it for long as a pastor in any American church today. Too bold. Too political. Too spicy. But I came to access one of the Bible's primary lessons on forgiveness through an agnostic comedian's memoir. Chelsea Davantez in *I Shouldn't Be Telling You This [But I'm Going to Anyway]*, describes how the Bible's concept of forgiveness is one she wishes she would have found sooner and might have made her a Christian if she had, "Vengeance is mine, says the Lord."[4] In other words, revenge isn't ours to exact; it is a cosmic event.

If you're not in a place to forgive the ones who hurt you, you don't have to, ever. But dear wayfinder, you deserve a blessing in your new life. You deserve release—not from accountability, but from anger and the insatiable desire to exact the justice that belongs to the universe. Embracing new life means letting go of the apologies you will probably never get from those who hurt you. The ultimate flex, when you know you've really gotten through the thing and made it to a new beginning, is when you can genuinely wish the ones who harmed you, well. X deserves love and a relationship with someone who cherishes him. He deserves freedom from his upbringing and childhood trauma. My former friends deserve soft places in their lives and people who will see them for who they are and what their hopes and dreams are. I deserve these things too. Holding my hands over my heart, I accept the lament of not being able to give that to one another, and a grin begins to form as I rejoice in what was on the other side of our ending for me.

---

4. So nice it's in there twice: Deuteronomy 32:35 and quoted in Romans 12:19

Wayfinding Practice: A Ritual for Forgiveness

Forgiveness is not something we do for other people. We do it for ourselves. When you are ready to release someone or an experience of harm, reclaim peace, return to alignment, and stop the cycle of self-harm from holding onto pain, here's a ritual for forgiveness:

Place a hand over your heart. Speak the name of the person who hurt you or the action that caused harm. End by saying: *I have carried this long enough. With an open hand and a protected heart, I release this burden. I choose peace over punishment.* Then drink a bunch of water because that shit takes energy.

Coping Skills for the Apocalypse

I think it is healing behavior, to look at something so broken and see the possibility and wholeness in it.

— *Adrienne Maree Brown*, Emergent Strategy:
Shaping Change, Changing Worlds

BECOMING AN EXPERT AT COPING SKILLS AND TRAUMA PROCESSING won't ever insulate you from the real systemic shithole that is becoming more evident by the day. We live in an unfolding apocalypse. Picture me with a handy dandy whiteboard on an easel, writing out APOCALYPSE in all caps and then separating the word by its roots: APO—(un) and CALYPSO—(cover) = Uncovering; Revelation. This is the time we are in when what was once hidden from our eyes is being revealed. That sinking feeling that the world is falling apart in our fingers? That's apocalypse. Truths are being made known when the average American gets to see how little taxes corporations pay year over year. Men in seats of power are being called out and down for their behavior. Perhaps the courts are holding our politicians accountable. What has been is being made known. Even Queer and Trans rights are not new phenomena, but the revelation of the people who have always existed but been hidden in our midst.

Our affair was unethical. Getting caught was an event within a landscape of apocalypse. Can I release myself from the guilt of my truth being made known and embrace it as part of the milieu of what we've all done to survive? All the clergy burnout experts will write chapters upon chapters about "Coping skills" and "Questions to reflect upon" but you can become an expert at coping skills and trauma processing, and none of those would insulate you from the real, systemic shithole that is becoming more and more evident. So what then? Do we just accept the way things are and sink deeper into it, biding our time for this reality to be revealed for the Gilead-like state that it is? Of course not. We must nurture and strengthen the spiritual muscle of hope. That doesn't mean paste on a Pollyanna grin and bear it. It means dig in deep to the things we cannot accept and change them, to paraphrase Angela Davis. For me that begins with speaking my truth and sharing my story. I will not stay silent in shame. I do not brag about my torrid affair, but I do own it. I left a marriage that wasn't working the hard way. And I would leave that marriage again. I wish I'd had the courage to say, "I can't do this anymore." But I understand and empathize with the me who didn't feel strong enough to do that. My first husband was a foot taller than me, in better financial straits than me, older than me, more educated than me. I thought I had to stay. I came from a family of people who stayed. But now I know, you can go. It will hurt, but it is survivable. And once you survive, you can thrive and in your shine, you light the way for others who live in the dark of shame and sorrow.

Coping skills will *soothe* you on the brambled path that is the way to liberation, but there is no substitute for digging in deep and deciding this stuff won't stand anymore. Are we teaching our future generations to be strong enough not to put up with the crap we chose to accept as true and right? The Hippocratic oath of humaning that us generational pattern breakers have undertaken is "Do no harm, but take no shit." I know we're dismantling the people pleasing (and trying hard to survive the kids we're raising to do no harm but take no shit), but are we also building them up for the endurance race that is a human lifetime?

Just as important as building a connection with our audience, every sermon, every post, every Powerpoint, comes the challenge of getting out successfully. A chess grandmaster knows that the first move is important, but the endgame is where it's won. Even if you started out in life dealt a not-so-good hand of cards, what matters of course is what you make of it. I was born with a magnificent inheritance of a charmed life, and squandered it as is part of the Fool/Hero's journey. But what matters is the endgame. In the end, every woman has the opportunity to transform into Sophia, or Woman Wisdom. After a time of trial and lessons learned, she has something to teach the rest of the world. Our hypersexualized, capitalist patriarchy would rather oversexualize little girls, limit adult women to child-bearing, mothering, or sex work, and then retire women past their sexual prime as old, fat, tired, lifeless and only good for the metaphorical glue factory. Womanhood is so much more diverse than this script. Girls can be curious, brave, adventurers; they have questions and imagine possibilities for themselves. Even my son, when he was around five or so, asked from the back seat, "Mom, can boys be pastors too?"

I refuse to be boxed in. I will be playful, curious, brave, generous, empowering but never just nurturing or just mothering. Can't we embody the full spectrum of humanity? The wilderness meant getting back in touch with the mother in me, making sure the pastor's kids had a theological education, not like the Cobbler's kids who have no shoes. My benediction each night was a forehead cross while saying the blessing, "May God bless you and keep you. May God's face shine upon you and grant you peace" as I willed those words for myself also. I learned in the wilderness how to make food from scraps, to make community wherever I could find it—in the neighborhood "Biking club" the kids started, with my college friends over Zoom after the kids went to bed. I thanked God every day that a pandemic happened right square in the middle of my most public of scandals. Going to the grocery store with a mask, sunglasses and earbuds was like a blessed anti-gravity chamber of anonymity during a personal shitstorm. I pray every person going through their own scandal in a small town would be blessed with a global mask-wearing shutdown. It gives time for the headline to move from the front page to the bottom of tomorrow's birdcage.

But in the wilderness, you learn to appreciate the scarce beauty of the cactus's one pink flower in a thousand miles. There is no lush undergrowth or canopy. Friendships disappear, thank you notes and sympathy cards become a means of reaching out across the void at someone.

In the wilderness, I purged my closet of my black dresses. I kept my 3 (4? 5?) favorites, but sold the rest to clergy sisters who were still "of the cloth" and needed the cloak of neutrality on Sunday mornings. I stepped out into a new uniform of life that includes big earrings, expressive bold colors, and soft, stretchy waistbands. I returned to my childhood love of overalls.

Sometimes the wilderness means going somewhere you've never been before, but with the tools you got from prior seasons; sometimes it is shedding the skin from the seasons that no longer fit you.

My kids and I played dress up, we embraced the sanctity of happy hour, where everyone has a beverage that brings them joy, and a tray of something based on fruit, cheese, nuts, and protein to keep us from losing our minds while dinner cooks. In the wilderness, we watched the seasons change from fall to the winter that froze time and tree branches, to spring that brought us out of our cozy places and into wind and sunshine, to blisteringly hot summer, where days stretched on forever and school might never come again. In that time I went to therapy, I read books, I mailed it in at work, and stretched every dollar. I applied for food stamps, but was just over the cusp of qualifying, which I still don't understand. The government-issued checks for parents during the pandemic and subsidized housing were the difference between us having a safety net and not. Even in all that turmoil, I couldn't claim "poor." Poor is a class, is a state of mind, is the bottom of someone's shoe. I was rising, but it's hard to rise if you don't have a place to rise *from*. The wilderness is like the autolysing stage for a loaf of bread—all the elements are there: flour, water, starter/yeast and salt, but they aren't working together yet. Like a tangled up necklace chain, I needed time, patience, and attention to the miniscule details so that the foundation I would be rising from had no cracks, no pasted over bits, no parts where I had slapped on a smile and denied my deep needs. A woman has to belong most deeply to herself.

Sometimes when I am with other women married to men, they say things like "Oh I don't know what to DO when my husband is out of town! I can't get through life without him! He makes my coffee/puts toothpaste on my toothbrush/takes out the trash/does any number of things for me." I smile quietly and think very loudly, "YES YOU CAN. YOU CAN GET BY WITHOUT HIM I PROMISE." The wilderness gave me that.

From its generative richness, I pass on the blessing of the wilderness, amended from St. Theresa of Avila's:

The world gets no body but yours,
No hands, no feet on earth but yours,
Yours are the eyes with which you look
With compassion on yourself,
Yours are the feet with which you will go miles for the sake of your
    cardiac health,
Yours are the hands, with which you will bless every mess in your
    home.
Yours are the hands, yours are the feet,
Yours are the eyes, you are Your Body,
You have no body now but yours,
No hands, no feet on earth but yours,
Yours are the eyes with which you look
With compassion on yourself.

Elaine Murray

The world has no body now on earth but yours.

It's like that scene in *Harry Potter and the Prisoner of Azkaban,* when Harry waits and waits for his father, whose patronus, the stag, will fend off the soul-sucking dementor's kiss. And he waits almost too long before he realizes the patronus is his own to cast. We must be our own lovers, our own heroes, our own servants, our own kings and queens. We belong, most deeply to ourselves, and this is beautifully, splendidly, scarcely, and abundantly enough.

Wayfinding Practice: An Uncovering Ritual

You'll need a piece of paper, a candle, and an object that symbolizes what you're releasing for this practice (like a ribbon, an article of clothing, a stone)

Name your apocalypse—what's being revealed in your life. Write down what patterns you're noticing about the world, about your relationships, about yourself. No need to self-edit. This is raw and real.

Shed what no longer fits you—what beliefs, habits, and coping methods have you outgrown? Choose a symbol of something you're ready to shed. Thank the object for being a support to you in the time you needed it. And release it (and by that I mean, literally get rid of it. You can burn or tear it, or just donate it to someone else).

Cast your own protective shield—remember a time when you really showed up for yourself. Hold your hand over your heart and bless yourself using the amended St. Teresa blessing from above or say out loud: *I belong most deeply to myself. I am enough. I am rising.* If you want, you can conclude with drawing an image of what a protective shield might look like for you as you face new revelations and embrace new life.

Conclusion

On Swearing Off Marriage & Organized Religion Like a Typical Millenial

A Lookback

IT'S 2020, AND A WEEK FROM TODAY IS SHOWTIME: MEDIATION. THE second mediation, in which I show up, not shell-shocked, but as a "Queen in pawn's clothing" as my friend, Susan says. I'm going to fight like hell for my kids, show the world, or at least this little tiny community of two attorneys, two mediators, and my former spouse that if they want to see what maternal strength is, it is a woman showing up to do no harm and take no shit from would-be intimidators.

Where does my story begin?

David Copperfield was born.

I was grafted. Like Hephaestus's armory, I think my bones were knit together in some holy place, that if you knew my mama, you would know that womb is less of a cushy, padded growing place and more of a lab where earthquakes are tested.

So it begins with being born: 1987, Mineral Wells, Texas. My conception, dear reader, was a post-Thanksgiving nap. I like to think I was born from a sexual expression of national gratitude. I'm not sure if birth order matters, but if you're into that kind of psychological analysis, I am the youngest of three girls—three lionesses, three priestesses, three demi-goddesses. Not that we have illusions of grandeur, it's just that each of us are epic heroes in our own ways. Move over Avengers, the Murray Girls are a particular brand of badass that the world didn't see coming.

But that youngest one? She's something else.

Before my memories begin, there was a neighbor across the street who cared for children. Nonnie had fostered countless children over her 70 some-odd years and on occasion would provide some relief for poor anxiety-ridden Liz Murray, stay at home mama of three girls managing a money pit with a workaholic husband.

Nonnie used to say to my mama, "This one. This Elaine is special. I don't know what she's going to give the world, but I can tell it's going to be something big."

Everyone needs a Nonnie—someone in your life who doesn't have to be but is your biggest fan. Everyone needs someone to recognize that the world is a richer, deeper, more beautiful place because you are in it.

I can even say this about my ex-husband. X is a gift to the world, a deeply broken one, but aren't we all in some way or another?

When I was four, I remember my mom mumbling "Quit being such a bitch" or something like that under her breath at me. Now that I've got two kids over the age of four, I wonder what they will remember of me. This book is a work of healing, healing from Postpartum Anxiety, healing from being in an abusive marriage, from ordination to a church that didn't have it in them to respect me, healing from an affair and healing into healthy relationships.

My haters tell me they "Hope I'll find healing" like they hope a leprechaun finds a pot of gold at the end of that rainbow they're chasing, knowing full-well that rainbows are tricks of light with no end.

I may not be a leprechaun, but I am much more magical, and healing, for me, is within reach.

My plastic surgeon, at the very last appointment after my

mastectomy said, "Miss Elaine, you are a healer. I've never seen anything like it. Your body knows how to heal." What he (and I) didn't know then, was that my soul did too.

How does a soul heal?

Prayer, one might say, but what is that?

A conversation with the Holy, with that deep, quiet place within us, the one who knows us and who will not be swayed by the latest self-care trends or whatever lame excuses and walls we put up to hide from this Divine.

The healing journey I am on is like riding a bicycle, it isn't just knowing how the handlebars work, then pedaling, then eventually adding in brakes. This healing journey has taken everything I know about anything from every corner of my life: English literature, the Bible, Celtic prayer, Tarot cards, Pagan crystals, cognitive behavioral therapy, networking, storytelling, preaching, wrapping first edition copies of *Old Yeller* in Fred Gipson's son's land surveying office. It has taken everything all at once. And I suppose that's my encouragement for others who find themselves at the bottom of a pile of shit-sandwiches trying to heal. In the words of Daddy Pat, "If you eat enough shit sandwiches, there's bound to be enough fertilizer in them to make you grow."

Going back to this comment from my plastic surgeon, and the anthem that's gotten me through some dark days, "Highwomen" by The Highwomen *"I was a healer/I was gifted as a girl/I laid hands upon the world…"* I recognize that title, "Healer" is not a unique testament to who I am, but a truth about something within **all of us**. The same instincts we develop that make us yearn for the surface when we've been underwater for too long and are running out of air are the ones that show us each next right step towards a healed existence.

A few folks who heard my story of struggling with marriage and parish ministry and my confession of turning to intimacy outside of marriage said the most important phrase in the healing process, "You survived." I am a survivor. I survived and have at least some wild hare of a healing instinct within me that would not keep my head underwater long enough to be snuffed out. I came up out of drowning. I came up out of the ambivalent toxicity of people who didn't care if I lived or died, who couldn't see past their own hurt to stop hurting me.

Survivors don't just get out alive. We heal. The soul does not stay in homeostasis, continuing to bleed all over everyone. We all have healing within us: the blood's ability to clot, the body's reflex to jerk the head up from too deep waters, the soul's meandering way to find air to breathe, connection to sustain it in the wilderness.

We find a plan and work the plan, even when the plan doesn't account for how you might find 15,000 more dollars hiding under a mattress every year. My plan began as "Find a place to sleep tonight" and then get through the day thirty minutes at a time. My parents all but force-fed me to put the six pounds I lost overnight back on my skin and bones. "Tears have been my food day and night," the Psalmist prays from the pit, and yes, sister, I am right there with you. I didn't think there was divorce in the bible, but there it is right in the agony of Psalm 42.

God hates divorce and after having gone through one, I know this to be true. But what the church often gets wrong, as well as abused spouses hiding in the shadows of relationships that no longer feed, nourish, or sustain them, is that God hates the *agony* of divorce—the tearing apart of relationship that was grafted together by covenant. When Jesus taught about divorce and the weeping and gnashing of teeth, he was **describing** a reality, not *prescribing* a future place of deeper suffering. God hates going through the anger, pain, tears, and hurt with us. God doesn't hate people who are in the middle of a divorce, or people discerning if divorce is the next right thing. God doesn't hate people who have been divorced. God is Immanuel—the One with us. I believe God gave X the courage to walk through the door of our home on L Street and say "We're getting divorced." That same God has written treatises with me in the midnight hours of ways to end well a marriage that was down to the embers.

We survived, God and I. At the end of the adventure when

you've survived the fire and brimstone and the utterly despairing loss of friends, the work continues. This is when survivors must continue to see this work through so that your survival doesn't make you who you are, but your *healing* does. Heal yourself, create spaces where others can heal. I see my children, beautiful, curious, kind, loving—and our bedtime prayers changed from asking God's help with this "Thing that's happening to our family" to thanking God for helping our family through divorce. They went from being scared to say it, too scared of what it meant, to being grateful for God's saving presence, for joy and hope in the midst of what we have been accustomed to calling "The breaking down of a family." Did our family perhaps become more ourselves through this legal proceeding than we were before?

Nancy Sherman, a Georgetown Professor of Philosophy who studies moral injury and PTSD in veterans describes, "In order to heal from shame, guilt, and betrayal, you have to own it. [The veterans] first own it themselves, then they own it with a peer group that understands what they've gone through and isn't going to judge," she says. "A key part of moral repair is acknowledging what you've done, and the more people you can acknowledge that with, the more safe people, the more you are going to heal from it."[1]

Hence the need to own my shit, my story, my guilt, and betrayal. I never wanted to hurt my children, my spouse, my family, or the church that formed me. But I survived. And I will not be a survivor who abuses. I will be a survivor who heals.

A Sunday afternoon bike ride wasn't a weapon of mass destruction unleashed on a village of innocents. It was a beacon of survival, a light in darkness. What do I wish I'd done to experience this light and joy? Gone to therapy is perhaps the easiest answer, though if you've ever sought therapy, talked to your insurance company (if you are lucky enough in the US to have insurance!),

---

1. "Healing a Wounded Sense of Morality" July 3, 2015, *The Atlantic* by Maggie Puniewska

found the list of people who have openings, gone through the process of finding one, meeting with them, figuring out rather quickly within the process of pouring your heart out that they will not be a worthy companion on the journey...then you know, resisting therapy is completely understandable.

What do I wish I'd done to survive? I wish I'd dived deep into the recesses of myself. Asked her what she needs—not let the distraction of fitness or a colleague who listens, who is in a pit also be the rock I would cling to. I wish I'd taken time for me. I wish I'd pilgrimed and listened to the God within who was speaking.

I did listen, but not in a way that was socially or ecclesially acceptable. Now I pay the price that patriarchy determines. I've noticed white males really don't like when the rest of us use the "P Word." Just because you're at the top of it, doesn't mean it isn't hurting you also.

A colleague shared with me that "Patience will be my frustratingly close companion in this chapter," and she's right. This story doesn't come out easily and in the meantime there are bills to pay, children to raise, love that needs to be shared.

There is an urgency to embracing new life. Brown children sit in cages who cannot wait for the rest of us to figure out our "New life." But here's another wrinkle I've observed: as privileged and self-absorbed as we, particularly straight, white, cis-gendered people can be with our navel-gazing self-actualization—if we don't listen to that deep, small, still voice within speaking us into new being each day, we will always burn out, always find ourselves tripping over our own woundedness to inflict, rather than help others.

The same God who created universes, invented trees, rocks, rivers, and dreamt up the life-cycle of a star and brought it into being thought the world needed one of you too. And the same still, small voice that prods *you* awake on each new day, and coaxes *you* through hard things with a gentle internal whisper of "It's gonna be ok. You got this." speaks Spanish within the heart of a mama, who holds her child's hand as they escape gang violence and trek across

Central America in search of a safer existence. The world is a hard place, and perhaps this refugee Mama knows that the place she is headed has people in offices far away working actively against her survival and thriving. All because her skin isn't the same color as mine and because her children, for some reason, don't deserve as many chances to thrive as mine do. It is when we listen to the small but mighty force of persistence within us that we are empowered to claim our shared humanity, and see beyond our "First world problems."

It sometimes feels like the world is actively, purposefully getting worse—like we are only a few unfortunate accidents away from tripping our way into a dystopian nightmare. Many a philosopher from around the world and across the decades attempt to explain our declining work ethic, rampant apathy, and failure of nerve.

They say loneliness is an epidemic. We are isolated from each other, even while piled up in crowded cities with shortages of time, money, and space. We are isolated even from ourselves, shattered and disconnected, mal-aligned between our values and our actions. We are isolated from the still, small voice inside of us pushing us towards life, fulfillment, service, and belonging.

Listen. Breathe. Close your eyes from the world outside of your body so that your soul sees what is inside you. Connect, first to yourself and that still, small voice and the rest will follow. David Lamotte's song "Crawl Inside" echoes through my crowded cavernous place:

Gonna crawl inside your heart
Gonna bring a whole bunch of paint
From the outside it's so beautiful
From the inside it just ain't
And I know this will be hard for you
But your graffiti's gotta go
I'm gonna crawl inside your heart
So you can see what we all know

From the end of World War 2 to the 1980s, institutions rocked. The church, the country club, Rotary, Kiwanis, you name it, we all joined them. It was an era of joining. Full stop, let's take a moment and feel how awesome that was and how powerful we felt because we had the most toys in our toy box, because we were at our winningest.

Post-modernity, divorce, scandals, the rise of the digital age, began changing us. Now fewer of us are getting married, identifying with a particular religion, buying into any of the bill of belonging goods that these groups were selling. Does it mean we've lost? Or we're losing? Or that society as we know it is toast?

By no means!

I teach my children about competition that there's two kinds of winning: winning at the competition itself and winning at competing. No one wants to give the award to the fastest person who upon finishing said to all the others: "Haha, suckers! Better luck next time!" And it's a beautifully broken thing for one who came in second (or dead last) to be able to immediately and gracefully say: "Congratulations!" And mean it to the winner.

We aren't playing a zero-sum game of life in which there is a winner at Millionaire Estates and losers at CountrySide Acres. For starters, we are in late phase democratic capitalism and retiring at all is questionable at best.

We're entering into a cultural reality in which winning well will be some of the most rebelliously beautiful work we do, a gift all year long. But losing well, winning at losing, is an exercise truly and appropriately lauded; it lifts the veil on the true reason we were striving in the first place—connection, humility, courage, joy.

When Therapist Pat asks me what I am doing for others because a forward, outward outlook is a rope that will pull me out of this pit when the darkness tries to swallow me, I say I am writing. I am writing this story, sharing what I see: hope in the midst of heartache, the contours of the foundation I feel since the structure I had built with everyone else looking for their picket fence, 2.5 kids and a dog promised by the American Dream. I'm sharing the truth that there is life outside of that, joy outside of that. Like Jonas, the little boy in Lois Lowry's *The Giver* who escapes with his memories on a bicycle, I too have peeked outside of the bubble. I survived and I believe there is joy outside of settling into the cultural scripts of what happiness looks like.

The first question of the Heidelberg Catechism is "What is the chief end of man?" in the 21st century paraphrase: Why are we here? And its answer: "To glorify and enjoy God forever." "Glorify" is a tricky word—it means to expand, lift up, make something or someone shine. As I come to terms with the sin of adultery, I know it was not an act or a pattern that glorified God. But I believe redemption comes through empathy, vulnerability, through sharing the story in a way that others too could see themselves as not above this, but as vulnerable human beings in need of connection and love too. Perhaps the decline of institutional joining is an indication that more of us are embracing the need for connection, not just through dues and membership badges but through need and gift, through gratitude and accountability, through telling another person, "This isn't easy."

To embrace new life is to join the ranks of belonging, first and most deeply to ourselves and from that connection to forge deep ties to others at various stages of goo, breaking free, and flight.

Wayfinding Practice: An Exercise for Connection When the World is Too Much

Find a quiet place, even just five minutes in your car.

Reconnect with reality by practicing the 5-4-3-2-1:

Name five things you can touch, four things you can see, three things you can hear, two things you can smell, and one thing you can taste. This will immediately ground you in the present. Then whisper or scream the answer to this question: **what feels like too much right now?**

Hold your hand over your heart and repeat as you breathe in and out: *I am here. This is now. And I am still breathing.* Then ask yourself, "What is true about me, even when everything else changes?" Take the answer with you as you return to the present moment, knowing that you belong in this world and you belong to yourself.

Of Sacred Flesh and Fat Grace

Sex, GLORIOUS SEX.

I tried to leave it out, truly. I did. But you can't write a spiritual memoir without writing about embodiment—and sex, in all its tangled, trembling forms, is the soul making itself known in skin.

People like to joke about the missionary position, roll their eyes, call it dull. But there is nothing boring about being seen. Nothing dull about mutual vulnerability—the kind of sacred exposure that happens when one body meets another and says, "Here I am. All of me." It may be the most radical act of spiritual trust: to look into someone's eyes while your body opens, connects, retreats, opens again. The world calls that "just sex." I call it communion.

Love is wild. Untamed. Savage even. But it is not selfish. Not when it's real. When we make love—not just have sex—we enter into holy ground. And yet, how many of us were taught to be ashamed of that ground before we ever stood on it? In "abstinence-only" purity culture, masturbation was framed as a failure. A secret. But I believe now that the body's wisdom should not be ignored or demonized. An orgasm can be like a good cry—a release of something deeply human and healing. This isn't about voyeurism or self-indulgence. It's about caring for ourselves as whole beings—spirit and sweat, tears and touch.

Still, vulnerability scares us more than anything. During my divorce, it was easier for X to read out loud the words I'd written about sex with someone else than to acknowledge that we'd stopped being vulnerable with one another long ago. There's a cruelty in that, but more than that, there's fear. He once said I was "too emotional" and that it scared him. If you're afraid of a woman's tears, it's not the woman who needs to change. What does that fear awaken in you?

When I fell in love again—unexpectedly, powerfully, spiritually —it was branded betrayal. Manipulation. A spider's web. "Poor Rob," they said. "She played him like a fiddle." But to have one's emotional and physical needs met in a willing partnership is not abuse. It is mutual grace. It is intention. Yes, it was messy. Yes, it cost things. But wasn't Jesus honest about what faithfulness would cost? Families turned against each other, communities torn apart. Following joy, following truth, following love—it's never the easy road.

Was it faithful? Maybe more than my first marriage. We prayed. We cried. We trusted. And, yes, we had sex. And it was sacred.

In the *Book of Common Worship* "Service of Christian Marriage," the statement on the gift of marriage reads, "This way of life must not be entered into carelessly, or from selfish motives, but responsibly, and prayerfully."

Which brings me back to X. "Saint X" one member of my family called him. My Jungle Gym first husband. Tall and gentle and endlessly kind. He let toddlers climb him like Everest and said "Sure!" more often than he should have. But kindness is not the same as connection. Niceness does not nourish a soul. It is the water, yes—but marriage is a garden, and gardens need more than water. They need light, nutrients, pruning. They need intention. And my first marriage—our sweet lima-bean experiment—outgrew the little baggie stapled to the kindergarten bulletin board. I didn't know how to keep it alive once it left the safety of the classroom wall.

Nice was never enough.

And so we divorce the kind ones. The good dads. The ones who made our families look perfect on Instagram. And we grieve what wasn't bad, but wasn't enough. And we live with the ache of that. With the agony of knowing that someone who idolized you wasn't capable of truly seeing you.

Because we want to be seen. Not worshiped. Not tolerated. *Seen.*

And I will teach my children this: be kind and brave. Kindness costs something; niceness does not. Bravery looks like crying in public, like telling the truth, like choosing not to shrink from life's hungers, even when people would rather you just quietly disappear.

When they ask me what ruined my marriage, or what ruined my career, or what ruined my life—I will say: nothing. Not really. Things have changed, yes. But nothing is ruined.

God is too big for that.

The bigness of God is absurd. Hilarious. Strange. Like that one year I asked for a telescope and got a microscope instead. God said, "Look closer," and I, disappointed and holding my onion skins, still remember the humbling invitation to pay attention to the small. God isn't grand the way we want Them to be. They're not in the pulpit thunder or even always in the bedroom lightning. God's in the belly folds. The ones we try to hide. The sweaty, fleshy folds of grace that keep us warm and smothered and fed, whether we like it or not.

God is a grandmother who feeds us too much and loves us too hard and doesn't care that we've messed up again. Because, beloved: grace is not interested in your performance. Grace is interested in your aliveness.

I don't know what the next chapter holds. There's no guaranteed arc, no bow neatly tying this up. I know there will be sadness and silence. I know I will raise my kids hard and well, that we will laugh and cry and go feral with affection. I know I will still have good sex with the man I love—and maybe none of it will look like "settling down," but maybe that's not what this life is for.

So I will follow joy. I will follow the one who makes my heart sing songs it's never heard before. I will find God in strange places —in orgasms and arguments, in courtroom dissolutions and class-room reinventions. And I will keep going.

Not because I am brave.

But because I am loved.

And love, at its wildest, says: *come just as you are, and stay until you remember who you were all along.*

Wayfinding Practice: Have Great Sex

I wasn't going to tell you to adopt a dog when your heart breaks, but I will invite you to enjoy the pleasures of your own body and optionally someone else's with their full unequivocal consent. We have all kinds of kooky messages about the "sins of the flesh" but I worship a God who grants us life and life abundant, resplendent with joy and delight in our created (and creating!) selves. I won't give you too much instruction here, just strip down and enjoy your beautiful, sexy body. It's okay to touch yourself. It's okay to giggle and let your body parts make noise. You are created in the image of God and that image is love. When I invited you to "have great sex"—that's sex that feels good to you and whoever else is participating. Sex is one of those beautiful activities that really has no purpose. Sure, you can make babies by having sex, but you can also not in lots of ways!

Healing & Witchcraft & Hope

GOD/DESS HAS BLOWN THE DOORS OFF THE SHELTER WHERE MY thoughtfully cultivated theology hid. Little ones learn the rhyme with interlaced hands, *"here is the church, here is the steeple; open the doors, see all the people..."* After leaving parish ministry, quite abruptly, my interlaced hands are free. Freedom is terrifying and thrilling and wonderful—like one of those roller coasters where your feet hang free and you wonder about the safety of those steel harnesses as you get thrown upside down in a loop-de-loop.

The heaviness of stones grounds me in such a flighty season. My cousin, La is a witch. Like Glinda the Good Witch, upon hearing that my heart was broken and life in shambles, she promptly sent me a big rose quartz heart, the size of my palm. I hold it and visualize my heart whole, beautiful, filled with love— even in this empty season. Years ago, she said, "When I didn't know who I was, you gave me a stone just like this (I did?!), and I held it every day as I began my journey to finding myself again." The rock is the beginning of a cairn, an ebenezer, signifying that I am a pilgrim on the way. It is a reminder of the love that surrounds me and how the people who matter most (for me, a rediscovery of the value family brings to my life) are here for us and love us. It's important—a kind of deep magic—to hear from those who have been where we are and who propel us with the courage to live into who we will become. Witchcraft has taught me to lean on the magic of reinvention, that there is always a deeper way to truly be ourselves and how we show up in the world. It's not always easy and it can be messy, lonely, devastating at times. The heart rock, the rose crystal, reminds me of the deep magic that held two sisters together (La's and my moms) during their seasons of wilderness, grief, and embracing new truths.

I used to laugh at candles and circles of stones. Today I wear a peridot on my neck and amethyst on my hand, carrying that quartz heart in my pocket. I relish the power a full-moon brings, and Friday the 13th has a peace of its own as if the universe gives us liminal space to grow if we so choose. My horoscope has become as necessary a part of my morning ritual as the study of a Psalm, because I do believe the natural world leads us to know the things of God. I sprinkle cinnamon in my coffee to welcome abundance. I light candles to remind of the presence of pure, divine light. It doesn't always have to be one way or using one script. There are many paths up the mountain.

There are days in which, no matter what system you cling to for light, life, hope, understanding, meaning, and purpose—none of those things are there and you find yourself in the darkest pit, wondering not only how you got there but if and how you will get out. It's the pit where you moan and tell your story weeping—it's where I believe Jesus said there would be darkness and gnashing of teeth. That wasn't some fiery furnace in the underworld, but a very real existential place that if you are a person of heart or depth, you have been there. The number one rule of life in the pit is this: keep going. The pit doesn't get to squelch you. You may need crystals, candles, to phone a friend, and get a home cooked meal, but on the pit days, keep going.

The second rule is: hope will return. Emily Dickinson called "Hope"

> *the thing with feathers -*
> *That perches in the soul -*
> *And sings the tune without the words -*
> *And never stops—at all -*

Wayfinding Practice: Exercise that Hope Muscle

We all have the ability to hope, but sometimes we let this spiritual muscle atrophy.

You've got broken dreams, you've been let down, the voice of sarcasm and cynicism has taken over that once small childlike curiosity you had? It's time to get fit.

You exercise hope both by looking forward and by looking back. Here's a little three part spiritual "workout" for growing in hope.

The Hope Squat: Make a list of the ways things have worked out well for you in the past (hope pushed up through hard circumstances), especially when you weren't sure or were down in the dumps (sunken low).

The Hope Plank: Sit in silence for as long as you can—60 seconds to start. Every time you have a thought or distraction, gently remind yourself with a mantra like "Trust that something bigger and wiser than me is at work right now."

The Hope Lunge: Imagine some ways the thing you want to be different could work out in the best possible way. Visualize healing, reconciliation, or a new beginning. Let yourself really feel what that would be like to live that reality.

Wrestling For the Blessing

"Walk with your head held high," Mama told me as I braced myself for my first school event post-scandal, post-whispers, post-whatever-version-of-the-truth-people-were-telling-each-other. Her words came to me like an ancestral command—straighten your spine, square your shoulders, and go face the people who think they know who you are. Because sometimes the holiest thing you can do is just keep showing up.

Living through the unraveling of your marriage in a town small enough to know the color of your couch cushions is a bit like that morning after the 2016 election. Everyone walking around shell-shocked, side-eyeing their neighbors, wondering, "Did you do this?" And if so—"Who are you, really?"

There's a specific loneliness in not knowing who sees you as a person and who only sees your mistakes. I used to think I didn't need a safety pin, some post-election talisman of solidarity. But I admit, in this season, I've longed for some signal—a secret hand sign, a nod, a kindness that says, "I know you're more than what they say. You're still here."

And I am. Still here.

It hurts to be misjudged. But you know what might hurt even

more? Knowing that some of the things people say about you *might not be entirely wrong*. That's the brutal blessing of owning your shit. You don't get to airbrush the photo or rewrite the script. You get to say: *Yes, I did that. And here's what else is true.*

Owning it doesn't mean wearing it as shame. It means reclaiming your wholeness with all your contradictions intact. You name what you did, what it cost, what it taught you, and how you're trying—daily—to be a person of integrity *after the fact*. Because grace isn't a get-out-of-jail-free card. Grace is the complicated miracle of staying in the story.

When people say I "Ruined someone's life," I wince—then I breathe. Because I know that ruin isn't always destruction. Sometimes it's excavation. Sometimes it's the earthquake that cracks open the old fault lines that were going to crumble anyway. It's not kind or comfortable, but it is necessary. My marriage did not die because I stopped loving my spouse. It died because we'd already stopped *seeing* each other long before anyone walked out the door. But I didn't die with it. And you, dear wayfinder, are not going to die from whatever ending you are navigating either.

Jacob wrestling with the stranger in the night from Genesis 32— has been my scripture-shadow, the mythic framework for much of my adult relationship with God and calling. For years, I thought Jacob was me and the stranger was God. Then I thought maybe the stranger was some divine messenger. But now, in this season, I know: I am Jacob. And the stranger I've been wrestling is a long-formed, shape-shifting image of who I thought I needed to please in order to be whole.

For a time that shadowy figure was X—especially during the legal untangling of assets, custody, calendars. The mediations. The passive-aggression with legal letterhead. The long silences. The exploding text threads. The relentlessness of parenting in two different households under the illusion of one united front.

For a time it has been the church, in all its unholiness—seasons of censure and nasty stares, letters circulated, charges filed, all but a scarlet "A" sewn on to all of my clothes. But the wrestling continued.

In the story, Jacob keeps wrestling until he comes away with a blessing—a new name, and even the changed gait from an injury to his hip. Blessings often don't arrive in the form we imagine or desire. Mine didn't come as vindication, or closure, or even under-standing. It came as identity. Just like Jacob, I got a new name and a clear sense of who I am and what I will and will not carry.

This is not a story of a ruined life. It's a story of an ending that became a new beginning; a reshaped life from the ashes of the former one. The difference matters because if I were ruined, the story would be over. But the story is not over. I'm still being writ-ten. Still breathing into the shape of my future. *Let me go. But bless me first.*

At the end of a worship service, the leader gives a "Benediction" —*bene* meaning "good" and *diction* meaning "word." It's a blessing to go forward from this place of encountering something holy to find and chase after holiness in the world beyond those doors. The Divine goes with you, behind and before, beside, above, and below. We can bless each other in our comings and goings, but the most powerful blessing is one we can give ourselves.

Wayfinding Practice: Blessing Yourself

Look in the mirror and make eye contact with yourself. Touch a finger to your forehead, your throat, and pause at your heart's center. Say these words:

I go into this day beloved.
I enter into this future that is arriving with hope,
trusting that the Divine/God/Source is at work within me
transforming my sight
opening to me the path of joy and least resistance.
I will encounter losses and I fearlessly name them.
I will discover opportunities for new life and I will embrace them.
I go into this day, this life, this world with a blessing.

Acknowledgements

"Thank you" are the two most important words to me and in my gratitude I must first acknowledge that "It takes a village" to raise an author, to publish a book, to do so many things worth doing in this life.

Many thanks to my writing buddy, the Reverend Kathleen Henrion, for excellent memes, shared joys and irritations at motherhood, and great sermon ideas and edits; my sisters, the E girls, for so many hours of Marco Polo listening and eye rolls, both for me, and the people whose stories you hold of how they hurt me and healed me. You are a blessing more numerous and light-filled than the stars we grew up beneath in the Texas Hill Country sky. The trinity of Pats—GOD! Thank you. Thank you for loving and listening and sharing your wisdom to guide my feet from an old life to a new one.

Big thanks to community of saints at Tehom Center Publishing, particularly Dr. Angela Yarber, whose book *Microaggressions in Ministry* was the first book I read two weeks into my first pastor job and somehow even then she was lighting the way for me to write, to pastor, to heal my way into new life.

Thank you to Meagan, Nancy, Susan, Quincy, Rebecca, June, Phyllis, Heidi, Elizabeth, Lynn, John, the people at Pipe Creek Presbyterian Church who have heard me preach some of this stuff and might actually read this book.

Thank you Mom and Dad for taking me in when I had nowhere else to go. For relentlessly standing by me in the goo and reminding me of my dignity. I may need that reminder again now that this thing exists in the world!

Biggest gratitude to Rob, to Ollie and Isaiah for letting me tell our story, for making life together so brutiful, and for not letting me shove this manuscript under a pillow, but gently prodding, "How's your book coming along?"

Thank you reader for being brave enough to navigate your way through life's many endings to its beautiful hard-won new beginnings.